BENEATH THE SURFACE, VOLUME 2

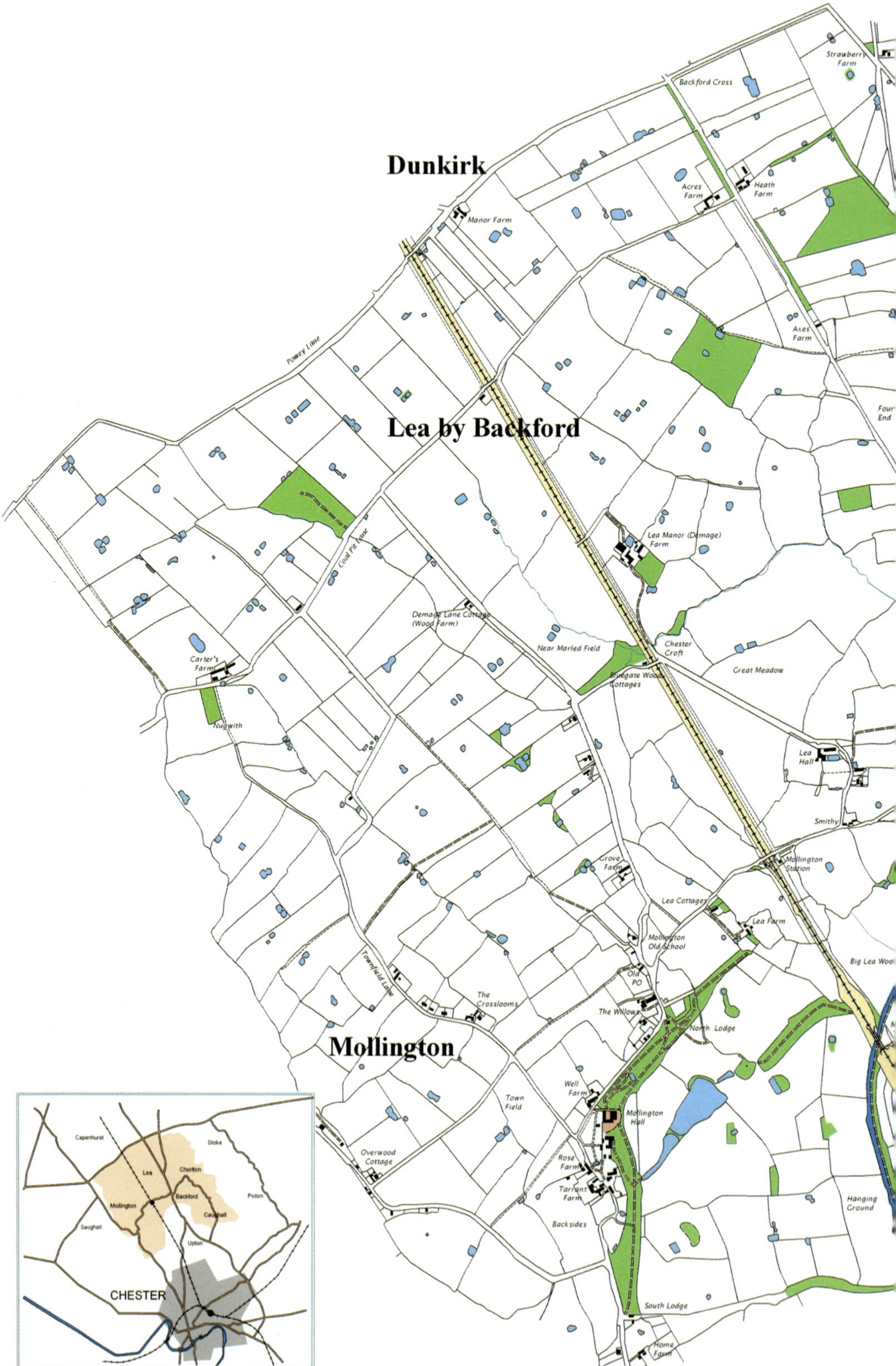

Dunkirk
Lea by Backford
Mollington
Backford Cross
Strawberry Farm
Acres Farm
Heath Farm
Manor Farm
Axes Farm
Four End
Powey Lane
Coal Pit Lane
Lea Manor (Demage) Farm
Demage Lane Cottage (Wood Farm)
Near Marled Field
Chester Croft
Great Meadow
Carter's Farm
Nugwith
Lea Hall
Smithy
Mollington Station
Grove Farm
Lea Cottages
Lea Farm
Mollington Old School
Old PO
Big Lea Wood
Townfield Lane
The Crosslooms
The Willows
North Lodge
Well Farm
Mollington Hall
Town Field
Overwood Cottage
Rose Farm
Tarrant Farm
Backsides
Hanging Ground
South Lodge
Home Farm
Capenhurst
Stoke
Lea
Chorlton
Mollington
Backford
Caughall
Picton
Saughall
Upton
CHESTER

Map of the Parish of Backford

including the townships of :
Backford
Caughall
Chorlton
Lea-by-Backford &
Mollington

This map was drawn by Malcolm McIvor in 2013 and based on the 1899 edition of the Ordnance Survey Map

Illustration Acknowledgements

In addition to acknowledgements noted in captions to illustrations, thanks are due to the following for permission to use illustrations and photographs :

Bonhams of Chester, page 42, 43; John Curtis, 36; John Hess, 142, 143, 144, 145, 150, 151, 152, 153; Malcolm McIvor, frontispiece map; Barbara Moth, 94, 95, 96, 97, 99; Carl Stagg, 214, 225; Judith Pickard, 216, 220, 227; Brian Webster, 241–249; Alan Whitham, 177; Michael Richardson, 5, 72, 73, 80, 82, 133, 134, 138, 180, 182, 189, 191, 193, 194; and various family members for photographs which appear in the War Memorial chapter.

Other illustrations come from the archives of the Society or are believed to be in the public domain and we apologise if any name has been omitted.

Beneath the Surface, Volume 2

Essays from the Cheshire Townships of: Backford, Caughall, Chorlton, Lea-by-Backford and Mollington

Backford, Mollington and
District Local History Society

First published in 2014 on behalf of the
Backford, Mollington and District Local History Society
by Scotforth Books (www.scotforthbooks.com)

ISBN 978-1-909817-16-6

Typesetting and design by Carnegie Book Production, Lancaster.

Printed in the UK by Short Run Press

Contents

Introduction

In 2008 the first volume of essays from the Backford, Mollington and District Local History Society was published. Nearly all the books have been sold and its success has given us the impetus to produce a second volume, once again based on the work of Society members, who continue to produce essays on a wide variety of topics of local interest.

The essays have been arranged in a rough chronological order, so that we start with the finding of a Roman coin, followed by a group of family-based stories covering the period from the late 17th century. In fact, there is much more family history in this volume than in the first. Those articles have required a greater depth of research, itself being made possible by the greater knowledge and experience of our members now. We feel that, partly as a result of these articles, the second volume more closely approaches a history of the parish.

However, there has been a variety of incidental history to report and the matter of Britain at war is topical and very important to include now. As factual features, we have included the catalogue for the 1937 sale of building materials from the demolition of Mollington Hall and published, for the first time, John Davies' 1953 History of Backford.

Does the second volume mean the end of our series? Perhaps not, because ideas for a third volume are already being considered and the necessary enthusiasm still exists.

Once again, we are pleased to thank Cheshire Local History Association for their generous loan to help with our costs. Thanks are also due to the writers of our essays and to those who have carried out editing and/or proof reading for us.

The Editorial Committee: John Hess, Michael Richardson and Brian Webster.

The Front Cover: Painting of St Oswald's Church, Backford.

The painting by Harold Hopps is of St. Oswald's Church, Backford in 1929. The original is held by the Williamson Art Gallery, Birkenhead, within a collection of Cheshire and Wirral works, and is reproduced here with their kind permission.

Note the more open view of the church and that the swinging entrance has been moved to the street corner.

Dorothy Carline, who died on 24th July 2010

By John Peter Hess

It is very sad to have to report the passing of such an important contributor to our local history, but such is the case. Dorothy Carline lived to a grand old age, and, as a result, had many recollections to call on – more than anyone else I have known.

Her article 'A Mollington Childhood', which appeared in the first volume of 'Beneath the Surface' in 2008, was a marvellous example of detailed and invaluable reminiscences, provided for us in very readable longhand. 'Parish Reminiscences' 2000, the production of which I was able to discuss with her at her home in Saughall, was another opportunity for her. I especially remember her description of Mollington Methodist Chapel in the 1920s, something no one else would have been able to give.

Her obituary, below, shows the strength and commitment of her family, something which is always a consolation in these times.

Obituary of MISS DOROTHY PRIMROSE CARLINE

THE funeral took place on August 9 of Dorothy Primrose Carline of Saughall, Mollington, who died at home on July 24, aged 98.

A service conducted by the Rev Brian Harris was followed by cremation at Blacon.

Dorothy, a retired personal assistant, was born in Mollington on Primrose Day (*19th April – Editor*) and had a happy childhood with her beloved younger brother Jack.

After attending the village school at age 11 she won a scholarship to the City and County School in Queens Park, Chester and at fourteen she joined the local Choral Society as a soprano. On leaving school she joined Williams and Williams in Chester, where she became a PA and helped run various staff societies, while also caring for her frail mother. She enjoyed growing fruit and vegetables up to the end of her life, caring for her cats, and keeping in touch with her many friends and relations. In retirement she helped run many village organisations in Saughall, including the Golden Link and Gardening Clubs, and after her funeral the Golden Link and WI laid on a splendid buffet in the Vernon Institute. Dorothy bequeathed her eyes to be used to help others to see.

Family Mourners: Doris Carline (sister-in-law), Kathleen Walker (cousin), Leslie Brown (son of cousin), Ian and Gillian Carline (son of cousin and wife), Jane, Darryl, David, Philip, Robert and Emma Lloyd (daughter of cousin and her husband and children), Hazel, Noel and Gillian Blundell (daughter of cousin, her husband and daughter), Susan Walker (goddaughter), Paul Smith (godson), Mr and Mrs David Siddorns (godson and wife), Dorothy Carline and Pamela Hosking (cousin's wife and her Moston daughter) and Heather Blundell (cousin's granddaughter (rep. by Hazel and Noel Blundell)) and many good friends and neighbours.

Organisations represented: Saughall Golden Link Club, Saughall Gardening Club and The Vernon Institute.

Floral tributes, sympathy cards and donations (£400 to Claire House Children's Hospice and £15 to British Heart Foundation) were all gratefully received.

A Rare Roman Coin from Mollington, Cheshire

By David Shotter
(Professor Emeritus, Dept of History, University of Lancaster)

In 2012, a local metal-detectorist made a lucky discovery of a very rare Roman coin – an *as* issued by the Roman Emperor, Nerva, in AD 97.[1] The find was made on private land in the village of Mollington, and was promptly reported to Vanessa Oakden, the Finds Liaison Officer for the area in the national Portable Antiquities Scheme. The findspot was close to the projected line of the Roman road which ran from the legionary fortress at Chester to the site of the multi-period 'emporium' at Meols, which is now largely lost off the north Wirral coast.[2] The coin is moderately well preserved, although it needs to be stabilised to prevent further deterioration.

The obverse face depicts the laureate head of the Emperor, Nerva, facing right; the legend reads: IMP NERVA CAES AVG P M TR P COS III [P P] ('The Emperor, Nerva, Caesar, Augustus, Chief Priest, First Year of his Tribunician Power, Consul for the third time, Father of the Fatherland'). The reverse face shows the standing figure of the god, Neptune, advancing to the right, holding a vertical trident in his left hand, and a ship's prow (*acrostolium*) in his right. At Neptune's feet (though not very distinct on this specimen) is a small reclining figure; some have identified this figure as Consus, an ancient Roman god associated with the storage of grain, who had a shrine beneath the Circus Maximus in Rome.[3] However, an alternative – and more convincing – interpretation is that the small figure is that of Triton, the son of Neptune and Amphitrite, who, on examples of the coin that are better preserved than this one, holds in his right hand a horn fashioned from a twisted sea-shell, which he blew to calm the waves.[4] The statuesque figure of Neptune on Nerva's coin is striking, especially when compared with the conventional treatment in mosaic art which depicts the god as a 'marine charioteer'. The legend on the reverse of Nerva's coin is NEPTVNO CIRCENS C[ONSTI]TVT S C, which seems to mean 'By Decree of the Senate: in Commemoration of the Games established in Honour of Neptune'.

The Neptune as from Mollington: © Vanessa Oakden and National Museums, Liverpool.

Nerva's establishment of games for Neptune – (the *Neptunalia,* which were held in July/August), seems strangely extravagant when compared with his general reluctance to spend money on public entertainment, which is noted in ancient sources.[5]

Although no specific connection is known between Nerva and Neptune, the striking of this coin-type nonetheless indicates that the god did have some relevance to Nerva's situation. Nerva had come to power in September of 96, following the murder of Domitian, to which Nerva may or may not have been privy. Although Domitian's murder was popular amongst senators, the people and the army had a much higher regard for him, and thus potential resentment towards Nerva. The new Emperor, therefore, needed to 'make friends' quickly, and Neptune's wide range of 'divine responsibilities' made him a sound choice for Nerva's attention.

First and foremost, Neptune was the god of the sea: as such, his protection will have been essential as men and material passed to and fro between the Continent and the province of *Britannia*; there are surviving inscriptions from Roman Britain which serve to demonstrate the perceived importance of the god's protective powers. Indeed, Carausius, the rebel Emperor in Britain in the late third century AD, described Neptune as his companion and guardian. The especial importance of Neptune in Rome's relationship with its British provinces may account for the fact that thirteen of the sixteen known examples of this coin appear to have been found in Britain.

For Nerva, Neptune held out further attractions: much of Rome's grain-supply was transported across the sea, and much that was locally grown needed a good supply of water to bring it to fruition. We know that one of the few building-projects of Nerva's short reign was a new granary complex in Rome.[6] Further, there were other coin-issues in the reign which highlighted the subject of the grain-supply. Thus, with Neptune's help, Nerva could pay attention to what the contemporary Roman satiric poet, Juvenal, rated as the two principal preoccupations of the Roman people – bread and circuses.[7]

Neptune's responsibility for inland water also came into play: it was Nerva who, in AD 97, appointed Sextus Julius Frontinus, a former governor of Britain, to the curatorship of Rome's aqueducts and waterways.[8] His treatise on the subject still survives. It was certainly not irrelevant to this that one of the periodic floods of the River Tiber had occurred at this time, prompting the need to reconsider the City's flood defences.[9] Thus, AD 97, the year in which Nerva appears to have concentrated his attention on Neptune, saw the issue (in mid-year) of the Neptune *as*, the appointment of Frontinus to look to Rome's waterways, improvements to the grain-supply and (in July/August) the inauguration of the new games to celebrate Neptune – without doubt, Neptune's year.

As already stated, this particular *as* is rare – so rare, in fact, that for a long time its authenticity was doubted by many numismatists.[10] However, the appearance since the 1920s of more examples of the coin has served to resolve these doubts. Even so, the coin remains rare: a total of just sixteen examples of it have been recorded since the first in 1766; of these, two have unfortunately disappeared without trace, one of which was seen in the eighteenth century in northern Italy, whilst the other was last seen in the late nineteenth century in Chester. However, fortunately, engravings of both of these have survived.[11]

The origins and locations of the extant coins can be briefly summarised: as already noted, the first to be recorded was found in Colchester in 1766. It was passed by the finder to his neighbour, Sir Charles Gray, who was a Trustee of the British Museum.[12] At some stage, it found itself in the collection of the family of the noted archaeologist, Sir Arthur Evans, who is of course best known for his excavations on the island of Crete. On his death in 1941, the coin was donated to the Ashmolean Museum in Oxford. Another example, which was bought and sold on a number of occasions in London during the nineteenth century, was eventually (in 1918) donated to the Fitzwilliam Museum in Cambridge by the Rev. E.C. Dewick, the son of its last owner. Since the mid-nineteenth century, the British Museum has acquired three examples: one of these was found in the River Thames, near London Bridge, in the 1830s,[13] whilst another was possibly a nineteenth-century discovery in Colchester.[14] The origin of the third of the British Museum's specimens is not known, although it was one of two examples which had at one time belonged to the collector, Frederick Walters. It is believed that the second of Walters' coins was sold at auction in Lucerne in 1932, and acquired by Berlin Museums; the origin of this coin remains unknown.

In 1980, workmen demolishing a wall in Tarascon-sur-Rhône (in Provence) found another example of the Neptune *as*; it was retained in private ownership, and unfortunately cannot now be traced.[15] Details of this coin, however, were recorded, and it was found to be slightly larger and heavier than the others. More recent enquiries have revealed six further examples: one was sold at auction in London in 1995, and subsequently became a 'promised gift' to Yale University Museum and Art Gallery,[16] whilst one each was located in the Corinium Museum at Cirencester and in Pontefract Museum in West Yorkshire. The origin of the coin in the Corinium Museum is uncertain, but it may well have been found in Cirencester in the nineteenth century, whilst the coin in Pontefract Museum derives from excavations in 1980 of Castleford Roman fort and *vicus*, in a level that was dated to AD 140–80;[17] this coin is thus the only example to have been recovered in a controlled excavation. A fourth example was purchased in London in the 1990s, and is now in a private collection in the UK.

The final two coins were sold at auction in 2003 and 2011, respectively in Munich and Vienna; the former is known to have been purchased by an Austrian collector, whilst the latter, which is thought to have been found in 'the Balkans', is now in a private collection in the United States of America. It is noteworthy that, whilst a large number of museums throughout the world were contacted, very few had an example of the Neptune *as*; indeed, most surprisingly, even the Capitoline Museums in Rome do not have one.

What significance, then, can we attach to these coins? First, they clearly divide into two groups: one group of fourteen coins have on their reverses Neptune advancing to the right, whilst the remaining two

– those sold at auction in Munich and Vienna – depict the god facing to the front. As we have seen, the coin sold in Vienna was probably found in the Balkans, although we have no knowledge of the origin of that sold in Munich. It seems likely, however, that it was found on the Continent. Of the fourteen coins on which Neptune is shown advancing to the right, one was found in France, although the provenances of the remaining thirteen lead back, certainly or probably, to Britain. Indeed, given the large numbers of Gallo-Romans who served in the administration or the army in Roman Britain, it is not impossible that the coin found in Provence also originated in Britain.

A study of the group of fourteen coins suggests that, with the possible exception of that from Provence, all were struck from the same die. It is less easy to decide where they were manufactured: whilst it is possible that they were made in Britain, their quality shows no sign of the clumsiness that characterises many of the bronze coins of the Emperor Claudius, found in Britain – made, perhaps, by elements of the Roman army in the province.[18] These coins, together with the two sold in Munich and Vienna, bear every appearance of having been struck by the mint in Rome. In this case, it would appear that the Rome mint

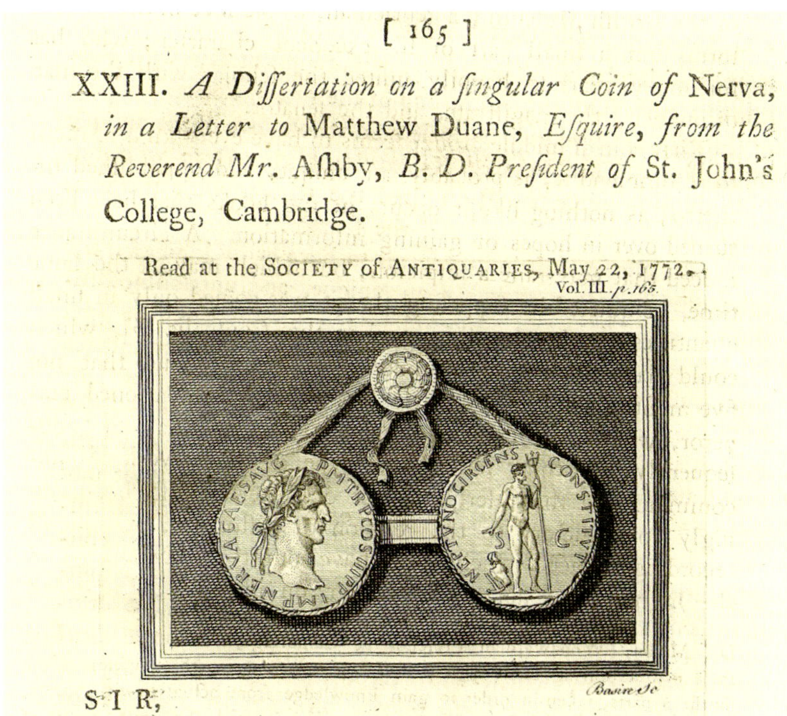
[165]

XXIII. *A Diſſertation on a ſingular Coin of* Nerva, *in a Letter to* Matthew Duane, *Eſquire, from the Reverend Mr.* Aſhby, *B. D. Preſident of* St. John's College, Cambridge.

Read at the SOCIETY of ANTIQUARIES, May 22, 1772.

Vol. III. p. 165.

SIR,

Engraving of the Neptune as found in Colchester in 1766. From Archaeologica, *3, 165–184 (1775)*

was striking batches of coins, which were not necessarily identical, for use in different provinces. It has, indeed, been shown in other studies[19] that the Rome-mint did produce supplies of 'small change' for use in individual provinces or perhaps groups of provinces. In the case of the Neptune *asses* of Nerva, we may suggest that, for whatever reason, the mint produced one set of coins perhaps for Britain and the western provinces, and another for the provinces of central and eastern Europe. It would seem likely that many more of these coins remain to be found, particularly since it has been suggested that batches of coins manufactured in the mint at Rome might run to many thousands.[20]

In view of the location of the discovery of the coin from Mollington, one wonders whether it might have been a talisman lost by someone whose business was maritime in nature. Before dismissing such a suggestion as fanciful, we might recall the ceremonial that accompanied the opening in May 2012 by the Countess of Derby of the Cruise Terminal at Liverpool Docks, and the description given of the event in *The Liverpool Echo* (30 May, 2012):

> One hundred years ago, *Mauretania, Lusitania* and their sisters sailed daily from this place. Today we welcome their beautiful daughter (sc. *Ocean Countess*), and ask Neptune and the river gods to wish her fair weather and following seas.

How often were such sentiments expressed during the Roman period in the Wirral and in other parts of Britain?

References

1. H. Mattingly, *Coins of the Roman Empire in the British Museum, Volume 3*, London 1966 (Nerva, no. 132 and p. 553).
2. For an assessment of the site, see Griffiths, Philpott and Egan 2007, 425ff.
3. Ogilvie 1969, 10 and 94.
4. Woytek 2008, 119ff.
5. Dio Cassius *History of Rome* 68.2,3.
6. Grainger 2003, 56f.
7. Juvenal *Satire* 10, 81.
8. Blake 1973, 274.
9. 'Victor' *Epitome on the Caesars* 13, 12.
10. De Loye 1984, 99.

11. De Loye 1984, 96; Watkin 1886, 227.
12. An account and illustration of the find are given by the Rev. G. Ashby in *Archaeologia* 3 (1775), 165–84.
13. Roach Smith 1841, 150.
14. De Loye 1984, 101–2.
15. De Loye 1984, 95.
16. Woytek 2008, 119.
17. Mattingly and Pirie 1998, 20.
18. Sutherland 1937, 10ff.
19. E.g. Walker 1988; Kemmers 2003; Van Heesch 2009.
20. Reece 2002, 122.

Bibliography

Ashby G., 1775: 'A Dissertation on a Singular Coin of Nerva, in a letter to Matthew Duane, Esquire', *Archaeologia* 3, 165–84

Blake M.E., 1973: *Roman Construction in Italy from Nerva through the Antonines*, Philadelphia (PA)

De Loye G., 1984: 'Les *As* de Nerva au type "Neptuno"', *Revue Numismatique* 26, 95–103

Grainger J.D., 2003: *Nerva and the Roman Succession Crisis of AD 96–99*, London

Griffiths D., Philpott R.A. and Egan G., 2007: *Meols: The Archaeology of the North Wirral Coast*, Oxford

Kemmers F., 2003: 'Quadrantes from Nijmegen: Small Change in a Frontier Province', *Schweizerische Numismatische Rundschau* 82, 17–35

Mattingly H., 1936: *Catalogue of Coins of the Roman Empire in the British Museum: III Nerva to Hadrian*, London

Mattingly H.B. and Pirie E.J.E., 1998: 'Catalogue of the Coins from the *Vicus*', pp. 18–22 in Cool H.E.M. and Philo C. (eds), *Roman Castleford: Excavations 1974–1985: Volume I, The Small Finds*, Wakefield

Ogilvie R.M., 1969: *The Romans and Their Gods*, London

Reece R., 2002: *The Coinage of Roman Britain*, Stroud

Roach Smith C., 1841: 'On the Roman Coins Discovered in the Bed of the Thames, near London Bridge, from 1834–1841', *Numismatic Chronicle* 1 4, 147–68

Sutherland C.H.V., 1937: *Coinage and Currency in Roman Britain*, Oxford

Van Heesch J., 2009: Providing Markets with Small Change in the Early Roman Empire: Italy and Gaul', *Revue Belge de Numismatique* 155, 125–42

Walker D.R., 1988: 'Roman Coins from the Sacred Spring at Bath', pp. 281–338 in Cunliffe B. (ed), *The Temple of Sulis Minerva at Bath, II: Finds from the Sacred Spring*, Oxford

Woytek B., 2008: 'Ein Unikaler Sesterz Traians aus dem Jahr 98 n. Chr. und sein Typologisches Umfeld', *Numismatische Zeitschrift* 116/117, 115–31

So Where does Moston Belong?

By David C. Russell

The ecclesiastical parish of Backford is listed as consisting of the townships of Backford, Caughall, Chorlton, Lea, and Mollington.[1] However, certainly as far back as the mid 16c Moston was, to quote Omerod, "conceived to form a part of the parish of Backford". The Moston inhabitants supported Backford church and appeared in the registers there.

In 1599, St Mary's on the Hill, Chester, claimed that Moston, and the tithes of part of neighbouring Chorlton, belonged to them. Although this claim was initially rejected, St Mary's continued to argue their case in the local court until, in 1603, it seems that they finally won their appeal. An entry in the Backford churchwardens' book[2] stated that "Moston appeared to have been lost," in spite of Mr Morgell (the diocesan registrar) indicating that in his opinion Moston belonged to Backford. In 1850, when Upton parish was created out of part of St Mary's, Moston became part of that parish.

A most important court decision does, however, seem to have been overlooked. During the Commonwealth period, Commissioners were appointed to examine parish boundaries in England and Wales in the interests of "the better maintenance and encouragement of ministers". Seizing this opportunity the inhabitants of Backford, Moston, and Chorlton petitioned the Commissioners to restore Moston, and the lost part of Chorlton, to Backford parish. All interested parties were consulted and the factors considered included the relative values of St Mary's and Backford, the amounts raised by tithes, and, perhaps significantly, that Moston was much nearer to St Oswald's, Backford than it was to St Mary's. The result was that in May 1656 a deed was drawn up by the Trustees[3] stating:

> *now and upon consideration had of the inhabitants of ... Backford ... Moston ... Charlton ... and hearing parties on both sides therein, we thinke fit and accordingly order by and with the approbation of his Highness ... signified 22 May ... that the said towneshippe of Moston and half towneshippe of Charlton from henceforth be*

> *severed and divided from* St *Maryes and ... be ... consolidated and united with Backford ...* and *that the same be held and enjoyed by the minister and incumbent of Backford for his better maintenance and livelihood according to the purport, true intent and meaning of the said Act and Ordinance.*

Why this order was not both carried out and maintained is unclear. The residents of Moston continued to support and attend Backford church but there appears to be no further statements in the Backford records that their parish boundary rights had been restored. Nor is there any evidence of the 1656 document being countermanded.

Although today Moston is included in the parish of Upton perhaps one might ask, where does it really belong?

References

1. Ormerod, vol. 2, p.362.
2. Backford Churchwardens' book 1603,
3. Minutes of the Trustees for the Maintenance of Ministers 22 May and 29 May 1656, Lambeth Palace Library and Records of the Church of England during the Commonwealth Period, catalogued under COMM.XII.c (Registers of the union and division of parishes 1655–59). See also *Calendar of State Papers Domestic 1655–56*, p.331.

The passage quoted here, and other passages relating to the Backford boundary issue are transcribed in *Lancashire and Cheshire Record Society*, vol 34 (1896), p.108,113,130,132–134.

HUNT–ROBARTES FAMILY TREE

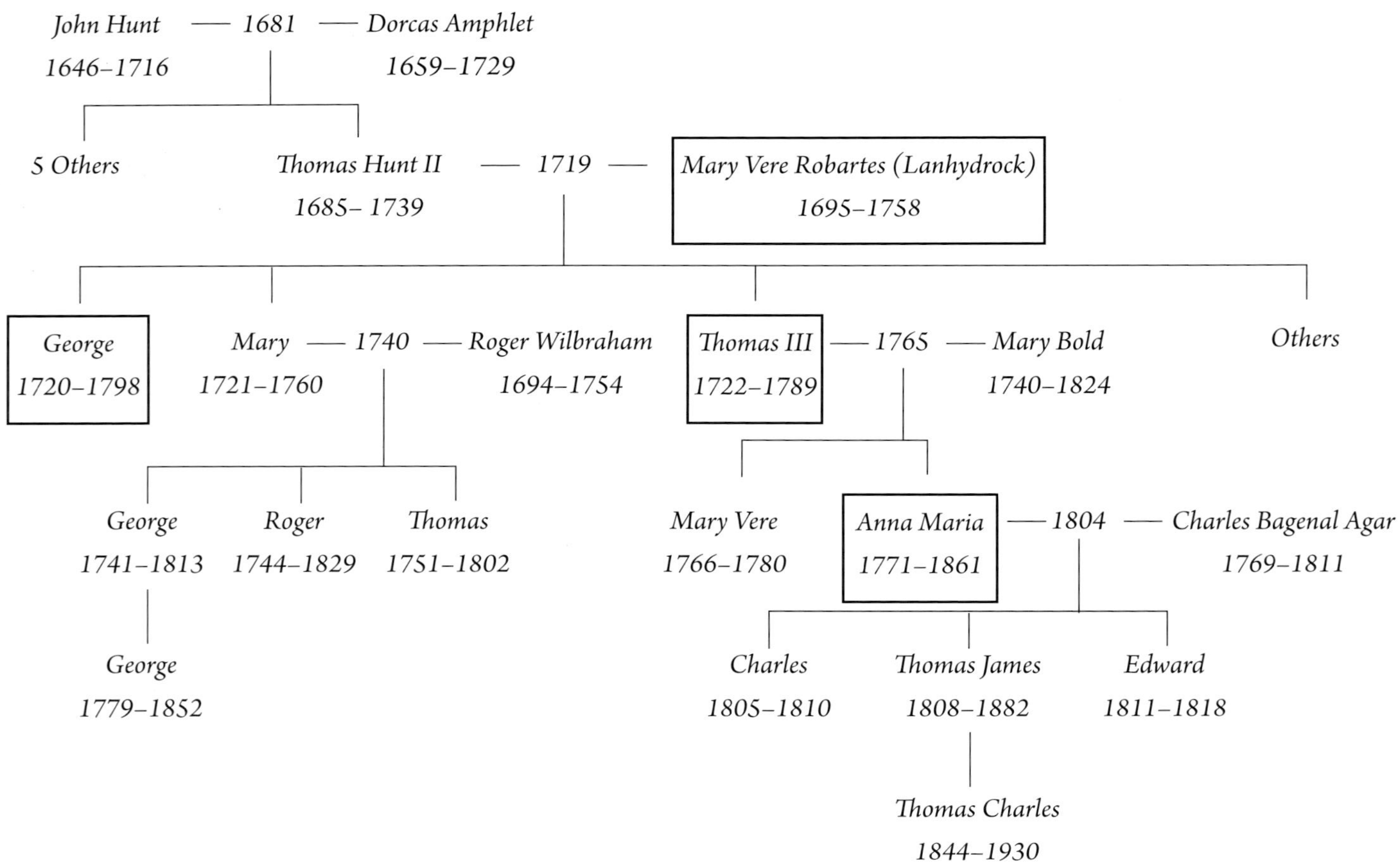

An Accidental Heiress: The Life and Times of Anna Maria Hunt of Mollington Hall

by Ann Marie Curtis

The year is 1792. Imagine a young woman, good-looking, intelligent, energetic, brought up by her aristocratic mother as a lady, and heiress to two fine estates. She is approaching her 21st birthday and the fashionable society painter, George Romney, has been commissioned to make a portrait for her coming of age. Polite society is buzzing with conjecture as to her fate in the marriage mart. She is a possible target for impecunious younger sons of noble houses or indeed heirs of impoverished, declining, noble families. However, Anna Maria is well protected from fortune seekers, both by her mother's aristocratic family, the Bolds of Bold Hall in Lancashire and by the lawyers of her late father's family, the Hunts of Mollington Hall.

Anna Maria was not originally destined for this life at the centre of London polite society or for the pivotal role which she eventually played in the life of two great families, their estates and the lives of their hundreds of dependants. Her paternal great grandfather, John Hunt (1646–1716), was a lawyer and landowner, based in Shropshire. His was an old family but John Hunt was not numbered amongst the highest of the aristocracy. In 1683 he moved to Chester and in 1699 he bought Mollington Hall, near Chester, then more of a hunting lodge, from Francis Leche. It was here that he and his wife Dorcas raised their family. His eldest son, Thomas Hunt II (1685–1739), inherited Mollington Hall and estate, together with numerous other pieces of land and lived there as a 'gentleman' i.e. a man who did not practise a profession, though he too had been admitted to Middle Temple in 1701.

Painting of Anna Maria Hunt aged 21 by George Romney. Reproduced by kind permission of The National Trust.

During this time the Hunt family had been acquiring more land, obtaining a good income from tenant

Painting of George Hunt. Reproduced by kind permission of The National Trust

farmers, and rising through Cheshire society. Then the first piece of the jigsaw leading to Anna Maria's eventual change in position, was put into place. Thomas Hunt II, in 1719, married Mary Vere Robartes, sister of the 3rd Earl of Radnor, owner of Lanhydrock House and its vast, lucrative estate, in Cornwall. The couple lived at Mollington Hall, with a town house in Bridge Street, Chester but did not have any grand expectations for their family, which consisted of George, Mary, Thomas, Elizabeth, Ann and Frances. Thomas Hunt II died in 1739 and was buried at the church of St. Mary on the Hill, in Chester, close to his daughter, Ann, who had died aged eight years. This was the parish church for Lower Bridge Street (west) in Chester and also for Mollington.

However, Mary Vere's brother had remained unmarried and died with no legitimate heir, in 1741, so Mary Vere Robartes Hunt inherited Lanhydrock. This was a considerable step up the society ladder for the Hunt family, who now owned the two estates of Mollington and Lanhydrock. A second piece of the jigsaw had been put into place. Thomas and Mary's eldest son, George Hunt (1720–1798), was heir to Lanhydrock and in his will Thomas Hunt II had also left Mollington Hall and estate to George. To his second son, Thomas Hunt III (1722–1789), he had left money and some lands in Cambridgeshire. Thomas Hunt III was to become the father of Anna Maria Hunt.

After George Hunt reached his majority, he inherited and made Lanhydrock his chief residence and sold Mollington Hall and estate to his younger brother, Thomas Hunt III. In 1747 Thomas was called to the bar, at the Inner Temple. In 1756 Thomas bought the manorial remainder of Mollington from the Glegg family of Gayton. Now, having extended his estates and become 'Lord of the Manor,' Thomas Hunt III set about rebuilding Mollington Hall as a Georgian mansion, in readiness for an advantageous marriage. Eventually, in 1765, he married Mary Bold of Bold Hall in Lancashire. A third piece had been added to the jigsaw.

Their two children were girls, Mary Vere born on 4th October 1766 and Anna Maria born on 29th March 1771. Mary Vere was baptized in St. Oswald's Church, Backford, Cheshire but Anna Maria was not.

She was baptized in the fashionable church of St. George, Hanover Square, London, as her father had purchased two town houses at nearby South Audley Street, in 1768 and the family began to spend more of their time in London.

Painting of Thomas Hunt III by Thomas Hudson. Reproduced by kind permission of The National Trust

The girls had an idyllic childhood, dividing their time between London and Mollington, with visits to Lanhydrock and to their cousins, the Wilbrahams, in east Cheshire. (Mary, sister of George and Thomas, had married Roger Wilbraham, of Townsend, Nantwich, in 1740 and the couple had three boys.) The Hunt parents appear to have been, unusually for the times, directly concerned with their children's welfare and upbringing. Then, suddenly, on April 30th 1780, Mary Vere died, aged 13. On 8th May, she was buried in St. Mary's Church, in Chester, the scene of most Hunt baptisms and funerals. There is no record in the church registers of the cause of death, though between March and October of that year, of the 47 burials 32 were for minors – an extremely large proportion, even for those times. This seems to point to a prevalent infectious illness, to which children were particularly susceptible. In Mary Vere's case, the fact of her baptism at Backford, rather than St. Mary's in Chester, may also suggest that she was perhaps a sickly child from birth. This tragic event supplied another piece to the jigsaw of Anna Maria Hunt's destiny. Anna Maria, who presumably had escaped or survived the illness, aged 9, was now an 'only child.' She appears to have been very close to both parents, physically and emotionally and needed to draw particularly on the support of her mother and the extended Hunt family during times ahead.

During these years, her Uncle George had been living at Lanhydrock. He entered into developments in Cornwall, becoming rich with tin and copper mining on his estates, representing the local seat of Bodmin as MP for over 30 years and reviving the house which had been almost empty since the death of the 2nd earl in 1723, the 3rd earl preferring to live abroad. However George Hunt never married. Another piece of jigsaw! As time went on, Anna Maria began to be unofficially acknowledged as the heiress, both of Mollington and Lanhydrock estates!

In 1789 Thomas Hunt III died. This was a blow to Anna Maria, who revered both her parents. It was also the time at which a young girl of

Anna Maria's station in life would perhaps be expected to be thinking about her presentation at Court, or at least, of 'coming out.' However, there is no evidence that Anna Maria was presented at Court. Certainly her mother would have been in a position to present her. However, protocol due after her father's death may have delayed it, or it may not have been deemed essential, particularly by Anna Maria, who was the sort of girl to have her own opinions about everything! The former Hunt family background was Parliamentary/Puritan/Non-Conformist and so Court matters were probably not deemed important. Newspaper recordings of such presentations are not complete and strict records have been preserved in the Royal Archives at Windsor Castle only from 1816.

Although her mother and eventually Anna Maria were to inherit Mollington Hall and estate, the estate was mortgaged up to the hilt, her father having arranged this mortgage to renovate and remodel the Hall as a Georgian mansion, fitting for his aristocratic bride. She and her mother decided to live in Upper Seymour Street, London and to lease both the houses in South Audley Street and the Mollington estate, the latter to John Feilden, a Manchester cotton merchant. Her mother inherited Thomas' personal fortune and had to make Anna Maria an allowance.

Four years later, 1792, we have fast forwarded to Anna Maria's 21st birthday. Her Uncle George had the Romney portrait done at his expense and was tacitly making known to the world that she was his

Photograph of 17th Century Gatehouse and Lanhydrock House. Reproduced by kind permission of The National Trust.

heir. There is a rumour that at this time she was about to become engaged to a nobleman. Certainly this sort of portrait was often made at an engagement. However, no engagement or marriage took place. The portrait was completed over a period of approximately 6 months, plenty of time to break off an 'unofficial' engagement!

Anna Maria also came into an inheritance of approximately £6,000 from a maternal relation, at this time. This was a substantial sum but not sufficient for her to repay the mortgage and consider living at and maintaining Mollington Hall, herself. So, Anna Maria and her mother decided to take action with regard to her inheritances. Her father's will was extremely complex. Her father had stipulated that Anna Maria must inherit Mollington estate after her mother's death and then, after that, Anna Maria's second son, if she had one, the elder son being expected to inherit Lanhydrock. They decided to get a bill passed in the House of Lords, enabling them to sell Mollington estate, and promising to make recompense from Lanhydrock, for assets lost. This was no easy undertaking, but eventually permission was given and Mollington estate was sold to John Feilden in 1796 for £15,000.

With finances now more secure, Mary Hunt and her daughter, Anna Maria, took up residence again at their more fashionable London town house, in South Audley Street. Then, in 1798, George Hunt died and at 27 years of age, Anna Maria inherited Lanhydrock. This also proved to be a poisoned chalice. Although Anna Maria gained the estate, her

Wilbraham cousins in Cheshire got most of George Hunt's money, shares in mines and arrears from tin, copper and timber dues. Her debts to the Wilbrahams were in the region of £68,000, which included her having to buy the contents of Lanhydrock house from them! She was left with these debts and a paltry sum of approximately £100 with which to run the estate!

She decided to cut her coat to suit her cloth. Until she had paid off her Wilbraham cousins and got the estate into credit, she had to cut non-essential expenditure. She refused to consider sponsoring a (Whig) MP for Bodmin. Her Uncle George and later her father Thomas, then her Wilbraham cousins, first George and then Roger, later followed by a John Nesbitt had formerly held this position. Although they represented the interests of the country landowner, in Parliament, they had had independent voices and were not known to be party hacks. Anna Maria decided that she could not support an MP and the seat was lost to the Hunt family and to Lanhydrock estate. She took advice from her stewards at Lanhydrock, taking measures which would improve the estate and investing in it when returns allowed. She dispensed charity to estate workers during times of county or national need and harnessed revenue in good times. Altogether, she was the main reason why the estate functioned as a viable unit until the start of the Second World War. In Cornwall, Anna Maria Hunt is regarded as something of a local saviour. Without her sensible measures, dedication to the improvement of the estate and in many ways a personally unassuming way of life, the economy of that part of Cornwall would have been adversely affected. She herself expressed great surprise in later life when she realised that she was able to finance quite expensive undertakings and was also able to allow herself luxuries!

Miniature of Charles Baganal Agar painted c1810. Reproduced by kind permission of The National Trust.

Throughout the early years, Anna Maria remained a spinster. Then, suddenly, on 15 November 1804, at the 'mature' age of 33, she married a 35 year old lawyer, Charles Bagenal Agar, at her mother's house in London, 76 South Audley Street, by special licence. Her husband was the youngest son of Viscount Clifden but he had only a very modest fortune and little expectation. The marriage settlements were drawn up. At this time a married woman's property became to all intents and purposes, that of her husband. In her settlement, Anna Maria stipulated that she should have a substantial sum of money from 'her' revenues, strictly for herself, to dispose of exactly as she pleased, with no interference from her husband. In addition she had £1000 per annum. Although her husband technically became Lord of the Manor at Lanhydrock, Anna Maria's always seems to have been a controlling voice. She was obviously not going to allow a man who had no knowledge of 'her' estate, to undo all the hard work that she had done.

The couple appear to have been very happy. Charles worked actively as a lawyer, and 3 sons in total were born to them. Unfortunately their eldest son, Charles, died aged 4 years and a year later, on 16 June 1811, Charles Bagenal himself died, at the family's London house, after he and Anna Maria had been married for only 7 years. He was buried in London but there is a memorial to Charles Bagenal Agar in the church of St. Hydroc, adjacent to Lanhydrock House. It was at that time a private estate church but is now an Anglican parish church. Their third son, Edward, was born a few months after his father's death but he also died when he was only 6 years of age. Only the middle son, Thomas James (1808–1882), lived to maturity. Anna Maria and her mother were the guardians of the child and Anna Maria worked tirelessly to keep Lanhydrock estate in good order, even into her 70s. Although remaining at her house in London, Anna Maria's mother, Mary, gave Anna Maria emotional support until she herself became even more seriously ill. Anna Maria had a connecting door opened between her house 1, Dean Street and her mother's adjacent corner house, so that she could look after her mother, at this time. Mary Bold Hunt died in 1824. Now Anna Maria was the sole economic and emotional support of her family.

After reaching his majority in 1829 her son Thomas James Agar theoretically took over the running of Lanhydrock Estate. However Anna Maria was consulted first on all matters, by the land steward William Jenkin and house steward John Cole, with her son's participation being purely nominal. However, after his marriage to Juliana Pole-Carew of Antony, Cornwall, in 1839, Anna Maria's son, Thomas James Agar, settled at Lanhydrock and took a greater and greater role in its development. Anna Maria spent more and more time at her house, in London, at 1 Dean Street, Park Lane, and died there on 3rd March 1861, at almost 90 years of age, 50 having been spent as a widow. She had left a wonderful thriving estate for her son and grandson and had carried out some important measures, not usually attempted by women. She was not buried in the family vault at St.George's Field Burial Ground Chapel, Bayswater Road, London, where her mother, husband and two small sons had been buried. In 1861, the year of her death, the cemetery was dug up and contents removed to Hanwell. The chapel in the cemetery was demolished later and a housing estate now stands on the whole site. Instead, The Honourable Anna Maria Agar (née Hunt) was buried in the crypt of the Anglican Chapel, at All Souls Cemetery, Kensal Green, Kensington, London, on 12 March 1861. Her house at 1 Dean Street is renumbered as 2, Deanery Street but the adjacent property of 76 South Audley Street was demolished in 1970 and a modern office block now stands on the site.

Her son, Thomas James Agar, was created 1st Baron Robartes of Lanhydrock and Truro in 1869. Due to a series of unfortunate deaths in the Agar family, Thomas Charles Agar, Anna Maria's grandson, also became 6th Viscount Clifden of Gowran, in 1899. Although he and his wife Mary had ten children, only one son and one daughter ever married. Of their six sons, one died in infancy, one died during the first World War, and three remained bachelors. Lanhydrock was given to the National Trust in 1953 by Anna Maria's great grandson, Francis Gerald Agar Robartes, 3rd Baron Robartes and 7th Viscount Clifden. Gerald, a bachelor, continued to live there until his death in 1966. His only married, younger brother had a daughter, who lived in Africa and was uninterested in maintaining Lanhydrock.

The present day village of Mollington lies approximately 4 miles north of Chester, between the A540 and the A41. It grew up around Mollington Hall and its grounds. The farms in and around the village were once part of its estate.

John Feilden first leased and then bought Mollington Hall and Estate from the Hunt family, in 1796. His descendents eventually sold it. The Hall and some parts of the Estate were sold to T. Gibbons Frost in the early 1900s. The remainder of the estate was broken up into lots and sold by auction in 1907. North and South Lodges, on Well Lane and Townfield Lane respectively, were renovated by the Frost family in 1907.

In the early 1930s the Hall and grounds were bought by Costains. The Hall was demolished by Costains in 1935, with the contents and building materials sold in 1937. Later, new suburban-type housing was built on the land. Today there are only a few traces left of Mollington Hall and its estate. The estate wall, which since 2012 has carried a Historic Blue Plaque, still runs alongside the south east side of Townfield Lane and the whole of the south side of Well Lane. The wall has been breached repeatedly to provide entrance drives to the houses built on the old Mollington Hall site. The back gardens of these houses contain the ha-ha of the old Hall, back walls of the old kitchens and some garden store houses etc. One garden houses the Italian urn which once stood in front of the Hall's main entrance. The old Hall's fish ponds and ice house are situated on land now titled Mere Farm (entrance on Townfield Lane). They can be seen from the path running alongside the Shropshire Union Canal, between the A540 and the A41. The North and South Lodges were sold separately and provide large, comfortable, family homes to this day.

However, not in Mollington, nor at Lanhydrock, nor in London, is there an extant memorial to Anna Maria Hunt Agar, this unusual, energetic and quietly heroic Georgian woman. Nonetheless, her legacy remains in each of these places, not least in the lovely George Romney portrait, made for her coming of age and displayed in Lanhydrock House.

Primary Sources

Parish Register of Chester, St Mary (Chester Record Office P20)
Parish Register of Backford (Cheshire Record Office P32)
Will of Thomas Hunt, d.1789, attested copy (Cornwall Record Office CL/1307)
House of Lords Bill to approve sale of Mollington estate, 1796 (HOL Record Office)
Burial Register of All Souls Cemetery, Kensal Green (London Metropolitan Archives)
City of Westminster Archives Centre, London

Secondary Sources

Beneath the Surface: Historical Essays from the Cheshire Townships of Lea-by-Backford, Backford, Caughall, Chorlton and Mollington (Backford, Mollington & District Local History Society, 2008)

Clarke, J.W. 'Mollington Hall', in *Chester Archaeological Society Journal*, vol.41 (1954)

Earwaker, J.P. *The History of the Church and Parish of St Mary-on-the-Hill, Chester* (London 1898) p.282–286, for the Hunt Pedigree.

Holden, P. 'New Light on a Georgian Townhouse', in *The Georgian Group Journal*, vol.17 (2009)

Howells, G. 'Anna Maria Agar: the Restoration of the Robartes Dynasty 1798–1844', in *Lanhydrock House Journal*, vol.5 (2005–6)

Trinick, M. and Garnett, O. *Lanhydrock* (The National Trust, 2006)

This article, in a slightly different form, was originally prepared for publication in the journal, *Cheshire History*, volume 50, (2010–11) p.61–70, and is published here with the kind permission of the editor of *Cheshire History*.

THE HUNT FAMILY TREE

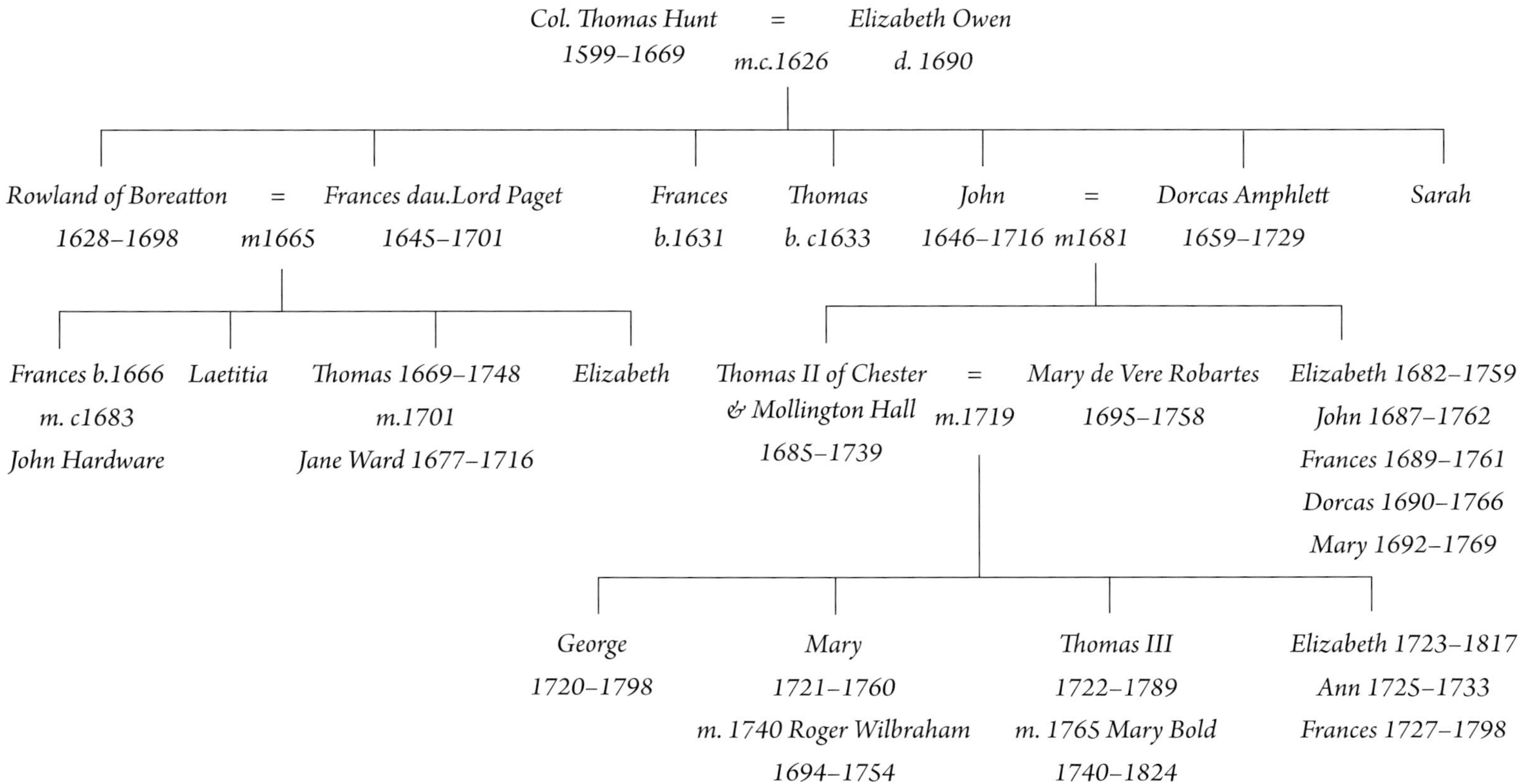

THE HENRY FAMILY TREE

Philip Henry
1631–1696

m1660

Katherine Matthews
1629–1707

John
1661–1667/8

Katherine Hardware
1664–1688/9

m1687

Matthew Henry
1662-1714

m1690

Mary
Warburton
1668–1731

Sarah 1664–1752
Katherine 1665–1748
Eleanor 1667–1697
Ann 1668–1697

Katherine
b1689

Elizabeth 1691–1692
Mary 1693–1693
Esther b 1694
Ann 1697–1698

Philip Henry
Warburton
1700–1760
MP for Chester
1742–1754

Elizabeth 1701–1752
Sarah 1703–1767
Theodosia 1708–1786
Mary b1711

The Hunts and the Henrys – The Story of the Linked Lives of two non-Conformist Chester Families

By Ann Marie Curtis

Thomas Hunt of Shrewsbury (1599–1669), a well respected lawyer, landowner and member of the Drapers' Company, was the father of three sons. Rowland 1629–1698 was the eldest, Thomas was born around 1635 and John 1646–1716, was the youngest. The sons had been educated at Shrewsbury School, which was at that time a bastion of Calvinistic education and they grew up during the time of the struggles between King Charles I and Parliament. The family as a whole were Puritans with regard to religion i.e. believed that the practices of the Church of England needed 'purifying' and were Parliamentarians with regard to politics. Thomas, and his father Richard before him, exerted their considerable influence in civic affairs, in order to make Shrewsbury a more godly society. Together with their similarly minded friends in civic circles, they were known as the 'godly party.' However the Hunts never seemed to adopt the more extreme forms of Puritanism followed by some later Parliamentarians.

Thomas Hunt trained the Shrewsbury Militia for the service of Parliament in 1642 and because of this he was declared a traitor by King Charles I. He was also suspended as an Alderman of Shrewsbury. When the Civil War broke out, Shrewsbury originally became a Royalist stronghold and Thomas Hunt may have left Shrewsbury to go to Bristol. This town was occupied by Parliamentary forces, to prevent the second port of the country falling into Royalist hands. This did however occur in early 1643 and Thomas Hunt returned to Shropshire, where his main military action was in the fortification and garrisoning of Wem, near Shrewsbury. Hunt acquitted himself well there in a skirmish in 1643[1] and was appointed Governor of Wem for nearly two years. When Shrewsbury fell to Parliamentary

forces from Wem, in 1645, Thomas Hunt was reinstated as an Alderman, given the rank of Colonel and later co-opted as M.P. for Shrewsbury after the removal of a Royalist sympathiser i.e. he joined the Long Parliament as a Recruiter. However, during 'Pride's Purge' of moderate Parliamentarians on 6th Dec.1648, Thomas Hunt was 'secluded' i.e. forbidden to attend Parliament. He therefore played no part in the decision to bring King Charles I to trial, or later, on 30th Jan. 1648/9 to execute him. The execution was witnessed, however, by a young Oxford student, Philip Henry, who was visiting his father, a senior servant in Whitehall, at this time. Although Henry's religious views were also Puritanical, and therefore opposed to those of the King, he apparently still found this experience a harrowing one.

Colonel Thomas Hunt.ca 1650

Under the Protectorate of Oliver Cromwell, Thomas Hunt was made High Sheriff of Shropshire in 1656 and in 1657 Lord Mayor of Shrewsbury. Colonel Thomas Hunt's eldest son, Rowland had been admitted to Gray's Inn, London, his father's old Inn, in 1646. This particular Inn of Court had been noted for accepting students from anti-establishment backgrounds but like the other three Inns, closed to new students during the Civil War. Under the Commonwealth and the following Restoration, Gray's did not recover as well as the other three Inns. Perhaps because of this, the middle brother, Thomas, was sent to London to train and work as a merchant.

After the Restoration of King Charles II in 1660, the Hunts lived quietly on their land and though they did not have to forfeit any of it, neither did they obtain any preferment. They did not seek positions at Court and would have been unlikely to obtain them if they had done so. However Colonel Thomas Hunt had already amassed enough money to buy and settle his eldest son, Rowland on the estate of Borcatton, Shropshire in 1667. His youngest son, John, was admitted to Gray's Inn of Court in 1666. John was called to the Bar there and later became an Ancient. John and Thomas Hunt had to make their own ways in the world, as they were not endowed with land in the same way as the eldest son, Rowland, had been.

During the Cromwellian period, Anglican bishops had been removed from office and many Anglican clergymen had been Puritan in outlook and practice. After the Restoration of the King, Restoration of the Church of England along former Anglican lines soon followed. In 1662 all clergymen had to sign the Act of Uniformity. About 2,000 Puritan ministers felt unable to do so and were deprived of their livings as a result. They became known as non-Conformists. These ministers included Rev. John Bryan of St. Chad's Church and Rev. Francis Tallents of St. Mary's Church, Shrewsbury. The Hunt family supported these non-conformist or Presbyterian ministers and although Colonel Thomas Hunt had died in 1669, we find that in 1673 the Shrewsbury house of Elizabeth Hunt, Colonel Thomas Hunt's widow, was used as a meeting place for Presbyterian congregations.[2] Apart from the years 1683–1687, when the meetings were suppressed, Bryan and Tallents preached alternately on Sunday mornings and evenings 'at common church hours' until the death of Mrs. Elizabeth Hunt on Oct 23rd 1690. Thereafter the meetings were conducted at Mr. Tallents' house in Shrewsbury, until, in October 1691, a meeting house was opened in High Street, for public worship. (By 1799 this church had metamorphosed into a Unitarian place of worship and was frequented by the Wedgwood and Darwin families. I wonder what Mrs. Elizabeth Hunt would have thought of this development.)

After graduation, Philip Henry (1631–1696) had become a minister at Worthenbury Church, near Wrexham but later refused to sign the Act of Uniformity or accept the Book of Common Prayer. He was therefore, in 1662 evicted from his post. He retired to Broad Oak, an estate near Whitchurch inherited by his wife Katherine. He appears to have made the acquaintance of Colonel Thomas Hunt during this period. Broad Oak was at a disputed five miles distance from Worthenbury. The Five Mile Act of 1665 banned non-conformist preachers from preaching within this distance of either an incorporated town (one with a mayor and corporation) or their former church. Philip Henry did preach occasionally in his barn or in the houses of other Presbyterians and was once fined for so doing. Refusing to pay, he was imprisoned for a few days and goods in kind were seized. However, in May 1672, Philip Henry received an unsolicited licence from Whitehall, permitting a room or rooms in his house at Broad Oak to be

Mrs Elizabeth Owen Hunt

used for Presbyterians to assemble for public worship and devotion. Perhaps King Charles II remembered the times when they had played together as boys in the Palace of Whitehall, where Philip Henry's father had been a servant.

In June 1675 Philip Henry is travelling home from London together with two other non-conformist ministers. He sends a letter to his wife describing the proposed route of their journey and mentions that they will be met partway by Mr. Hunt's brother who will accompany them further.[3] It was common to travel in company at this time due to dangers of physical or human origin. Philip Henry could be referring here to either of the younger Hunt brothers, Thomas or John, as their new companion.

Philip Henry gave religious instruction to his children and found Matthew, his second son and the only one to survive childhood, an exceptional pupil. Originally Matthew (1662–1714) spent a very short time at Whitchurch Free School and then was taught Hebrew, Greek and Latin by his father. As time went on a private tutor was engaged, most notably William Turner, who lived with the Henry family. Eventually, as Philip thought that there were too many worldly temptations at university, he decided to send Matthew, aged 17, to be tutored in Islington, London by Mr. Doolittle, a non-conformist minister and teacher. In a letter home to his sisters in 1680 Matthew asks for his love and service to be given to Mr. Thomas Hunt 'if hee bee not gon home'.[4] It would seem therefore that even though Colonel Thomas Hunt had been dead for over ten years, the two families were still on visiting terms. The Thomas Hunt mentioned is most likely to have been the middle son of deceased Colonel Thomas Hunt.

Rev. Philip Henry © National Portrait Gallery, London

It is mentioned in 'The Life of Philip Henry' by Rev. Matthew Henry that his father continued to spend one Lord's Day in four with the family of Rowland Hunt of Boreatton. Perhaps the close relationship between the two families is best illustrated by this excerpt from the Life of Philip Henry by J. B. Williams, in which Philip Henry's attitude to his children is described. 'When they had been for a week or a fortnight Kindly entertained at Boreatton, as they were often, he thus writes in his Diary upon their return home; 'My care and fear is, lest converse with such so far above them, though of the best, should have influence upon them to lift them up, when I had rather they should be kept low.' For, as he did not himself, so he was very solicitous to teach his children, not to mind high things; not to desire them, not to expect them in this world.'

John Hunt of Mollington ca 1680

John Hunt married Dorcas Amphlett at Clent, Worcestershire in 1681 and moved to Chester around 1683 to follow the legal profession. John Hunt had premises on Lower Bridge Street, Chester and also bought Mollington Hall, 4 miles north of Chester, in 1699. There do not appear to have been any well-defined non-conformist congregations in Chester when John Hunt first arrived here. In any case, such persons would have been legally prevented from setting up their own church. Elizabeth, the eldest child of John Hunt, had been christened at Clent in 1682, but all the rest of John and Dorcas Hunt's children were christened at the Anglican Church of St. Mary on the Hill, Chester. This does not however infer that they necessarily performed any more than minimal duties to the Church of England.

Mrs Dorcas Hunt Wife of John Hunt ca. 1680

In 1683 Matthew Henry inherited the estate of Bronington, Flintshire, from his maternal grandfather. Whilst there, he seems to have visited frequently with Rowland Hunt of Boreatton, Shropshire. Rowland advised him to study law, as non-Conformist ministers were still somewhat restricted in their preaching and other religious practices, at this time and a living of some sort must be earned. Matthew Henry was admitted to Gray's Inn on 6th May 1685.[5] It is easy to speculate that Matthew Henry had been sponsored by either Rowland or John Hunt. Both these Hunt brothers had been admitted and called to the bar at Gray's Inn and John was elected as an Ancient at Gray's in 1688, only three years later.

It is interesting that whilst studying at Gray's Inn, Matthew Henry visits Mr. Baxter, an old Puritan minister friend of his father, Philip. Baxter had also been the minister at Wem whilst Colonel Thomas Hunt was governor there. In a letter to his father in 1685, Matthew states that Mr. Baxter observed that 'of those gentlemen who were with him at Wem, he hears none whose sons tread in their fathers' steps but Colonel Hunt's.' It is obvious that many other former Puritans have by now become Anglican. The few who have not done so have largely become Presbyterians.

Matthew Henry preached in his father's neighbourhood in vacations in 1686 and visited Chester, on business for his father, in January 1687. Several former Puritan Anglican clergymen, who, like Matthew's father, had been evicted from their livings, had already settled in Chester in the 1660s and from then onwards Chester began to become a centre of non-conformism. These former Anglican clergymen included Mr. John Wilson from Backford, Mr. Crook from St. Michael's, Chester and Mr. Jonathan Hervey. Lady Catharine Booth had made her house in Chester available to John Wilson for preaching purposes and it is possible that people from the Backford congregation went to hear him.[6] Sadly, John Wilson died rather prematurely, in 1672. Matthew Henry would still however have found in Chester a reasonable number of persons ready to listen to his preaching and to take part in discussions with him. Matthew preached in private houses during his visit and impressed so much those Cestrians who heard him, that he was asked to settle in Chester as a minister. He decided to return to Gray's but promised to come back to Chester at a future date, probably anticipating the likelihood of Toleration for non-Conformists being soon granted. Before his departure for Gray's Inn, however, Mr. Philip Henry delivered an address (sermon) at Boreatton on the occasion of his son Matthew and Thomas, the only son of his friend Mr. Rowland Hunt, leaving the area to take up residence in London. Indeed both young men were going to London to study the law. Matthew was to return to Gray's Inn and Thomas Hunt was to begin to study law at Middle Temple.

Thomas Hunt was admitted to Middle Temple on 12th February 1686/7 and was called to the bar there on 18th May 1694. However, Matthew Henry did not stay very long at Gray's. He was ordained privately by six non-conformist ministers on 9th May 1687, in London and began his ministry at Chester on 2nd June 1687. The Declaration of Indulgence promulgated in this year, by King James II, enabled non-conformist ministers to now preach without hindrance. Matthew still preached largely in private houses or halls and his reputation and congregation size grew. It is here that he met up again with John Hunt Esq.

The Hunt family introduced Matthew to the Hardware family of Peele Hall, near Mouldsworth, in the parish of Tarvin. Mr. John Hardware, son of the family, had married Frances, daughter of Rowland Hunt of Boreatton. Apparently through their connection with the Hunts of Boreatton, Matthew Henry's sisters had become friendly with John Hardware's younger sister Katherine and had already marked her out as a suitable bride for Matthew. They were obviously able to gauge their brother's preferences well, because Matthew married Katherine Hardware, in Tarvin Parish Church of St. Andrew, on 19th July 1687, only six weeks after becoming acquainted with her! The newly-weds then boarded in the Chester house of Katherine's parents. Sadly Katharine died in childbirth on 16th February of 1688/9. Their daughter was named after her. Later, in July 1690, Matthew married Mary Warburton, daughter of Robert and Elizabeth Warburton of Hefferston Grange near Weaverham, a bride suggested by his former in-laws. Mr. and Mrs Hardware then retired to another of their properties, Bromborough Court Estate, Wirral. Matthew and Mary Henry had a family of nine children, which included just one son, Philip, named for his grandfather.

In 1689, the Act of Toleration brought in by the next King, William of Orange, enabled Protestant, non-Anglican communities to build their own churches, chapels or places of worship, which should be registered. Broad Oak Chapel, fashioned from an outbuilding at Broad Oak House, was registered and Philip Henry preached there every Lord's Day until he died in 1696. A meeting house was built for Matthew Henry in Crook Lane, Chester, in 1700 and John Hunt is listed as a trustee of the Chapel and as one of the most important contributors, giving a donation of £20. Richard Amphlet Esq. (possibly John Hunt's father-in-law or some other relation of his wife, Dorcas née Amphlet) also made a donation of £5. In 1707 a gallery was added to cater for members of another non-conformist congregation, that of Mr. Jonathan Hervey, who had become too frail to preach. Many of Hervey's congregation already came to the Crook Lane Chapel and when the two congregations formally amalgamated the number of adherents rose to 350.[7] Jonathan Hervey died in 1708.

Matthew Henry's Chapel, Crook Street
Cheshire Records Office Ref. 224939

During his ministry in Chester, Matthew Henry travelled widely within the county, preaching to non-Conformist congregations in the villages and small towns. He actually lived in Bolland Court, Whitefriars, Chester, (Mr. Bolland being a member of his congregation) and the 'double decker' summerhouse in the garden there is said to be the site where his sermons were composed and also his prodigious output of theological works. Henry's 'Exposition of the Old and New Testament' is still regarded as a definitive work in theological colleges. Sadly the area is now the domain of dentists and solicitors and the summerhouse has disappeared.

The Hunt and Henry families appear to have remained on friendly terms throughout this time. On 31st Dec. 1701, Matthew Henry records in his diary that the year has been a very good one for him with not so many 'afflictions' as in some years. However, he states that 'The greatest (affliction) has been the death of my dear and honourable friend Madam Hunt of Boreatton'.[8] This lady could be the widow of Rowland Hunt of Boreatton who had died in 1698. There is also at least one reference in Matthew Henry's diaries, to having taken supper with the Hunts at Mollington.[4] Normally Henry only mentions by name members of his own family or the families of other non-conformist ministers.

In 1701 Thomas Hunt of Boreatton, son of Rowland Hunt (deceased) and for a short time fellow law student with Matthew Henry, married

Jane Ward in London. The couple settled at Boreatton and Jane Hunt became friendly with the family of Matthew Henry. Jane kept a diary and often mentions non-Conformist gatherings and Matthew Henry's preaching.

Later the death of another 'worthy good' friend is mentioned in Matthew's diaries. It is that of Mrs. Hunt, wife of Mr. Hunt, merchant, London. This could be the wife of Thomas Hunt, middle brother of Rowland and John. Mrs. Hunt died on 20th Jan 1711, 'much lamented'.

Matthew Henry © National Portrait Gallery, London

So far, the Hunt family have influenced Matthew Henry's decision to study law, one member of the family even accompanying him. They were also instrumental in his coming to Chester after ordination. Once here, they introduced him to his first wife and later John Hunt was a prime mover in building a chapel for him. In 1708 Matthew Henry was invited to minister at the Silver Street Chapel in London. Apparently John Hunt encouraged Matthew to go there, but he did not do so. However, in late 1712 there was a renewed invitation and this time Matthew Henry did go to London.

Even so, there was one last religious service which Matthew Henry performed for the Hunt family. In the diary of Mrs. Hunt of Boreatton, she states that on 3rd May 1712 she is staying at Chester at the house of Mr. Henry. She states that tomorrow there will be the Lord's Table at service. She confides that she desires to partake and has been encouraged to do so by Mr. Henry. The entry for 4th May 1712 is couched in very abstruse and poetic language. However it appears to convey that she was indeed admitted to the Lord's Table and found it a spiritually uplifting experience. This Mrs. Hunt of Boreatton would of course have been Jane, wife of Thomas Hunt of Boreatton, son of the deceased Rowland Hunt.

Later, Mrs. Dorcas Hunt, wife of John, is registered as being admitted to the Lord's Table in Matthew Henry's old chapel by the next incumbent, John Gardner, on 3rd January 1714. This would indicate that Dorcas had been attending the chapel regularly as an adherent but was not received into full membership until just before that date.[7] This date in January would be the first time that she had received Communion in that chapel whereas her husband, John Hunt would have been a full member for most of his life. Even after leaving Chester, Matthew Henry is having an influence upon the Hunt family.

Later in 1714 Matthew visited his beloved Cheshire and died here, at Nantwich on 22nd June. He was buried with great dignity in the chancel of Holy Trinity Church, Chester (now Chester Guildhall), close to the remains of his first wife Katherine, née Hardware and his three daughters who died in infancy. This church was adjacent to his former chapel in Crook Lane. (His second wife, Mary, was also later buried there in 1731.) Matthew Henry's funeral was attended by many city clergy and local dignitaries.

John Hunt died two years later and one of his personal bequests to his wife was 'all Mr. Henry's exposition of ye Old and New Testament.' John Hunt was buried in St. Mary's, where most members of the Chester branch of the Hunt family were baptised and buried, including later, in 1729, his wife Dorcas. Most of the Hunts of Boreatton are buried in Bass churchyard, Shropshire.

Both branches of the Hunt family remained lawyers and land owners, however their religious affiliation diverged in subsequent generations. The Boreatton branch remained non-Conformist for a few more generations. However, the Chester branch quickly gravitated towards Anglicanism. We can assume that as the children of John and Dorcas Hunt were brought up in a non-Conformist family, they were fairly well aware of the differences between Presbyterian and Anglican theology. However, Thomas Hunt II, the elder son of John Hunt, chose to have all his children baptised in the Anglican Church, at St. Mary's, Chester. By this time it would have been legal to simply report the birth of a child of a dissenter family, rather than to have the child christened, unless the parents so wished. However, the children of Thomas Hunt II were actually christened at the parish church of St. Mary's, Chester. Moreover, Thomas Hunt II also requested in his will that his children should be brought up in the 'Moderate Principles of the Church of England'.[9] This would seem to suggest that this branch of the Hunt family had decided to become bona fide members of the Church of England. Later, the descendants of Thomas Hunt III inherited Lanhydrock Estate in Cornwall and sold the Mollington Estate. They moved to Lanhydrock and later endowed Anglican churches in Cornwall. One female descendant married an Anglican clergyman who was given the living of St. Hydroc's Church adjacent to their Lanhydrock stately home.

Philip, Matthew Henry's only son did not enter the non-conformist ministry but chose instead to have a legal education at Lincoln's Inn. He was admitted on 3rd April 1721, using his mother's maiden name of Warburton, and was called to the bar on 8th June 1727. After his mother died in 1731 he inherited Hefferston Grange. In 1733 he became a Freeman of the City of Chester. Later he became Attorney General and Recorder for Chester. Later still he decided to enter politics and was M.P. for Chester from 1742 until 1754. Although he had been adopted unopposed as Tory member for Chester, he rarely voted with the government and was regarded as 'Opposition' when he was re-elected in 1747. Broad Oak Chapel, had been used only for monthly lectures since 1707, when a Presbyterian Chapel had been built for the congregation at Dodington, Whitchurch. In 1746 Philip Henry Warburton ordered his grandfather's chapel at Broad Oak to be demolished and largely on account of this, is described in the register of the Presbyterian Chapel of Dodington as 'an enemy of all righteousness.' Warburton did not stand for re-election to Parliament in 1754, never married and died at his home, Hefferston Grange, Cheshire in 1760.

A split then occurred in the congregation at Crook Lane. Those opting to remain there later joined the Unitarian Church and those more true to Matthew Henry's ideas left. At first they used a civic meeting hall in Common Hall Street, Chester but in 1777 founded their own Independent Chapel in Queen Street, off Foregate Street, then a thriving part of town. In 1806 the chapel became a founder member of the Cheshire Congregational Union.

The original Matthew Henry's Presbyterian (later Unitarian) Chapel survived until 1962 when redevelopment to give the Forum precinct and car park caused it to be demolished. The church was relocated to Nevin Road, Blacon and many artefacts were taken there, amongst them a 300 year old wooden pulpit and associated railings, memorial tablet, organ, communion table and stained glass windows, one of which depicts Matthew Henry. In 1989 the building was bought by Evangelical Christians and renamed the Matthew Henry Evangelical Church. The artefacts from Matthew Henry's original chapel, including the pulpit from which he probably preached, are still retained within the building.

Matthew Henry Independent Chapel, Queen Street.

The Queen Street Independent (later Congregational) Chapel was demolished in 1978, when Tesco was built. If you go along Queen Street to the back entrance of Tesco, pass by, do not go in! After 20 yards you will see a remarkable sight on your left hand. There, incorporated into the back wall of Tesco's car park, is the neo-classical façade of the (Matthew Henry) Independent (later Congregational) Chapel. This is surely the only Tesco store in the country to incorporate a church! There is no blue plaque here or in Whitefriars. Can this be an oversight on the part of our civic authorities?

Members of the Hunt family of Chester and Mollington are buried in the churchyard of St. Mary's Chester. However this church is no longer used as a parish church and can only be visited during an event open to the public or by special permission from CWaC. Their former home of Mollington Hall was demolished in 1937. However in August 2012, an historic blue plaque was placed on the Estate Wall which had surrounded the Hall and gardens.

In 1962, the tri-centenary of his birth, a memorial to Matthew Henry was installed on the Grosvenor roundabout, Chester. If you care to place your life in danger from the Chester traffic, you may examine it in detail.

References

1. 'The History of Wem' by Samuel Garbet. The state of Wem during the Civil War.
2. Register of High Street Church, Shrewsbury 1692–1812. Shropshire: Parish Registers, Nonconformist and Roman Catholic Registers, Shropshire Records Office, Shrewsbury
3. DMD/0/1 Henry family letters, Cheshire Records Office.
4. 'Matthew Henry and his Chapel, 1662–1900' by H.D. Roberts.
5. Records of Gray's Inn, London.
6. 'Beneath the Surface' by Backford, Mollington & District Local History Society. Non- Conformity in the Backford area, by Arthur Poulton.
7. Unitarian Records Archive, Subscription Book for Matthew Henry Trinity Street Chapel – ZDM H/1 Cheshire Records Office.
8. 'Memoirs of the life, character and writings of the Rev. Matthew Henry' by J.B. Williams.
9. Will of Thomas Hunt, Cornwall Records Office, Truro. CL/1307.

Other Primary Sources

Admission Records of Gray's and Lincoln's Inns of Court and those of Middle and Inner Temples.

Parish records of St. Mary on the Hill, Chester.

Secondary Sources

Dictionary of National Biography, London. Smith, Elder & Co 1891.

Earwaker's Hunt Family Tree.

'Heavenly' Henry, The Life and Times of Philip Henry 1631–1696 by David Hayns.

The Lives of Philip and Matthew Henry, by J.B.Williams.

The Victoria County History: History of Chester.

FEILDENS OF BLACKBURN AND MOLLINGTON *(Family members closely associated with Great Mollington)*

Henry Feilden d1742 = *Elizabeth Sudell* d1738

Ann b1722 | *Mary* b1723 | *Randal* b1725 | *John* = *Starkie* b 1726 (No Issue) | *Catherine* b1730 | *Mary* b1732 | *Robert* b1734 d1735 | *Joseph* = *Margret Leyland* b1736 d1792 | *Henry* b 1738

Henry (1765–1815) = *Fanny Hill* m. 1790 Witton House, Blackburn | *John Feilden* b1769 d1859 Married 1795 High Sheriff 1803 Mollington Hall 1797 = *Elizabeth Loxham* b1770 d1823 (Father: Rev. William Loxham of Longton) | *Cecily* b1766 d1822 | *William Randle Bt* b1772 d1850 (Feniscowles) = *Mary Haughton Jackson* | +3s1d

John-Joseph b1798 d1798 | *Priscilla* b1801 m1842 d1871 = *John Townshend* of Hem and Trevallyn | *Elizabeth Ellen* b1805 m1854 d1897 = *George Becher Blomfield* Canon b1801 d1885 | *Margaretta Dorothea* b1810 d 1892

Joseph b 1792 d1870 = *Frances Master* m1817 | *William* b1794 | *Henry* b1798 d1801 | *Randle Henry* b1802 d1870 = *Phoebe Arbuthnot* m1825 | *John* b1804 d1865 | *Margaret* | *Cecilia*

Randle Joseph b1824 d1895 Lt-General & MP = *Jane Campbell Hozier* m1861 | *Henry Master Feilden* b1818 d1875 = (1) *Caroline Mosely* (2) *Hannah Fox* | +7s5d

Cecil William Montague b1863 d1902 Unmarried | *Percy Henry Guy* b1870 m1902 d1944 = *Dorothy Louisa Brand* Dau. of Viscount Hampden of Glynde | *James Hartley Gilbert* b1867 d1944 | *Katherine Josephine Dolores* b1864 d1954 | *Randle Joseph Francis Campbell* b1862 d1886

The Feildens of Great Mollington

By Carl Stagg and Brian R Webster

We start the story of John Feilden, squire of Mollington, in Blackburn Lancashire.[1] There he was born into one of the landed gentry and cotton magnate families, the Feildens of Blackburn. Joseph Feilden (Snr) 1736–1792, the male Feilden heir and his wife Margret (née Leyland) co-heiress of William Leyland, brought up their family in Blackburn. Henry was their eldest son (1765–1815), the second son was John (1769–1859), and it is the latter who is our main point of interest. There was also a third son William Randle (1772–1850) who became a MP and Baronet. Their sister Cicely was born in 1766; later she married and had nine sons and six daughters.

The Feilden family can be traced some way back but their full influence in the life of Blackburn and environs is more fully marked when in 1721, Thomas Belasyse, fourth Viscount Fauconberg, sold his Lancashire estates and disposed of his manor of Blackburn to William Baldwin, Henry Feilden and William Sudell, this was the temporal moiety of the manor of Witton.

The ecclesiastical moiety was leased by the Archbishop of Canterbury, and in 1758 Joseph Feilden is named as "one of the farmers of the Rectory of Blackburn". A large portion of the Rectory Glebe was sold in the eighteenth century to Henry and John Feilden. Later in 1853, Messrs. Joseph and John Feilden surrendered 467 acres of the Glebe to the Ecclesiastical Commissioners, retaining the residue of the estate on the payment of £20,000.

Henry and John Feilden's predecessors are said to have commenced purchasing lands in Blackburn in 1690. Samuel Bower of Highgrave also acquired numerous messuages here in the latter part of the 18th century, which are said to have been sold after his death in 1793 to Mr. Henry Feilden of Witton House.[2]

Henry, father of Joseph, built his house in Church Street, Blackburn, opposite the Church gates, and it still has on its front the initials " H F E " (Henry and Elizabeth Feilden), and the date "1728". It was recorded that "Henry Feilden, of Blackburn, gentleman, removed from Bath, died, in 1742 aged 49" and was buried in Blackburn Church, in April that year.

The same Henry Feilden, born in 1693, may be regarded as the founder of the fortunes of the Blackburn family. He married Elizabeth Sudell from one of the other land-owning families of Blackburn in the same year of 1721 that he bought Witton Manor and then having five sons and four daughters with her. After childhood deaths the second son, John (1726–71) inherited the estates. He lived until 1771 with no issue, so his oldest surviving brother Joseph was the next male in line; Joseph was John Feilden's father.[3]

The main family residence was the Old Hall of Witton[4] which stood on a bank of the River Darwen near the Blake water, at the south-east corner of the Witton Park.

Joseph died in 1792. His eldest son was Henry (1765–1815) the elder brother of John. He was engaged in the cotton trade as a "chapman" as well as being a great landed proprietor. As a landowner and a chapman along with his brother John, he shared in the rapid increase of wealth which the construction of canals and roads, and the expansion of trade, brought to England in the eighteenth century. It had become the custom before the end of that century for both the landed gentry and the new-rich spinners and ironmasters to convert their home farms into parks, build commodious new houses to supersede the old manor-houses, and surround the parks with stone walls.

Before the Industrial Revolution, Blackburn was little more than a village, but in the hundred years between 1750 and 1850 the population increased tenfold and Blackburn became one of the great cotton weaving centres of the world.

Until the late 18th century handloom weaving, in tandem with small-scale farming, was the mainstay of the local economy. Handloom weavers would take their completed cloth-pieces to the warehouse of a manufacturer who would supply them with the raw materials. 'Putters out' took the finished cloth and supplied the raw materials. It wasn't until the Industrial Revolution and the invention of the power loom that the situation began to change. The damp Lancashire climate, a local supply of coal to power steam engines, a plentiful local supply of building stone and access to skilled weavers meant that Blackburn was ideally placed for an expansion in cotton spinning and weaving. As the industry grew, manufacturers' warehouses became mills.[5]

A new aristocracy of mill owners appeared and employment shifted from the land and home based spinning to purpose-built mills. The first purpose-built spinning mill in Blackburn was constructed in 1797, and by 1824 there were 24 mills. The number of spindles in Blackburn reached 2.5 million by 1870.[6]

About the end of the 18th century, more than half of the ancient township of Witton was enclosed to form Witton Park. It has as its background one of the most prominent landmarks of Blackburn, viz. Billinge Hill. It was on the south side of Billinge Hill that Henry Feilden, lord of the manor of Blackburn, built his new house Witton Hall in the grounds of Witton Old Manor just outside the township boundary, on the banks of the river Darwen, and in the township of Witton. He laid out the spacious grounds around the house as park and pasture land, and the bleak hill of Billinge he planted with trees, which became a noted sanctuary of bird life under natural conditions. The frontage of the house is towards the Preston Old Road, where a carriage drive, with lodge and gates, connected it with the outside world by means of a bridge over the river.[4]

In 1847 a series of folio volumes was published, entitled "The Mansions of England and Wales", illustrated with "views of the principal seats". Witton House, though not so pretentious as many of the other "mansions", finds a place in this work, where it is described as follows: "Witton House, somewhat less than two miles west of Blackburn, in that parish is the seat of Joseph Feilden, Esq. The mansion, which was built by the father of the present proprietor, about the year 1800, is very elegant stone edifice in the Grecian style. It is constructed of cream-coloured freestone, richly veined, and has in the centre of its eastern front a portico supported on columns of the Doric order. The principal apartments are enriched with several paintings by the best modern masters."

Henry was engaged in the cotton trade as a "chapman". Chapmen were merchants distributing the finished cotton products in support of the booming cotton trade of Blackburn and Lancashire. Henry died in 1815, aged 50, leaving his manors, capital and lands to his two brothers

John Feilden

John and William Randle Feilden in trust, with his wife Fanny being paid an annuity of £1500. So by descent and purchase, the Witton estates became vested in Joseph Feilden (1792–1870), "old Joe"(eldest son of Henry) and his uncle John Feilden (of Mollington Hall).

John Feilden, the second son of Joseph Feilden (the elder) and Margaret Leyland[8] of Witton Hall was born in 1769. His father Joseph died in 1792 and he inherited part of his father's Blackburn estates. In 1795, at the age of 26, he married Elizabeth Loxham.[1]

John was not his father's direct heir and could not then take up the family seat at Witton, so he had to find a suitable home in which to live with his wife Elizabeth. It was at this time that Mollington Hall was for sale; Mary Hunt (née Bold) was finding it difficult to run the Mollington estate and her London houses following the death of John Hunt(III) of Mollington Hall in 1788. Also her daughter Anna Maria had inherited the Lanhydrock estates in Cornwall from George Hunt, her uncle. The purchase of Mollington Hall was not a straightforward matter as the title was complicated by a raft of leases and an entailment to the male heir Thomas Wilbraham, the nephew of John Hunt. It is recorded that the sale was in 1797 at a cost of £15,000. It took an act of parliament in 1802 and various undertakings by the Hunts for a solid title to be confirmed.[7]

With the purchase of Mollington Hall in 1797, John Feilden established his branch of this prominent Blackburn family as the leading family in Mollington for more than a hundred years. As already mentioned, two years earlier John had married Elizabeth Loxham,[9] daughter of Reverend William Loxham of Longton, Rector of Bethnal Green and shortly after moving to Mollington their first child was born. Unfortunately it was not the happiest of experiences and their son John-Joseph died[10] before reaching his first birthday. Their second child, born in April 1801 was christened Priscilla in May 1801 at St Oswald's, Backford. In 1842 Priscilla married John Townshend,[11] son of John Stanislaus Townshend of Trevallyn House in Rossett; there were no children from this marriage. The second daughter of John Feilden and Elizabeth Loxham was born on 4th December 1805 and on

17th January 1806 was christened Elizabeth Ellen[12] at St Oswald's Church in the neighbouring township of Backford. Their final child was born on 15th August 1810 and baptised Margaretta Dorothea at St Oswald's Church, Backford on 11th October of the same year.

Elizabeth Feilden

Among the announcements in the London Gazette dated 5th February 1803[13] was one appointing John Feilden as High Sheriff for the County of Chester for the year 1803; a few years later he was appointed Acting Magistrate for the Hundred of Wirral and shortly afterwards Deputy Lieutenant for the Palatinate of Chester.[8] However, unlike his youngest brother William (later Sir William) for many years M.P. for Blackburn, John appears to have favoured the quiet life with little publicity. A search of the archives of The Times newspaper produces only the one mention of John as an individual when appointed High Sheriff; there are three or four records of John with other members of the Feilden family relating to their joint mill ownership in and around Blackburn.

The family's period of stability in Mollington was ended abruptly with the death at the age of 53 of John Feilden's wife Elizabeth in 1823,[9] leaving him with three teenage daughters to raise. Elizabeth's will[14] specified "*I request my Body may be respectably interred without pomp at Backford Church and a suitable white marble monument placed therein to its memory*" and her wishes were carried out.

John Feilden owned Mollington Hall for sixty two years and he planned and made a number of changes to the estate and the Hall. He improved the access to the property from the Chester turnpike, added a new kitchen and installed an acetylene gas plant[15] to name just a few. In addition, in 1802 he purchased the adjacent manor of Lea thus significantly increasing the overall size of the estate. In 1839, when the Chester to Birkenhead railway line was being planned to cross part of his land, unlike many other landowners, John Feilden invested in the project despite the obvious impact on the estate, for example, the need to re-site the North Lodge. It is reported that as a keen sportsman, he did express concern that the noise from the locomotives might disturb his game!

Despite his obvious pride and commitment to his Mollington Hall estate, it is difficult to determine just how much time he and his family spent there. The 1841[16] and 1851[17] census data for Great Mollington show that there were no Feildens anywhere in the village although there are groupings of servants as might be expected if the Feildens were only temporarily absent from the Hall. In 1851, John, Elizabeth Ellen and Margaretta were to be found[17] at an address in Ryde on the Isle of Wight. John had a close family association with the Isle of Wight since at this time his nephew, Randle Henry Feilden, was Rector of St Lawrence's church at nearby Bonchurch. Randle Henry was later named as one of the trustees and executors in John Feilden's will.[18]

In 1854, Elizabeth Ellen Feilden became the third wife[19] of George Becher Blomfield, a Canon of Chester Cathedral, Rector of Stevenage and brother of the Charles James Blomfield, Bishop of London. John Feilden died in 1859 just short of his ninetieth birthday; his will named his nephews Joseph and Randle Henry Feilden, sons of John's brother Henry Feilden, as trustees of his estate and executors of the will. In a later codicil John's oldest daughter, Priscilla Townshend, was added as a third executor. The will puts the control of the estate in the hands of the trustees but allows his three daughters, Priscilla, Elizabeth Ellen and Margaretta Dorothea, the use of the Hall and other properties in Cheshire but stresses that all monies and effects received under the will are for the personal use of the three daughters and must not follow the rules of coverture and come under the control of any husband they might have already or in the future. Following John's death, from the census data the Hall appears to have been rented out. Elizabeth Ellen is with her husband in Stevenage in both the 1861[20] and 1871[21] censuses while in 1861 Margaretta is with the family of her sister's late husband the Townshends in North Wales – her location in 1871 has yet to be ascertained. Living in Mollington Hall at both of these censuses is a cotton broker named Frederick Lyon and his family; Mr Lyon gives as his occupation Corn Broker (1851 when living in Litherland), East India Merchant (1861), Gentleman and J.P. for Cheshire (1871) and finally Justice of the Peace Cheshire (1881) having by then moved to Milverton, Warwick.

John Townshend died at the family home, Trevallyn House, Rossett, early in 1861[11] and his wife Priscilla continued to live in that area; the 1861 census shows her at Trevallyn House which was by then the property of her brother-in-law, Major-General Henry Dive Townshend who had inherited the house from John. By 1871 she is in a property close by in Burton (Denbighshire); she died later that same year. John and Priscilla Townshend are both buried in the churchyard of Rossett Church.

By the time of the 1881 census,[23] the Feildens are back in residence in Mollington Hall with George Blomfield named as Head of the household and in the company of his wife Elizabeth Ellen, his sister-in-law Margaretta Dorothea Feilden (incorrectly named as Blomfield) and Alice Royds, one of George Blomfield's granddaughters from his first marriage. The Times newspaper on 26th December 1885 reported the death on 24th December of George Blomfield at the age of 86 and added "the reverend gentleman attended the funeral of the Dean of Chester; he then contracted a severe chill and was seized with bronchitis and died on Thursday". In his will,[24] George Blomfield requested that the funeral should be conducted in the plainest manner and at least expense "without any needless articles of display and that no hat bands or scarfs [*sic*] be used".

The 1891 census[25] shows the two Feilden sisters were still living at Mollington Hall, however, the following year Margaretta Dorothea died.[26] Her will[27] had been written almost forty years before she died and most of the clauses were, by 1892, redundant since both her father and her sister Priscilla were then dead. Apart from a few small bequests to relatives, the bulk of the will can be summarized as "keeping it in the family".

Elizabeth Ellen Blomfield, the last remaining member of the John Feilden branch of this influential northern family, remained resident in Mollington Hall until her death in 1897.[28] Her last will and testament[29] was written only about six months prior to her death and in many ways reflects the fact that she was the final member of this part of the Feilden family. Her bequests to members of both the Feilden and Blomfield families are sizeable and in particular when compared with those made by her father forty years earlier. John stipulated sums of fifty or a hundred pounds for his nephews and godchildren, whereas Elizabeth Ellen bequeathed sums of one or two thousand pounds to similarly related family members. Bequests to staff members are also noticeably different; John left ten pounds to his butler, Jesse Hutchings while Elizabeth bequeathed one hundred pounds to her butler Robert Dean and also stipulated that this money should be paid "free of legacy duty".

Mollington Hall

In addition she bequeathed an annuity of eighty pounds to Robert Dean plus a further annuity to him of twenty six pounds to take care of her two dogs "Ginger" and "Mischief"! And again she directed that all annuities be paid "free of legacy duty". Perhaps there was a difference in the quality of these two butlers or maybe it was their lengths of service; Robert Dean, born "Hazelbury Somersetshire",[23] is shown on the 1871 census as a footman in the Blomfield household in Stevenage, he had been elevated to valet in the Mollington census of 1881 and to butler by 1891 so he did serve the family for a number of years.

As the final member of John Feilden's family and under the terms of his will,[29] Elizabeth directed that the Mollington estate should pass to Captain (later Major) Cecil William Montague Feilden, the grandson of her first cousin Joseph Feilden and second, but eldest surviving, son of the then late Lieutenant-General Randle Joseph Feilden and his wife

Witton House

Jane Campbell Hozier.[30] Cecil succeeded his father to the family seat of Witton Park in 1895 but he is reported as preferring to spend what leisure time he had at Mollington Hall which he allegedly described as a "pleasant little estate". However, he had little time to enjoy his place in Cheshire as the British Army was involved in the Boer Wars. The census of 1901[31] names only two servants as present at Mollington Hall and in that same year in the issue dated 27th September the London Gazette announced the award of the D.S.O. to Major Cecil William Montague Feilden of the 2nd Dragoons (Royal Scots Greys) "In recognition of services during the operations in South Africa". On 18th February 1902, the final year of the Boer Wars, Cecil was wounded at Klippan in South Africa and died[32] the next day aged 39. He is buried at Heidelberg, a suburb of Johannesburg and a memorial stone is in St Oswald's Church, Backford. Cecil willed his Mollington estate to his brother Lieutenant Percy Henry Guy Feilden, and the Witton estate to his other brother, Captain James Hartley Gilbert Feilden.[33] In November 1902, Percy married The Honourable Dorothy Louisa Brand, daughter of Viscount Hampden of Glynde[34] and initially made his home at Mollington Hall. However, in September 1906 he sold the Hall to Thomas Gibbons Frost, son of Sir Thomas Gibbons Frost and moved to Crawstone Hall, Cokethorpe, Witney, Oxfordshire; the latter Hall became an Independent Day School in 1957[35] and one of the six school houses is still named Feilden House.

References

1. W.A. Abram, "A History of Blackburn, town and parish", published 1877 by J.G. & J. Toulmin.
2. Victoria County History, "A History of the County of Lancaster, Vol. 6", J. Brownbill.
3. Blackburn Times, 22nd March 1930.
4. http://www.cottontown.org/page.cfm?pageid=528
5. http://www.spinningtheweb.org.uk
6. http://en.wikipedia.org/wiki/Blackburn
7. Paper presented by Paul Holden to the Women's History Network Conference at Southampton University, 2nd–4th September, 2005.
8. "A Genealogical and Heraldic History of the Commoners of Great Britain and Ireland etc. Vol. 2", by John Burke.
9. "The History of the County Palatine and City of Chester", by

George Ormerod, 2nd edition.
10. International Genealogical Index, Church of LDS see also ref. 5.
11. "Townshends of Trevallyn" by Lewis H Hughes (1998).
12. "Pedigree of the family of Feilden, of the County of Lancaster" by Ralph Assheton (1879).
13. London Gazette, 5th February 1803.
14. Last Will and Testament of Elizabeth Feilden, Cheshire Records Office.
15. J.W. Clarke, J. of Chester Archaeological Society Vol. 41 (1954).
16. Census for England and Wales, 1841 (6th June 1841), Office for National Statistics (ONS).
17. Census for England and Wales, 1851 (30th March 1851), ONS.
18. Last Will and Testament of John Feilden, Cheshire Records Office.
19. Monumental and other inscriptions in the churches of Stoak, Backford, and Thornton-le-Moors in the County of Chester, J P Rylands.
20. Census for England and Wales, 1861 (7th April 1861), ONS.
21. Census for England and Wales, 1871 (2nd April 1871), ONS.
22. Registered at Wrexham, December quarter of 1871 Vol.11b, page 197.
23. Census for England and Wales, 1881 (3rd April 1881), ONS.
24. Last Will and Testament of George Becher Blomfield, Cheshire Records Office.
25. Census for England and Wales, 1891 (5th April 1891.
26. Registered Chester, June quarter of 1892 Vol.8a, page 268.
27. Last Will and Testament of Margaretta Dorothea Feilden, Cheshire Records Office.
28. Registered Chester, June quarter of 1897 Vol.8a, page 275.
29. Last Will and Testament of Elizabeth Ellen Blomfield, Cheshire Records Office.
30. Baptisms at St Mark the Evangelist in the District of Witton, Blackburn 15th Nov 1863.
31. Census for England and Wales, 1901 (31st March 1901), ONS.
32. "The History of the Second Dragoons: Royal Scots Greys" by Edward Almack.
33. http://www.headington.org.uk/history/famous_people/feilden.htm People of Headington, Oxford. Katherine Feilden.
34. http://en.wikipedia.org/wiki/Henry_Brand,_2nd_Viscount_Hampden.
35. http://en.wikipedia.org/wiki/Cokethorpe_School.

The Forgotten Estate of Moston Hall and the founding of The Dale

By David C. Russell

Moston Hall, in the civil parish (formerly the township) of Moston, is situated to the west of Liverpool Road and the A41, a little over two miles north from the centre of Chester. The township has always been small and its boundaries unaltered, enclosing 275 acres, of which some 240 acres historically formed the Moston Hall estate. At the end of the eighteenth century the estate recovered about 70 acres of its former land which earlier had been sold off, and added a further 20 acres extending into the adjacent townships of Backford, Lea and Upton. For half a century up to 1871 the Moston estate was at its largest, and intact. Then a process of dismantling and other changes began which has considerably transformed the original estate; but it has not exactly disappeared.

Although references to Moston stretch back to the Middle Ages, the later hall has remained almost entirely hidden away from public view. This is partly due in modern times to it having being largely screened by trees and bounded to the west and north by canal and railway. In addition, there is no public access through the present estate which since 1939 has been wholly or partly owned by the Ministry of Defence and is now referred to as 'The Dale'. From 1940 to 1964 the author lived in a cottage adjacent to Moston Hall and still lives nearby. This article is an attempt to tell the story of Moston from early times to the present day.

In the beginning

Moston is not mentioned in Domesday Book. But it may have received its name in Anglo-Saxon times, the term 'mos-' or 'mors-tun' suggesting a marshy place or wetland meadow, with or without human settlement. It is an apt description. The land rises from the valley which geographers often refer to as the 'Deva spillway' whose stream historically separated the hundreds of Wirral and Broxton and which in medieval times was still liable to frequent flooding and was only easily traversed at nearby Backford.

Moston's early history up to 1600

The earliest known reference to Moston dates from about 1123, in a charter of Ranulf third earl of Chester confirming various grants of land that had been made to the monks of St Werburgh's Abbey, Chester, in the years since the abbey's original foundation charter was granted by Hugh Lupus in 1093. One entry reads:

> Ricardus de Cruce dedit unam mansuram in Cestria in vico apud pontem, et partem terrae quam habuit in Morcetone et vellet monachus fieri.
>
> Richard de Cruce gave one dwelling-house in Chester, in the quarter near the bridge, plus a parcel of land which he had in Moston, when he decided to become a monk.[1]

The Chartulary of St Werburgh's contains another document dating from the abbacy of Thomas de Capenhurst (1249–65) recording that the abbey was donated land 'in Morston' by Richard de Ledsham, when he entered the monastery.[2]

In 1303, in a *Quo warranto* ordered by King Edward I, the monks of St Werburgh's reasserted their claim to Moston and their right to 'the usual privileges of infangtheof, wayf, stray, and chattels of natives and fugitives, and view of frankpledge for this manor, at their leet of Upton'.[3] They renewed the claims during the reign of Edward III, in a long and detailed *Placita* (Plea) dated 1358, in which Moston is mentioned four times: three times as 'Morston' and once as 'Moreston'.[4]

From 1378 to 1390 a Thomas de Moston was keeper of the Dee corn mills near the bridge in Chester,[5] and several other 'de Mostons' occur in late medieval records of Cheshire and Lancashire. But they tend to be connected with the much larger township of Moston near Middlewich, or Moston north of Manchester, and we cannot be certain that any of them are linked with Moston by Chester.

St Werburgh's Abbey was dissolved by King Henry VIII in January 1540 and became the cathedral of the new diocese of Chester in July 1541. In the valuation of the assets of the monastery, before they were conveyed to the Dean and Chapter of the cathedral, the entry for Moston was written thus:

> Moston longe Medowe infra parochiam de Backford – viij[51, 6]

'Infra parochiam Backford – below the parish of Backford'. A possible misinterpretation of the word 'infra' as meaning 'within' may have had certain awkward repercussions in later years, as we shall see. Meanwhile, in 1541 Dean and Chapter became the legal freeholder of the township, for a time at least. What happened over the next half century is a story complicated enough to be worthy of its own volume, and whose lurid details were superbly disentangled by Archdeacon R.V.H. Burne in his history of Chester Cathedral (1958), under the heading 'the rape of the cathedral lands'.[7]

The story was all part of the nationwide scramble for land following the Dissolution of the Monasteries. In Cheshire the setting up of the new diocese and transfer of assets of St Werburgh's Abbey to the Dean and Chapter of Chester Cathedral was met with dismay by greedy local gentry who had hoped to get something for themselves. In 1553 Sir Richard Cotton of Combermere saw his opportunity. Possibly based on (malicious if not false) charges brought by former clerk to the Cathedral Chapter, William Glasier of Lea by Backford, that the Dean and others had been misappropriating cathedral property:

> Dean Cliffe and two of the prebends were imprisoned in the Fleet, by the procurement of Sir Richard Cotton, comptroller of the King's household, and under intimidation granted to him most of their lands in return for a fixed annual payment of £603 17s 0d, although the rents of the properties amounted to over £700.[8]

The Dean spent twenty days in prison and was released on 6 March 1553. After that, he and his successors spent almost the whole of the rest of the sixteenth century in a protracted struggle to regain the cathedral lands.

So what happened as far as the township of Moston was concerned? In 1553 after suffering this extortion it was in Cotton's possession. In 1556 Sir Richard died and was succeeded by his son, Sir George Cotton. Dean Cliffe died in 1558 and his successor initiated proceedings for the recovery of the freehold. In the meantime, Cotton, 'knowing the weakness of his case', conveyed Moston and other properties to various of his fellow Cheshire gentry. Moston was purchased by Hugh Cholmondeley of Cholmondeley, with the exception of a small portion which appears to have been acquired separately by William Glasier of Lea, perhaps as a reward for his informing against the Dean. (Incidentally, Glasier was a sheriff of Chester in 1537 and mayor in 1551.)

In 1575 Dean Longworth discovered a providential flaw in the cathedral title deeds: the word 'Chester' had been omitted, thus rendering the deeds null and void, so the cathedral lands were still Crown property and could not have been legally conveyed to anyone by the Dean and Chapter. So in 1576 the case was placed before the Privy Council and all parties concerned eventually surrendered their rights to the Queen, paving the way for her to grant whatever award she willed.

Meanwhile the Privy Council commissioned a separate enquiry to discover any lands that might be being 'concealed', having been prompted to do so by two unscrupulous locals, Francis Hitchcock and Lancelot Bostock. In September 1577 a certain Peter Grey was commissioned to find the said lands and on 8 March the following year the Queen granted him a lease of 'Boughton, Bull's Farm, Upton, Wervin, the Longe Meadowe in Backford, Moston, Salghton, Tilstone Fernall, Tarvin'. The next day Grey conveyed the lands to Hitchcock and Bostock who had obviously been in collusion with him.[9]

At the end of 1579, Letters Patent detailed and confirmed the grants that were made by Queen Elizabeth with respect to the main case placed before the Privy Council. Moston was included as follows:

> [30 Nov 1579] Eliz R ... grants to William and John Glasior, gents, the manor of Ley, alias Lee, by Backford, & the vills of Ley, Whitby & Overpoole, with tenements in Moston, Upton & Boughton ...[10]
>
> [19 Dec 1579] Eliz R ... grants to sir Geo. Calveley kt, George Cotton, Hugh Cholmeley, Thomas Leighe, Henry Maynwaringe, John Nuthall, and Richard Hurleston, esquires, the manors ... late part of the possessions of the dissolved monastery of St Werburgh ... and further grants to the same all lands, royalties, and other privileges of the said abbey, in ... Moston [etc].[11]
>
> [22 Dec 1579] Eliz R ... grants to the dean and chapter as follows ...

> £4 10.10. issuing from lands in Moston, in the holding of Ralph Rogerson.
>
> £4 10.10. issuing from lands ibidem, in the holding of John Ashton.[12]

Rogerson and Ashton were under-tenants of Hugh Cholmondeley. It seems that both Dean and fee-farmers were oblivious to the separate enquiry and its outcome concerning 'concealed' lands, as six months later, in July 1580:

> Her Majesty granted again all the said lands to the fee farmers and the rents to the Dean and Chapter, they not regarding or making any account of her Majesty's former grant of the same lands ... made two years before unto Peter Grey.[13]

Hitchcock bided his time in order to exploit the situation as fully as he could. In 1583, after his co-colluder Bostock had died, he decided to take possession of Moston and other lands granted in 1577, in due form of law. All the fee farmers concerned found their leases were in danger and almost without exception bought up his title. Consequently Cholmondeley, as well as the Glasiers, paid out for the title to their lands in Moston.[14]

This situation pertained to the end of the century. Then, according to Ormerod, in about 1601 John Ashton sold his share of Moston to John Morgell of Chester, who soon afterwards also purchased Ralph Rogerson's share.[15] This is pure guesswork on Ormerod's part, since he did not know that the land was actually owned by Cholmondeley and that Ashton and Rogerson were merely under-tenants. In the Cholmondeley family records there survives the evidence of what actually took place:

> ... Bargain and sale by Sir Hugh Cholmondeley to Hugh Dod of Chester, gentleman, of ... 2 meadows called the Long Meadows, formerly of the dissolved Monastery of St Worburgh, in Moston near Backford ... Signed and sealed Hugh Dod 19 Jan 41 Eliz. [1599].[16]

Shortly after this – we do not know exactly when – the lands purchased by Dod were conveyed to John Morgell of Chester. This did not of course include the relatively small part of Moston which remained in Glasier hands and never became part of the Moston estate. Morgell's acquisition of these 240 acres in Moston circa 1601 may be said to mark the beginning of the Moston Hall estate as it existed into the twentieth century. And the fact that he had an interest in Moston should not be met with too much surprise, since he was actually related to Hugh Dod through marriage.

The Morgells at Moston Hall 1601–1718

John Morgell (c.1549–1636), alias Morgan, was descended from an old Warwickshire family and entered Gray's Inn in 1569.[17] We do not know exactly when he arrived in Chester, but his name appears in legal proceedings connected with the diocese at least as early as February 1586, when he witnessed the ratification of the infant marriage of Joan, only child of William Chaderton Bishop of Chester, to Richard Brooke of Norton Priory, on their 'having reached the age of discretion' (12 and 15 years of age respectively).[18] In 1598 or thereabouts, he was appointed Registrar of the diocese, a key position which he held for the remainder of his life.

In 1588 he married Margery, daughter of William Dod of Chester who was a younger son of the Dod family of Edge. Margery was already a young widow. The marriage entry in the register of St Oswald's, Chester, reads:

> [1587/8] John Morguile & Margerie Pecocke, Jany. 14.

Margery's first husband, Richard Peacock of Nether Whitley (Great Budworth), had died the previous March.[19] The Morgell pedigree names six children born to John and Margery, the eldest being Ralph (b.1588/9), who with three younger brothers Edward, William and Thomas survived into adulthood. Morgell also had a natural son James 'to whom he gave 60 shillings per annum out of his office'.[20] But the pedigree fails to mention a daughter Elizabeth whose marriage 1 January 1623 is recorded in St Oswald's register. Margery Morgell died 8 December 1598 at the age of 43 (possibly giving birth to their last child) and was buried in the south transept of Chester cathedral, where her husband placed a memorial that was noted by William Webb circa 1623:

> Perpetuæ pietati sacrum Margaretæ Dod ... Johann. Morgel generos. Diocesios Cestren. regar. Principalis, uxori charissimæ mœstissimus posuit.

> In perpetual gratitude for Margery Dod … the honourable John Morgell, Principal Registrar of the Diocese of Chester, filled with sorrow for his most beloved wife, has erected this sacred [monument].[21]

There is no firm evidence that a substantial residence already existed at Moston when John Morgell purchased the estate. The Backford church registers record a handful of burials of persons 'of Moston' between 1591 and 1595 who may well have been cottagers working the land and living in isolated dwellings or more possibly in a hamlet on or near the site of the future hall. Whatever the case, it looks as though John Morgell set about building the first Moston Hall as a country house befitting his family's rising status. In 1622/3 it was described in Webb's itinerary of the county:

> Next to Wirvin, upon the sand brook, is Moston, not long since purchased and beautified with a neat house of brick by Mr John Morgel register of the diocess of Chester.[22]

This first Hall was eventually taken down and replaced by another in the early nineteenth century, at which time Ormerod recollected that:

> It was a tall building, with a front terminating in five gables, and stood on a pleasant knoll, in the middle of a large ley for cattle, which occupies the greatest portion of the township.[23]

Before its dismantling, the hall was uniquely captured in a drawing by Chester artist John Musgrove dated 1810, which, if it is an accurate representation of what he saw, shows marked signs of Georgian restoration and alteration.

Morgell's interest in Moston appears to coincide with his involvement in an interparochial boundary dispute between Backford and St Mary on the Hill, Chester, the precise circumstances of which are unclear. Before the Dissolution, the parish of Backford belonged to Birkenhead Priory whereas St Mary on the Hill and various lands outside Chester, including Moston and part of neighbouring Chorlton, belonged to St Werburgh's Abbey. But for some reason, now lost to history, at some point after the Dissolution and the setting of the bishopric of Chester, Moston was (to quote Ormerod's subtle choice of words) 'conceived to form a part of the parish of Backford'.[24] However, in 1599 a claim was put forward by St Mary's that Moston belonged to it. This was initially discountenanced by the county sessions in July of that year. But St

Mary's continued to argue what one can only assume was a justifiable case, and in the end Moston was confirmed as a detached portion of the Chester parish. And so it remained (except for one brief period to which we shall come later) until 1882 when St Mary's chapel-of-ease established at Upton in the 1850s became an independent parish with Moston within its boundaries. In the midst of this earlier controversy, an entry appeared in the Backford church warden's book for 1603, which read (as quoted by Ormerod): 'Mr Morgell paid 10s for a church ley, and did acknowledge that in his opinion, Moston did belong to Backford.'[25] If that was indeed Morgell's opinion, clearly his influence was not brought to bear on the final outcome.

In 1606 Morgell's position as Principal Registrar of the diocese of Chester was officially secured, as were careers in the registry for his offspring. The details were noted a century or so later in bishop Francis Gastrell's *Notitiae Cestriensis*:

> An. 1606. A Patent was granted to Joh: Morgyll, for his own life and ye life of his two sons.
>
> An. 1630. Another Patent granted to John Morgyll, for ye lives of his three sons, before the sealing whereof he enters into Articles with the Bp. not to intermeddle wth the Deans Rurall or their Acts, or to do any thing in prejudice of ye said deans or their Registers.[26]

The 'two sons' were Ralph and Edward; the third, included in 1630, was William, who entered Gray's Inn in 1614 and remained there, setting up his own chambers, so never actually returned to work in Chester. It is Edward's name that features most prominently in the work of the diocesan registry during their father's lifetime. The following is an interesting example cited in connection with a diocesan visitation to Furness:

> Proceedings of the court held [24 March 1622] for Furness Deanery at Cartmel parish church, before Thos. Stafford LLB, commissary of John Bridgeman bishop of Chester, and in the presence of Edward Morgell, notary public. Concerning four persons who 'disguised themselves in womens habitt for the keeping of a sumeringe at Hawkshead'.[27]

Edward lived near the cathedral in Chester. He predeceased his father in March 1634 and was buried in the cathedral. John Morgell himself died at Moston Hall on 27 November 1636 and was buried in the family vault in St Oswald's, Backford. Moston was inherited by his eldest son and heir, Ralph, then 47 years old.

Ralph also succeeded his father as principal registrar, and continued in office until his death in 1678. His position was reconfirmed in 1662:

> An. 1662. A Patent for principall Regis. was granted to Ralph Morgyll, Jere. Fuller and J. Tibbols for their lives ...[28]

The Civil War and Commonwealth period had meanwhile intervened. The Morgell family remained staunch Royalists and were amongst the closest supporters of Bishop Bridgeman in August 1642 when he headed up a group of city leaders in taking Chester for the king. When Bridgeman was expelled the following year the diocesan infrastructure ceased to function, the Registry included, for nineteen years, until after the Restoration of the Monarchy. Amazingly Ralph Morgell senior was still there to set things in motion again as far as the Registry was concerned.

Ralph himself, two of his sons and a nephew all feature in the local accounts of the Civil War. In December 1643 Ralph was involved in the relief of Hawarden Castle that had been taken by the Parliamentarians, as noted in the city council records:

> At a council holden at the council-chamber within his Majestys Castle at Chester this first daye of December 1643, we whose names are hereunto subscribed ... [have] hereby ordered, that on the morrow, by the break of day, 300 citizens and train-bands, together with their proper officers, and the companies of captains Thropp and Morgell, do march to the assistance of the King's forces now at Hawarden.[29]

The reinforcement duly arrived at Hawarden, mounted an attack on the castle the next day and early in the morning of 4 December the Parliamentarian garrison surrendered. Subsequently Morgell and Thropp, both aldermen of Chester, were formally issued with their commissions by the king at Oxford, 27 May 1644.

In 1645, during the siege of Chester, Ralph's eldest son Henry was the subject of a prisoner exchange, recorded in a letter sent to Cheshire Parliamentarian leader Sir William Brereton by the Royalist governor of Chester, Lord Byron, on 1 Nov 1645:

> Know I am content to exchange Jas. Gerard, prisoner in Chester,

> for Hen. Morgell prisoner in Tarvin; and on sight of Morgell at Chester discharged, Gerard shall forthwith be set at liberty.[30]

Six days later, Henry's younger brother Edward – both men carried the rank of lieutenant – was killed while on guard near the Wolfgate.[31]

At the beginning of February 1646, Ralph[32] Morgell was one of six Chester city commissioners who refused to surrender and sign the treaty between Byron and Brereton.

Ralph's nephew, another Edward (son of Edward the registrar who died in 1633) compounded 'for delinquency in bearing arms against Parliament' on 30 March 1646.[33] He was fined £100. A year later he still owed £80 and his estate at Little Christleton was to be sequestered in the event of non-payment. On 15 November 1650, £20 was still being sought from him.[34]

Ralph's brother William Morgell of Gray's Inn, London, was assessed at £200 on 14 August 1644, following an Order in Parliament to dispose of the chambers in the Inns of Court belonging to delinquents. However, he was eventually discharged from the sequestration (ordered on false information that he was in arms against Parliament in Cheshire) on account of the fact that he was 'now living privately in co. Bucks, and it is deposed he has not been in arms and that he opposed the Commissioners of Array'.[35]

How Moston Hall itself fared during the Civil War we do not know. Upton Hall, adjacent to the Moston estate, was taken and occupied by the Parliamentary forces,[36] and they laid waste nearby Bache Hall.[37] But with no evidence to the contrary it would appear that Moston itself emerged unscathed and life returned to normality after the Restoration.

However, 'normality' may also have had less fortunate repercussions, at least as far as the parish of Backford's interest in Moston was concerned. The question of the parish boundary had come up again during the Commonwealth period. Commissioners were appointed to survey parish boundaries across England and Wales in the interests of 'the better maintenance and encouragement of ministers'. This provided a new opportunity for Backford parish and the inhabitants of Moston (and the half of Chorlton that was still in St Mary's parish) to petition for a boundary change, if they were to be sufficiently endowed to support a minister. After due consideration and consultation with all the parties involved, on 22 May 1656 'His Highnes and the Councell (ie. the Lord Protector and his Privy Council) [did] approve thereof and confirme the same.' A week later a deed was drawn up detailing the arrangements:

> Whereas the rectory of Maryes in Chester is of the yearely vallue of 100[51] ... [while] the parish of Backford [is] of the yearely vallue of 39[51] ... and whereas the moiety of the towneshippe of Charlton and the towneshippe of Moston are within the parish of Maryes in Chester and [are] above 2 miles distant from the parish church of Maryes and within one quarter of a mile of the parish church of Backford, and the tythes of the said rectory of Maryes arising from Moston and moyety of Charlton are of the yearely vallue of 11[51] and noe more, and the said towneshippe may with convenience bee divided from the said parish of Maryes and united to the said parish of Backford as by a survey thereof taken by virtue of a commission under the Great Seale of England in pursuance of an Act ... and Ordinance of his Highness the Lord Protector for the better maintenance and encouragement of Preaching Ministers ...
>
> ... now and upon consideracon had of the peticon of the inhabitants of ... Backford ... Moston ... Charlton ... and hearing parties on both sides therein, wee thinke fit and accordingly order by and with the approbacon of his Highness ... signified [to us on] 22 May ... that the said towneshippe of Moston and halfe towneshippe of Charlton
>
> from henceforth be severed and divided from ... St Maryes and .. be consolidated and united with ... Backford ... and that the same be held and enjoyed by the minister and incumbent of Backford for his better maintenance and livelyhood according to the purport, true intent and meaning of the said Act and Ordinance.[38]

Two months later, on 1 August 1656, the Trustees appointed John Wilson, a graduate of Brasenose College, Oxford, as minister of Backford, with the instruction that the yearly sum of fifty pounds (£39 + £11) be granted for his maintenance out of the tithes and profits of the augmented benefice.[39] Consequent on the Restoration of Charles II, the scholarly Wilson was ejected from his living in 1662 for refusing to assent to the Act of Uniformity, and he retired to Chester where he acquired a considerable following as a Dissenting minister and devoted himself to writing until his death in 1672. Meanwhile, Moston found itself back in the parish of St Mary on the Hill, quite when and how we do not know. But despite this turn of events, Moston's unofficial bond with Backford was set to continue.

The Backford church registers, as most others, are incomplete for the Civil War and Commonwealth period. We can only guess that Ralph's son and heir Henry Morgell died and may have been buried there sometime before 1660. But in 1686 the burial of Henry's widow was recorded thus: 'Mrs Cath. Morgan, Widow, of Moston, buried' – evidence perhaps that the Morgan alias had not ceased to be used.

Preserved on the wall of the nave of Backford church are six splendid painted memorial boards,[40] three of which are Morgell monuments. The earliest, inscribed in Latin, is to Ralph Morgell's wife Margaret who died in 1627 after bearing him at least eight children. The other two record:

> Raph Morgell of Moston ... Esq ... Registrar of ye consistory court of Chester ... He died ye 14 january 1678 aged 56 yeares. He left ye poor of Backford 10^{50} ye use of it to be given in bread yearely for ever. Blessed are ye charitable.
>
> Rafe Morgall gent. & Eliz. his wife, who had issue Rafe William & Elizabeth Morgall. He died Nov. ye 27 1683 she died May ye 9th 1683. They gave five pounds to ye parish of Backford ye use of it to be given to ye poore on good friday in money for ever.

The age of Ralph senior is grossly incorrect. It was probably intended to be written as 86, though he was in fact 88 or 89 when he died.

The three children mentioned in the third memorial were the fifth and last generation of Morgells to live at Moston. Their mother was only 25 years old when she died, and six months later the children were orphaned whilst still infants. For three years, no doubt, their grandmother Catherine held the reins, until her death. Ralph, who was heir to the Moston estate, died in childhood, and William died unmarried in 1708, leaving their younger sister Elizabeth the sole heiress. She eventually found herself a suitable husband in the person of Henry Bennet of Chester whom she married circa 1715/16 and they lived at the Bennet residence in the parish of Holy Trinity in the centre of Chester. In 1718 she apparently sold (or leased?) Moston Hall to Methusalem Jones of Underdale, near Shrewsbury.[41] However, four years later, in 1722, it was back with the Bennets.[42]

The Bennets at Moston Hall 1722–1789

Henry Bennet was baptised 12 September 1686 at Holy Trinity, Chester. His was a long established family of Chester merchants actively involved in the affairs of the city. Henry's father, also Henry, had served as a sheriff of the city in 1681 and was mayor in 1698.[43] The son followed in his father's footsteps, becoming a sheriff of Chester in 1709 and serving as mayor in 1716,[44] about the year of his marriage to Elizabeth Morgell.

The first six children of their marriage, of whom three died in infancy, were all baptised at Holy Trinity Church: Elizabeth in 1716, Sarah 1717 (died), Jane 1718 (died), Sarah 1719, Henry 1721 (died) and Jane 1723. In 1722 the family 're-acquired' Moston Hall, and presumably settled there shortly afterwards. The next child, Ann, born in 1728, was baptised at St Mary on the Hill, the 'official' parish church of Moston. Their last child, Mary, born in 1730, was baptised at St Oswald's Backford – a familiar progression in the light of what the Morgells had elected to do the previous century. The Bennets also rented a family pew at Backford.[45]

In 1734 Bennet served as sheriff of the county of Cheshire.[46] He died in 1741, in his mid-fifties, and was honoured with a memorial in St Peter's church at the very hub of Chester's commercial and political life:

> a citizen who did honour to this city,
> a merchant who improved and extended its commerce,
> a magistrate who ruled it with dignity and justice;
> a lover of his country and a friend to mankind.[47]

Bennet's five surviving daughters were the co-heiresses of the Moston estate. The eldest, Elizabeth, married the prominent Welsh judge, John Williams (1700–87) of Bodelwyddan Hall, Denbighshire. The two youngest, Ann and Mary, both married in 1760: Ann to John Townshend of Hem House, Denbighsire and Mary to his cousin Sir Ellis Cunliffe who was MP for Liverpool and in 1759 was created 1st Baronet Cunliffe of Liverpool. Sisters Sarah and Jane remained unmarried and lived on at Moston. After Sarah died in the mid-1780s, it was decided that the estate should be sold. This happened in 1789, although it appears from her will signed at Moston in 1800 that Jane was provided with accommodation there for her remaining years.

The Masseys at Moston Hall 1789–1871

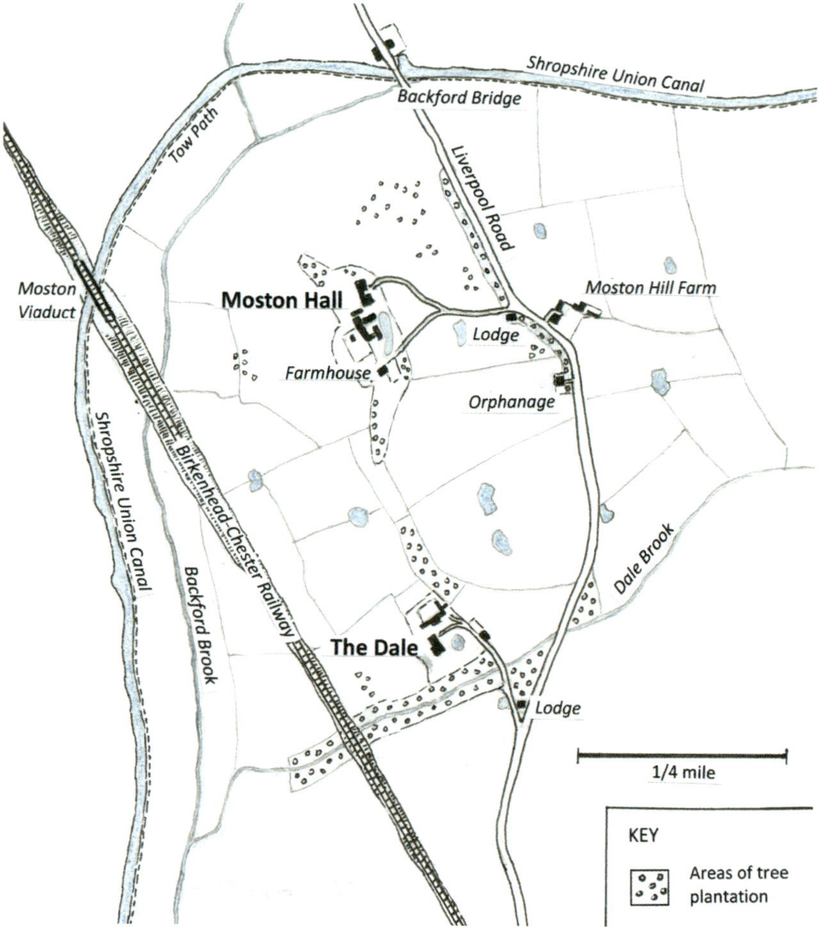

Moston Hall in 1810, drawn and etched by John Musgrove of Chester. Reproduced by courtesy of the descendants of William Massey of Cornelyn, Anglesey and Oriel Ynys Môn

Richard Massey and his wife Eleanor. (Courtesy of the Massey family archives, Oriel Ynys Môn, Anglesey)

The purchaser of Moston Hall in 1789 was William Massey, a Chester attorney. Details are sparse with regard to Massey's life before 1789, but he is almost certainly the William Massey born in 1740, a younger son of Richard Massey (Massie) of Coddington, in which case his mother's Denbighshire family was connected through marriage to the Williams and Townshend families. So there was a link of sorts which perhaps explains why Jane Bennet was able to see her years out at Moston.

In Chester, Massey had a substantial town house in Northgate Street. He appears not to have married, and Ormerod's pedigree of Massie of Coddington states unequivocally that he died without issue. However, he did have a natural son, Richard, who is identified by Ormerod as the heir of the Moston estate. And Massey's will, drawn up in 1803, also names a natural daughter, and two mistresses neither of whom were mothers of either Richard or his half-sister.[48] Richard Massey's inheritance was to be considerably more than what his father had purchased in 1789, for in the 1790s William Massey added almost a hundred more acres to the estate. Significantly this included some 33 acres purchased in 1791 from Roger Barnston (1749–1837) of Chester, which some years later was to become the desired location of a new house, The Dale.[49]

During the last decade of the eighteenth century and the beginning of the next, Massey probably undertook some major renovation and improvement work on the old house which may account for a number of Georgian features that appear in the 1810 drawing. The designing and landscaping of the gardens almost certainly dates from this time, since in his will drawn up in 1803 Massey requested that the house, buildings, gardens, plantations and pleasure gardens 'all be kept in good order'.[50]

Massey was quite a sporting gentleman. In 1802 he appeared on the card for the Chester Races riding in sweepstakes against such eminent persons as Lord Grey, Lord Camelford, Sir William Watkins Wynn and Sir Thomas Mostyn.

The Massey sisters. (Courtesy of the Massey family archives, Oriel Ynys Môn, Anglesey)

The greatest impact on Moston Hall during this period was undoubtedly the construction and opening of the Wirral section of the Ellesmere Canal running between Chester and the Mersey at Netherpool (Ellesmere Port). The canal company first met in 1791, obtained Parliament's approval for their plans in 1793, and the canal was completed and operating by 1796. It closely skirted the Moston estate to the west and north, following the low level contours of the Deva spillway already coursed by the Backford brook. At the north it touched, but nowhere passed through the estate boundary. The Moston land was intact and its privacy preserved, but from the raised knoll on which the hall was set, its residents will have seen cargo-carrying flat-boats and busy passenger craft passing by.

Shortly after the opening of the canal, Massey purchased a 16 acre strip of land in the townships of Lea and Backford which had ended up on his side of the water. Then some twenty years later his successor incorporated a 4-acre strip along the Upton boundary to develop the Dale plantation and provide a lodge house at the southerly approach to the estate. With these acquisitions the Moston estate reached its largest expanse.

William Massey died in 1806 and was buried in the family vault at Coddington, leaving Moston Hall and other property to his natural son,

Richard (b.1890). In about 1815 Richard Massey set about building a new hall and dismantling the old house: in 1816/17 Ormerod noted the house built by Morgell 'has been recently taken down'.[51] The nucleus of the present Moston Hall must have been completed by about 1820, as John Hanshall wrote in his *History of Cheshire*: 'The old hall of Moston was taken down about five years ago ... A small house has lately been built on its site by the present proprietor.'[52]

The relative quiet of life at Moston must have been disrupted by the arrival of the railway. The Chester and Birkenhead Railway Company was incorporated in 1837 and its proposed line was approved by Parliament later that year. The route lay across fields in the western part of the Moston estate, passing within 500 yards of the hall, and Richard Massey will have been well compensated for the 8 acres of land lost, if not for the 38 or so acres between the railway and the Backford brook isolated from the rest of the estate. Where the line crossed the valley through which the canal and Backford brook ran, this necessitated the major construction of the Moston Viaduct. The line was officially opened on 23 September 1840 and undoubtedly the residents of Moston observed the locomotive 'Wirral' making its first journey from Birkenhead to Chester.

In 1816 Richard Massey had married Eleanor (b.1795), daughter of Abraham and Mary Ball, at Holy Trinity, Chester. The family they brought up at Moston Hall included William (born 1817), Eleanor (1819), John (1821), James (1823) and Maria (1825). The Hall was staffed by half-a-dozen servants, including a housekeeper, lady's maid, house-maid, footman and groom. Moston Hall Farm, housing a farm manager and his family was built some 200 yards south of the main house, with a large variety of brick barns and other outbuildings stretching back towards the hall's stabling and coach houses. A lodge was built at the southern approach to the estate, on the main road leading to and from Chester.

At the time of the 1851 Census a total of 14 persons were resident within the township of Moston, the Massey family accounting for 5, plus 7 servants at the hall, and farmer John Bellis and his wife at the farmhouse. At the lodge (in Upton township) was Moses Lancely 'keeper of game' with his wife and 7 children, their eldest boy working on the farm. The Lancely family were already living at the lodge in 1841, but by 1861 they had progressed to the farmhouse.

The Masseys' eldest son William (1817–1898) was educated at Harrow and matriculated at Cambridge in 1835. He excelled as a sportsman, in the university cricket team 1837–39 and the MCC 1839–42, and rowed for Cambridge in the winning boat race crew in 1840. In 1841 he was admitted to Lincoln's Inn and was called to the bar in 1850. Later the same year he married a distant cousin, Margaret Henrietta Maria Massey (1826–1899) daughter of the late William Massey (d.1838), barrister, of Poole Hall near Nantwich.[53] The marriage took place at St Mary's Acton, and the couple initially set up home in Paddington, London. His mother-in-law, Mary Massey, lived with them.

She (Mary Massey) was the only daughter and heiress of John Goodman of Plas Porthamel, Anglesey, and her Anglesey property was a welcome retreat for the family. A year or so before she died, William and Henrietta decided to make Anglesey their permanent home, moving initially to Porthamel, then using their resources to build a grander house, Cornelyn, near Beaumaris. Their four children were born at Cornelyn: sons William Glynne in 1858 and Francis in 1860, and daughters Edith in 1862 and Gwenddolen in 1864, in which year William Massey was appointed High Sheriff of the County of Anglesey. The sons pursued army careers; and the girls, who with brother William Glynne remained unmarried, became well-known as 'The Massey Sisters' for their collecting and painting some 500 specimens of the flora of Anglesey.[54]

Returning to the Masseys at Moston Hall, of Richard and Eleanor's other children, John appears to have remained at home helping to manage the estate, whilst James pursued a career in the army. The two girls also remained at Moston. Maria, the youngest of the family, died in 1848 at the age of 22. Richard Massey himself died in 1861 and his wife Eleanor in 1869. The two sons John and James died in 1862 and 1870 respectively. All were buried in the Massey family grave at Backford churchyard.

Moston Hall in 1871

With brother William settled permanently in Anglesey, in 1871 Eleanor Massey junior was the only surviving member of the family living at Moston, with an estate increasingly difficult to manage. She sold the 50 acres of farmland across the Liverpool Road to Edward Holt Glegg of

Backford Hall who set it up as Moston Hill Farm, and decided to lease the hall itself. From an advertisement placed in the *Liverpool Mercury* 23 October 1871 we get a good description of Moston Hall and its outbuildings at the time:

> CHESTER – MOSTON HALL. To be Let, Furnished, This most desirable Family Mansion, standing on its own grounds, about two miles from Chester. It contains an excellent entrance hall, 26 feet by 18 feet; drawing room, 31 feet by 20 feet; two sitting rooms, one 17 feet by 16 feet, the other 22 feet by 15 feet; housekeeper's room, kitchens, sculleries, &c; twelve best bed and dressing rooms, nine servants' rooms. The outbuildings consist of two six-stalled stables, four loose boxes, saddle rooms, coach houses, &c. Very good gardens, with conservatories and vineries. An abundant supply of excellent water. For further particulars and cards to view apply to Messrs, Brown and Lamont, upholsterers, Chester.

We do not know the exact history of the Moston gardens. They certainly existed in the early days of Massey ownership, as evidenced in William Massey's will of 1803, and they were clearly flourishing when the property was advertised in 1871. The view from the hall was over lawns edged by flower borders and shrubs. In one corner stood a large cedar of Lebanon. Beyond the lawn, at a slightly lower level, was a tennis court with a sandstone pavilion, and to the north of this was an enclosed sunken woodland grotto with meandering paths.

There was also a large walled kitchen garden. Against its interior northern wall was a lean-to glasshouse some 30 feet in length with hot water pipes heated by a coal-fired boiler situated outside the wall. There was another greenhouse, freestanding, about 45x24 feet. The rest of the walled garden was divided into plots separated by paths and low box hedges, for vegetables and salads. Against the walls were apple and pear espaliers. Outside the walled area was a traditional outer or 'slip' garden providing space for more vegetables, with cold frames and small heated frames with their own coal-fired boilers.

Stretching beyond, and completing the pleasure gardens, were woodlands with paths for family and visitors alike to enjoy, walking or riding. Many of these features, including the walled garden, still existed in the 1950s.

The Dale, built by Eleanor Massey in 1874. Photograph ca. 1940 in collection of the Cheshire Regimental Museum and used with permission.

Moston Hall and The Dale 1871–1938

Shortly after the advertisement was placed, an offer to purchase was received and accepted. The buyer was Captain James Swetenham of the Hermitage, Cranage, near Holmes Chapel. Swetenham had served with the Buffs Regiment in India and was now Adjutant of the Cheshire Rifle Volunteers, and he and his family took up residence at the hall.

Rather less than a quarter of the original estate, basically the south-western portion, was retained by the Masseys, and Eleanor built herself a fine house in the upper field above the Dale, naming it appropriately 'The Dale'. She kept the original lodge house and former entrance drive to Moston Hall as her access to the main road, while a new entrance lodge and drive had been provided for the hall itself.

At The Dale, Eleanor managed to retain a measure of the former grandeur of life at the hall, her retinue of servants still including a coachman and footman, and the 'Bothie' in the garden housing a couple of lads to maintain the grounds. She also preserved the memory of her family by installing a large stained glass window on the north wall of the nave of Backford Church, overlooking the family grave, in 1896. Inscribed on it are the names of her parents and her deceased siblings Maria, John and James. She also donated an oak desk to the church for the purpose of securing and displaying Backford's 1617 chained Bible.[55] Earlier, in 1868, Eleanor and her mother had donated a brass eagle lectern to Holy

Trinity Church, Chester in memory of her grandparents Abraham and Mary Ball.[56]

Eleanor died in 1902 and her nephew and executor William Glynne Massey finally disposed of the family's remaining property at Moston. He sold the 38 acre strip of farmland between the railway line and Backford brook to Chester City Council. The Dale and its grounds were bought by Reginald Potts who moved there from The Oaks, at what is now Upton Golf Club.

Meanwhile Moston Hall itself remained in the possession of the Swetenham family. James Swetenham died at Moston in December 1891, age 66, a notice to that effect appearing in *The Western Mail* 15 December. Shortly before that his wife Esther planned and built a little cottage orphanage on the Liverpool Road just a few yards south of the entrance lodge. Run by Miss Gatt, a lady from Sunderland, and a female assistant, this catered for about ten girls between the ages of five and fourteen: some from the local area and others from as far afield as London, Bury St Edmunds, Cardiff, and Dublin.[57] By 1911 Miss Gatt had removed to Bedfordshire and the cottage ceased to function as an orphanage, although it retained that description until it became 'Parkholm' under new ownership in 1920.[58] In that year, Esther Swetenham, then in her eighties, sold Moston Hall to Edwin Ramsay Moodie (1868–1954), a captain

Present Moston Hall, begun by Richard Massey in 1817 and added to during the 19th Century. (1930 photograph in the possession of the author)

with the Cunard Line Shipping Company who on occasion was at the helm of the Mauretania, and she moved into Chester where she died in 1922.

Research still needs to be done on Moston in the three decades preceding the Second World War. According to Kelly's Directories of Cheshire, Moston Hall was still in the ownership of Moodie in 1923, but by 1928 was sold on to George Gordon Lockett. The Locketts were there until it ceased to be in private ownership.

Moston estates purchased by the War Office 1938–40

On 19 October 1938 The Dale was conveyed to the Secretary of State for War for £11,000, and on 1 January 1940 the Moston Hall estate was also acquired by the War Office, for £19,000. Having come once again under single ownership, the area was re-allocated for two distinct military purposes and establishments: the Dale Camp and the Moston Military Hospital.

The Dale Camp

Taking its name from The Dale, in September 1940 the Dale Camp became the home of the Cheshire Regiment which moved there from its former garrison in Chester Castle. The house became the officers' mess. New roads were laid out and new buildings went up, mostly single storey wooden huts and a few Nissen huts. Two-storied brick buildings included the Sandhurst block, providing accommodation and cooking facilities, a large gymnasium, Guard Room cum offices, and some married quarters.

A cricket field, football pitches and running track were laid out. This, together with the retention of some woodland and original fields, meant that the valuable sense of space that had formerly characterised the estate was not immediately lost. The gardens and fields indeed played a significant part in the agricultural and horticultural war effort by producing thousands of pounds' worth of food stuff.[59]

Female members of the ATS (Auxiliary Territorial Service) exercised an important role in the early days of the Dale Camp, as clerks, telephone operators, mess orderlies and so on. Although originally quartered in the Sandhurst block, they were soon re-housed in nearby huts which it was suggested should be fenced off with barbed wire. Apparently Lt Col B.Y. Hayes-Newington, as he then was, demurred at this proposal as it implied that the fence was deemed necessary to keep his soldiers away from the ATS. But he eventually agreed on the understanding that the purpose of the fence was to keep the ATS in their huts![60]

For the ordinary soldier life was marked with a series of bugle calls from reveille to last post, interspersed with drill on the squares, tackling the obstacle course, and rifle and machine-guns practice on the range. In the officers' mess things may have been more peaceful, but not without peril, for the junior subalterns. At dinner, proposing a toast to 'the King' instead of 'His Majesty the King', or sending the port in the wrong direction, could incur an instant fine of five shillings.[61]

On the northern fringe of the camp, looking towards Backford and Lea across meadows and the canal, but almost completely hidden, was a pillbox outlook-post: not the normal concrete construction but the rarer Allan-Williams turret which was dome-shaped, made of steel, and revolved over a circular pit. All traces of it have now disappeared.

It would take a separate essay to list all the changes that have occurred at the Dale Camp, or list the many regiments who have succeeded the Cheshires there over the years down to the present day. Since the Ministry of Defence was created in 1946 and the functions of the War Office were transferred to it in 1963, it has been MOD property. New roads and married quarters have been added, old buildings replaced, while the original woodland and open spaces of the old estate have virtually disappeared.

The Military Hospital and the Deva Hospital Annexe

Built at the same time as the Camp, the military hospital on the eastern side of the estate adjoined the Liverpool Road and included Moston Hall itself. Apart from two or three new brick structures the rest of the buildings, including all the wards, were single-storey wooden huts. The medical staff comprised officers and orderlies of the Royal Army Medical Corps together with members of the QAs (Queen Alexandra's Imperial Military Nursing Service, in 1949 renamed the Queen

Alexandra's Royal Army Nursing Corps). The matron and other senior staff resided in the Hall.

Patients, being treated for wounds received on active service and for general sicknesses, would often arrive at the hospital in convoys of ambulances and other military vehicles. They were then given blue uniforms to wear. For recreation there was a library, and the Army Kinema Corporation (AKC) provided a weekly film show. In the early years, German and Italian prisoners of war would be seen, escorted, working in the grounds.

By 1961 the military hospital had closed down and most of the site was transferred from the MOD to the Ministry of Health and became

Moston Hall, front 2009

Moston Hall, rear 2009

The Sunken Garden in 2009. Photographs of Moston Hall and garden by courtesy of 1st Battalion The Royal Welsh

The Dale Entrance, 2010

Entrance to the Dale Barracks, 2010.

the Moston annexe of the Deva Hospital at Upton (the former Upton Mental Hospital). The wooden-hut wards were updated and converted for use mainly as a 'no locked doors' mental health unit. There was accommodation for some 370 beds and mixed-sex wards were introduced.[62] The hospital also incorporated a school of nursing. This unit was gradually phased out with the development of the West Cheshire / Countess of Chester Hospital on a new site in the late 1970s.

Moston today

With the final closure of the hospital in 1982, the property was transferred back to the Ministry of Defence and incorporated into what is now The Dale Barracks. It is presently the home of the 1st Battalion Royal Welsh (Royal Welch Fusiliers).

Today no traces remain of The Dale house, demolished and replaced by modern housing, although the layout of the streets to some extent follows some ancient features such as the original entrance drive to the old hall. Now even the original barracks have been largely replaced by more modern buildings. Some of the early married quarters have been sold off and are now privately owned.

Moston Hall itself still stands, enlarged and slightly modified, and is used as the officers' mess by the present battalion. The lawned area still exists to the garden front of the hall, together with the tennis court and the remains of the sunken wooded grotto. The former walled gardens and rest of the pleasure gardens have been built upon, and there are no traces of the old stables, farm or other buildings associated with the hall. The nineteenth century entrances to Moston Hall and The Dale can still be identified on the Liverpool Road.

On the eastern edge of the site are the Fox Barracks, housing the Territorial Army C (Cheshire Yeomanry) Squadron, the Royal Mercian and Lancastrian Yeomanry. It is also the headquarters of the Cheshire Army Cadet Force.

Today the former country estate of Moston Hall with its gardens is all but forgotten. Yet it exists in a different form, and is known by a name that originally came from just one corner of the estate – the Dale.

References

1. Latin transcription in Ormerod, G. *The History of the County Palatine and City of Chester* (Helsby edition, 1882) vol.1, p.19. English translation by Tony Foster.
2. British Library Harley MSS 1965, folio 29. Also see Ormerod, vol.1, p.282 and vol.2, p.546.
3. Ormerod, op.cit., vol.2, p.818.
4. The Plea is fully transcribed in Ormerod, vol.1, p.285–288.
5. Thacker, A.T. and Lewis, C.P. (ed) *Victoria County History: A History of the County of Chester*, vol.5, part 2 (2005) p.107.
6. Transcribed in Ormerod, vol.1, p.274.
7. Burne, R.V.H. *Chester Cathedral: from its founding by Henry VIII to the accession of Queen Victoria* (London 1958) p.24–26, 72–82.
8. Burne, p.24 (quoting Ormerod, vol.1, p.254).
9. Burne, p.79.
10. Transcribed in Ormerod, vol.1, p.289.
11. ibid., p.288–289.
12. ibid., p.290.
13. Harley MS 2071, folio 146 (quoted in Burne, p.79).
14. ibid, folio 147.
15. Ormerod, vol.2, p.818.
16. Cheshire Archives: DCH (Cholmondeley of Cholmondeley)/A/176 and 182.
17. Foster, J. (ed) *The Register of Admissions to Gray's Inn, 1521–1889* (London 1889), col.42: admissions for 1569, listed on folio 615 of the original register.
18. Chetham Society, vol.31 (1853) p.136.
19. Parish Registers of Great Budworth (Richard was buried 8 March 1586/7).
20. Earwaker, J.P. *The History of the Church and Parish of St Mary-on-the-Hill, Chester* (London 1898) p.277 (Morgell pedigree).
21. Full Latin transcription in Ormerod, vol.1, p.195 (the memorial had disappeared by Ormerod's time: vol.1, p.297). Note that the name Margery correctly transposes to 'Margareta' in Latin. English translation by Tony Foster.
22. Published in Daniel King's *Vale Royal of England* (London 1656).
23. Ormerod, vol.2, p.818.
24. Ormerod, vol.2, p.362.
25. Cheshire Archives: P32/1/1 (Backford parish registers) folio 46.

26. Gastrell, F. *Notitia Cestriensis* (part 1) ed. F.R. Raines. Chetham Society, vol.8 (1845) p.24.
27. Cited in George, D. (ed) *Records of Early English Drama: Lancashire* (Toronto 1991) p.26.
28. Gastrell, p.24.
29. As transcribed in Poole. J. *The History of Cheshire* (Chester 1778) p.550–551.
30. Dore, R.N. (ed) *The Letter Books of Sir William Brereton*, vol.2 (Record Society of Lancashire and Cheshire, vol.128, 1990) p.201.
31. *Journal of the Architectural, Archaeological and Historic Society for Chester and North Wales*, vol. ... (1921) p.246.
32. His name appeared incorrectly as Richard Morgell in Poole's 1778 *History of Cheshire,* and was subsequently taken as such by Hanshall, Hemingway et al, following Poole.
33. Green, M.A.E. (ed) *Calendar of the Proceedings of the Committee for Compounding with Delinquents: Part 2, 1643–1660* (London 1890) p.1159.
34. Green, M.A.E. (ed) *Calendar of the Proceedings of the Committee for Advance of Money* (London 1888), vol.2, p.813.
35. ibid, vol.1, p.404.
36. Ormerod (1882) vol.2, p.820.
37. Ibid, p.776.
38. Minutes of the Trustees for the Maintenance of Ministers, 22 May and 29 May 1656, in the Lambeth Palace Library Records of the Church of England during the Commonwealth Period, catalogued under COMM.XII.c (Registers of the union and division of parishes 1655–59). The passage quoted here and the other minutes relating to the Backford boundary issue are fully transcribed in *Lancashire and Cheshire Record Society*, vol.34 (1896) p.108, 113, 130, 132–4. See also *Calendar of State Papers Domestic 1655–56*, p.331.
39. *Lancashire and Cheshire Record Society* , vol.34, p.147.
40. For a detailed description of the boards see Hess, J.P. 'Backford's Memorial Boards' in *Cheshire History*, vol.47 (2007) p.34–39; reprinted in *Beneath the Surface* (Backford, Mollington and District Local History Society (2008) p.49–62. Inscriptions are fully transcribed in Ormerod (1882) vol.2, p.371–372.
41. Interestingly, Methusalem Jones was a very close acquaintance and 'brother in religion' of the Hunts of Boreatton, one of whom had purchased and settled at Mollington Hall in 1699, only a

stone's throw away from Moston Hall, which may partly explain the transaction.

42. Ormerod (1882) vol.2, p.818.
43. ibid, vol.1, p.215.
44. ibid.
45. Hess, J.P. *St Oswald's Church in the Parish of Backford* (1998) p.34.
46. ibid, p.73.
47. The full inscription is given in Ormerod, vol.1, p.323–324 (but note that Ormerod-Helsby has misprinted the date as 1747). The memorial is still in situ, but difficult to see, being high on the north wall and almost hidden between organ pipes and a modern partition wall.
48. Cheshire Archives: DBC 1102/1/1 (Probate and estate of William Massey, 1803/1812).
49. Cheshire Archives: D1301/4/1 (Barnston Deed dated 16 Dec 1791, relating to sale of land in Moston).
50. Cheshire Archives: WS 1803 William Massey of Moston Hall.
51. Ormerod, vol.2, p.818.
52. Hanshall, J.H. *The History of the County Palatine of Chester* (Chester 1823) p.323.
53. They shared a great-great-great grandfather, Roger Massie of Coddington.
54. Smith, J. And Lazarus, M. *The Wild flowers of Anglesey: collected and painted by Edith and Gwenddolen Massey* (Oriel Ynys Môn 2004).
55. Mentioned in Kelly's Directory of Cheshire, 1902, p.47.
56. Ormerod, vol.1, p.330.
57. Census returns for 1891 and 1901.
58. Cheshire Archives: ZRGC/33: Cheshire Poor Law Union valuation list for Moston 1909–21.
59. See Crookenden, A. *The History of the Cheshire Regiment in the Second World War* (1949).
60. Quoted in Lt Col Bertram Yorke Hayes-Newington's obituary in *The Oak Tree* magazine of the Cheshire Regiment, 1984.
61. Letter from a former serving officer, to the Cheshire Regimental Museum.
62. For more details of this hospital see Murphy, S. *The Best is Yet To Come* (2004).

This article, in a slightly different form, was originally prepared for publication in the journal, *Cheshire History,* volume 51, (2011–12) p.65–94, and is published here with the kind permission of the editor of *Cheshire History*.

Acknowledgement

I thank all who have helped me with this project. They include the Cheshire Military Museum, The 1st Battalion Royal Welsh (The Welch Fusiliers), the MOD Defence Estates Property Directorate, John Smith of Oriel Ynys Môn, Tony Foster for additional research and advice, including the maps, and Michael Richardson for his photography.

The Story of Gibbet Mill

By Michael Richardson

Soon after the formation of our Local History Society, we received a number of photographs which had come to light when old files were being discarded from a local solicitor's office; amongst them was one titled "Backford Windmill" (fig. 1). However, there is no evidence for there ever having been a windmill at Backford and efforts were made to establish exactly which mill was the subject of the photograph. The most likely candidate was thought to be Saughall (Gibbet) mill on the A540 Parkgate Road and the current occupants of the adjacent Mill Farm felt that the photograph was almost certainly of Gibbet Mill. This has been confirmed by comparison with a photograph taken in April 2003 (fig. 2) which shows the extra windows added when it was converted into a residence in the 1970s.

Although the mill is actually in Saughall parish it is of interest to us because of its connections with the Carter family who can be traced back to the 1600s in Mollington. Before considering their involvement with the mill it may be helpful to look at its earlier history. Burdett's map of Cheshire dated 1777[1] describes it as "A new Mill" but it may well have existed for some time before the date of the map as this also refers to "The New Channel" of the River Dee which had been constructed between 1732 and 1737, some 40 years before the date of the map.

Fig. 1 Backford Windmill.

It is therefore quite likely that the mill had been built before 1750 when it was the scene of an incident in August of that year when four Irish harvesters were

Fig. 2 Gibbet Mill April 2003

travelling to Parkgate on their way back to Ireland. At a spot some three miles from Chester, three of them attacked the fourth and killed him; after this some versions of the story have them drinking in either Saughall or Shotwick. They were caught and, before the assize trial, one of the murderers gave evidence against his companions, so that they were found guilty and hanged at Boughton in September. On the same day the two bodies were hung up from a gibbet made on an ash tree where the footpath that runs to the north of the mill meets the Parkgate Road and this has led to the name "Gibbet Mill" which endures to this day. Although different versions of this story have circulated for many years, it has been found that reports of the incident and of the trial appeared in *Adams's Weekly Courant* (which later became the *Chester Courant*) for 4th and 11th September 1750 and these reports are transcribed as an appendix to this chapter. Unfortunately the edition of 2nd October is not available so we don't have any reliable report of their execution and subsequent hanging from the gibbet near the mill.

Nothing more is known about the mill for almost 80 years, until an announcement in the *Chester Chronicle* of 25th April 1828 for an auction to be held at "Saughall Mill, on the Parkgate Road, 4 miles from Chester, on Friday 2nd May, of the whole of the outdoor stock &c &c, the property of Mr Joseph Whaley, who has left the mill". This was almost certainly the Joseph, son of Samuel and Margaret Whaley of Capenhurst, who was baptised at Shotwick on 22 April 1795.[2] He was recorded as a miller when he married Mary Smith at St Peter's Church in Liverpool in 1820[2] and their son Joseph was baptised at Shotwick on 23rd October 1823. After leaving the mill he seems to have returned to Liverpool, where he was recorded in the 1851 census as a widower living with his son Samuel and his second wife Eliza. Then, in March 1846, there was another auction of farming stock at the mill because "Mr Whaley ... is leaving the Mill" – could this have been one of Joseph Whaley's sons? It's rather odd as we know (see the next paragraph) that the miller at that time was James Ellison. Perhaps this can be explained by the fact that the mill and adjoining farm may have been managed independently of each other.

The tithe apportionments for Shotwick parish (1843)[3] record that the Rev Richard Richardson (of Capenhurst Hall) owned much of the land in the area; the mill and farmhouse, together with seven fields totalling approx 30 acres were occupied by James Ellison; two of the fields to the north of the mill are named as "Gibbett [*sic*] Field". Bagshaw's Directory for 1850 lists James Ellison, corn miller, Saughall Mills whilst the 1851 census names him as James Ellinson, and describes him as 'miller and farmer of 60 acres'; he had been born in Wavertree ca 1804. Ten years earlier the census recorded him as John Ellieasen, born in Scotland, though examination of other entries suggests that the enumerator had problems with his spelling as at least three variants of Margaret appear in the four pages covering Capenhurst township and the miller's daughter is listed as Ellieathebh, surely the most unusual spelling of Elizabeth ever seen !

White's Directory for 1860[4] lists Thomas Williams at Saughall Mill though the 1861 census records him as a farmer and the next entry includes James Caddick as a 'miller' (probably living at one of the mill cottages). Interestingly, that census entry gives the address as 'Gibbit Mills'. In the 1871 census Thomas is recorded as 'farmer and miller, 42 acres, 1 farm servant & 1 miller'; working for him was John Clark, a 'journeyman miller' who lived on Parkgate Road.

The next miller appears to have been William Urmston, who is listed in the 1878 Post Office Directory.[4] The 1881 census records him living at Capenhurst Old Hall with his parents while his assistant was probably Samuel Davies who was living with his parents on Parkgate Road and was listed as a 'miller' in the census. William Urmston and his parents are buried in Capenhurst churchyard and their gravestone records that William died on 29th April 1892 aged 52, and his parents John and Ellen in 1891 and 1878.

In the late 1880s, the mill appears to have passed to William Carter who is listed in Kelly's Directory[4] for 1892 and 1896 as 'miller (wind & steam), farmer & threshing machine owner'. The Carters lived at the eponymous "Carter's Farm" on Coalpit Lane, Mollington and an account of the history of the family can be found in our first volume of local history.[5] John Carter (1773–1838) and his family were there from about 1809 and after his death his eldest son John (1799–1875) continued to farm there while his second son William bought Upton Mill in 1839 and through marriage with the Dean family built it up into a large and thriving milling and baking business which eventually became part of Allied Bakeries. A younger son Robert was a baker and grocer in Saughall from the 1850s onwards.

William's son, also William (born in 1843), had served as a miller with his father in Upton and took over the Gibbet mill some time before 1891 as he is recorded as the miller in that year's census. A newspaper report of Shotwick Fête in 1888[6] records that the "attendance included … Mr & Mrs J Carter & party, Saughall Mill" and also mentions that William Carter of Saughall Mill was the treasurer. Apart from running the mill the Carters managed an active dairy farm and won prizes for their butter at the Cheshire Dairy Show during the 1890s.[7] The 1901 census records William as "threshing machine proprietor" while his son Horace was described as "miller". William died in 1912 and Horace married Emily Cash in 1913 and they had three children, Hilda (born 1914), Horace Noel (born 1916) and Emily (born 1920). Horace continued to operate the mill until the night of 29/30th October 1927 when a violent Atlantic storm swept across Britain, causing widespread damage in the Chester area. Although the mill machinery had been steam-powered for some twenty years or so the sails had been retained as a feature and with the force of the gale they had been set in motion.[8] The friction of the wooden brakes started a fire which spread to various parts of the mill. Because the telephone wires had been damaged in the gale, Horace Carter had to drive to Chester to raise the alarm, where there were further difficulties contacting sufficient crew to man the fire engine, which eventually arrived at the mill at about 3.30 a.m. The fire was brought under control and prevented from spreading to adjoining buildings, but the mill never operated again and Horace died suddenly a few months later, in January 1928; he had been on the council of the Vernon Institute in Saughall and had served on Great Saughall Parish Council for many years.[9] The family is buried at Capenhurst church; the gravestone (fig. 3) records their deaths:

Fig. 3 Grave of Horace Carter.

Horace died 25th Jan 1928 aged 52
Emily died 13th Oct 1949 aged 73.
Noel died 7th May 1992 aged 75
Lall Martin died 26th Sept 1994 aged 79

Fig. 4 Drawing of the mill by Bertha Moreton.

The mill was listed in 1952 for its special architectural and historic interest[10] and soon afterwards was sold by Noel Carter, together with the adjoining farmhouse, to Mr and Mrs James Jones, who ran it as a 55 acre dairy farm and called Saughall Mill Farm since then. By this time the mill had fallen into disrepair, as depicted in the 1957 drawing by Bertha Moreton (fig. 4) but Mr & Mrs Jones were unable to get planning permission to restore the mill and Chester Rural District Council said that it was not of sufficient historical interest to warrant repairs. In 1956, Norman Ellison ("Nomad" of the BBC programme *Wandering with Nomad*) visited the mill to enquire what was happening to this local historical landmark.[11]

Eventually, in 1960, Mrs Jones sold the mill with a small plot of land to Messrs James Parker & Son, a local building firm, who were successful in getting permission to convert the mill for residential use; the cost of strengthening the building and replacing the sails (almost £2000) was met by Chester RDC.[12] However, disaster struck again in 2004 when the sails were badly damaged in a gale and a company experienced in mill restoration was called in to carry out the making and fitting of the new sails.[13]

References

1. Early Cheshire Maps on www.cheshirehistory.org.uk.
2. Parish Registers, searchable on www.findmypast.co.uk.
3. Cheshire Tithe Maps, searchable on maps.cheshire.gov.uk/tithemaps.
4. Trade directories in Chester History & Heritage, St Michael's Centre, Bridge Street.
5. *Beneath the Surface*, Backford, Mollington & District Local History Society, 2008.
6. Cheshire Observer, 30 June 1888.
7. Cheshire Observer, 21 October 1893.
8. Cheshire Observer, 5 November 1927.

9. Cheshire Observer, 28 January 1928.
10. Listed Buildings Register, searchable at list.english-heritage.org.uk.
11. Cheshire Observer, 18 August 1956.
12. Cheshire Observer, 29 November 1968.
13. Personal Communication, Mr F Parry.

Appendix:

Adams's Weekly Courant, 4th September 1750

Chester, Sept 4. *On Wednesday the 19th August, a barbarous Murder was committed about three Miles from this city, on the King's Highway leading from hence towards Parkgate. ----- Three Irishmen, who call themselves Garret Delaney, Edward Johnson, and John Caffrey, having been at Harvest-Labour in the South, were travelling along with their Countryman Bryan Molloy, an elderly Man, towards Parkgate; when the three former assaulted Molloy on the great Road, about Noon, and beat him most unmercifully with their Sticks, and when he was almost dead, they dispatch'd him, by striking a Reaping-Hook into his neck, under his ear, and cutting him in the Wind-pipe. They took from him two fresh new Guineas and seven Shillings in Silver, and a Bundle of Clothes tied up in a Hankerchief, and then hid the Body in a Ditch, and went away to Shotwicke, a little Town about a mile from the Place. When they were gone, a Labourer, who was in an adjoining Field, and heard the Cries of the poor Man, and the Sound of the Blows, but durst not shew himself to the Ruffians, came forward and soon discovered the Body, and alarming the next Village, the People went immediately to Shotwicke, and found the three Fellows drinking in an Alehouse, where they had just changed one of the new Guineas. They were secured in a Barn that Night, and the next Day brought to Chester, and after proper Examinations, were committted to the Castle. When they were apprehended their Sticks were bloody, some stains were on their Clothes, and on one of their Shoes. The nephew of Molloy, swore to the bundle of Clothes found with the three Men, that they were the Property of his murder'd Uncle.*

Our Assizes began Yesterday, so that these inhuman Miscreants will in all Probability, be soon brough to Justice.

On Sunday one of the three Men sent to the Justice who committed them, to offer himself as an Evidence against his two Companions.

Adams's Weekly Courant, 11th September 1750

Chester, Sept 8. *This Day ended our Assizes, when John Caffery, one of the three Irish Ruffians, mentioned in our last, was admitted on Evidence against his Comrades Garrat Delaney and Edward Johnson, alias Murray, who were found Guilty of Robbing and Murdering Bryan Molloy upon the King's Highway, about three Miles from this City, on Wednesday the 22nd August last and are sentenced to be executed upon the 26th Inst and afterwards to be hanged in Chains, in the great Road leading from Chester to Parkgate; which, it is hoped, will be a Terror and Warning to their Countrymen, who have of late committed many Villainies in that Part of the County.*

The Historic Designed Landscape of Backford Hall

By Barbara Moth

Background

Cheshire Gardens Trust undertook the research and recording of the historic designed landscape at Backford Hall as part of an ongoing project to record the parks and gardens of the historic county of Cheshire. News that the hall was to be vacated by Cheshire West and Chester Council in September 2011 prior to sale gave some urgency to the task. Considerable assistance was provided by John Hess who received material from Des Carroll, a former employee at Backford Hall, and from Sid Hawes, long time caretaker of the property.

There is no mention of Backford, 'ford by a ridge',[1] in Domesday, but it is understood that lands at Backford were given to the Massies, Barons of Dunham Massy, at the Conquest or shortly thereafter.[2] By descent it became part of the estate of Richard de Mascy of Sale and then belonged to Edward de Mascy of Tymperlegh.[3] In 1571 Henry Birkenhead purchased Backford from Thomas Aldersey. By 1605 Backford had become the residence of the Birkenhead family.[4]

In 1704 Thomas Birkenhead died without issue and the property was divided between his nieces Frances Birkenhead, married to John Glegg of Irby, and Deborah, wife of William Glegg of Grange (re married to Lieut-Col Charles Crosbie).[5] The 16th century mansion was taken down by John Glegg and replaced with a new brick mansion.[6]

In 1816 both parts of the estate were vested in Major-Gen Birkenhead, inheriting from his grandmother Frances Birkenhead and succeeding to the second portion on the death of Deborah (without issue) in 1795.[7] The grounds were laid out by John Webb.[8]

The Tithe Map ca.1842 (Fig.1) indicates that Birkenhead Glegg owned most of the parish of Backford, through which passed the Chester to

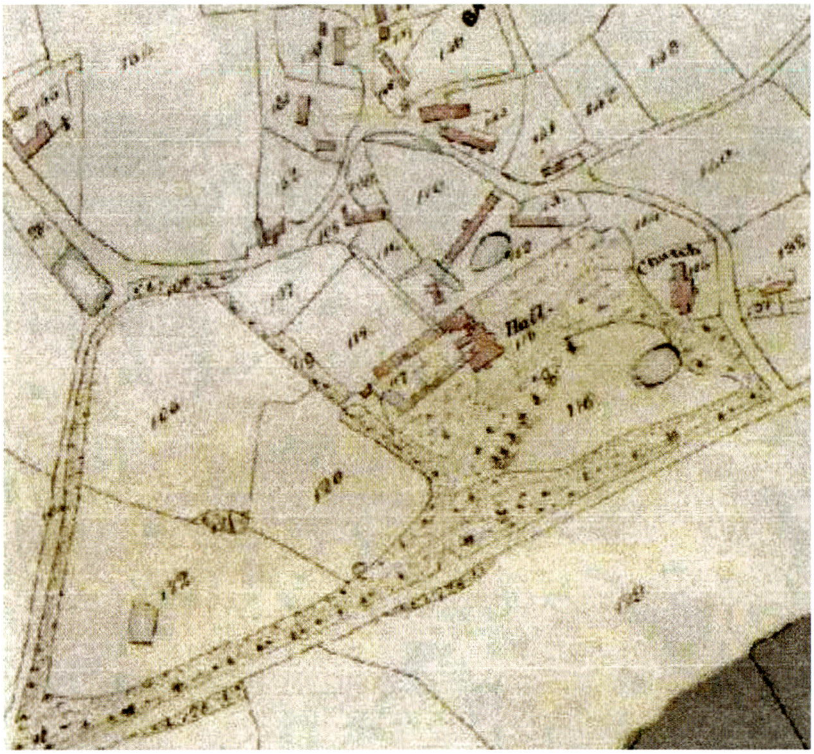

Fig. 1 Tithe Map c.1842 showing the 18th Cent. Backford Hall with grounds by Webb.

Birkenhead turnpike.[9] ‘Backford Hall, offices, buildings, yards, gardens and plantations’ are shown immediately east of the road, the plantations encompassing a meadow with an oval pool. Immediately north of the hall and outbuildings is a walled garden and garden, while to the east and south east are a house, buildings, yard, orchard, pasture, stock-yard and garden occupied by William Mason. The hall and environs, including the church of St Oswald and dwellings and gardens occupied by Thomas Hughes and Samuel Lewes, are bounded by an irregular winding lane passing through the village of Backford. There is a path between the church and hall. Three fields north west of the Hall are enclosed by woodland belts and circumscribed by a path. The northern boundary is defined by a road or lane.[10]

In 1843 Baskervyle Glegg died leaving Backford to his brother Edward Holt Glegg and cousin Lee Porcher Townshend in trust.[11] Edward Holt Glegg married in 1845.[12] A contract between John and William Walker of Birkenhead (builders) and Edward Holt Glegg of Backford

Hall, June 1st 1845, was drawn up for the erection of a mansion at the cost of £10,700.[13] Edward Holt Glegg, his daughter, son, nursemaid and other staff are recorded as resident at Backford Hall in the 1851 census and again in 1861 when Edward's wife Margaret and other staff were also present.[14] The new hall in neo-Elizabethan style was designed by John Cunningham,[15] and is dated 1863.[16] The lodge adjacent to the entrance from the Chester to Birkenhead Road is also dated 1863. The coach house, with the same diaper brickwork as the house, is dated 1853. Ormerod says "The grounds of the new Hall were laid out by Gray of London, the landscape gardener, in 1857, when the new Hall was built.[17]

It is understood that John Cunningham's original house was destroyed in a fire and then rebuilt, which would account for the discrepancy in dates. Beneath the forecourt is a large brick-lined tank which collected roof drainage from the front of the hall, creating a reservoir. It was probably constructed following the fire.[18]

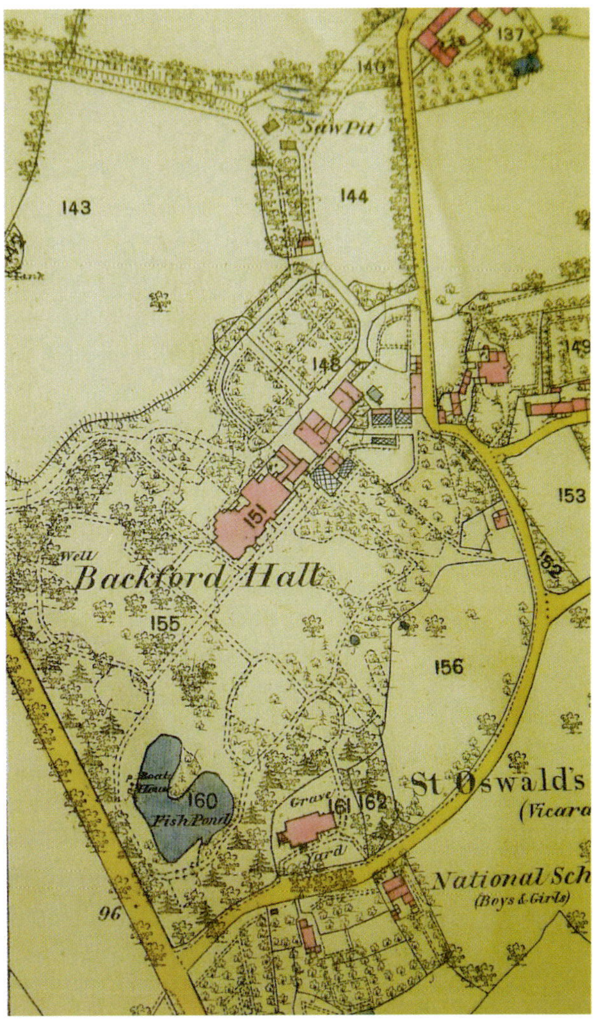

Fig. 2 First Edition Ordnance Survey 1875 showing Backford Hall by John Cunningham (1863) and grounds by Gray of London.

The First Edition Ordnance Survey ca.1875 (Fig. 2) records the new hall and the changes that had taken place since the Tithe Map ca.1842. It indicates that the new Hall occupied a similar position and south west/northeast alignment to the old hall but that all the outbuildings were now disposed to the north east, allowing unobstructed views to and from the two principal elevations of the hall. The main approach to the hall from the Chester–Birkenhead Road is now flanked by the lodge and reconfigured to create a curving drive to the forecourt north west of the hall. The meadow with pool has been incorporated into the pleasure grounds. The pool appears to have been extended creating a promontory and has a boathouse. There is a network of paths throughout the pleasure grounds. The path around the fields north of the Hall is retained. The road bounding the hall and grounds has been rationalised into a smooth curve and then straightened to the north, allowing additional ground to be encompassed within the hall grounds. Areas north and east of the hall include two gardens with curved walls, a conservatory, glass-houses and areas of regular tree planting, possibly an orchard. A small building shown on the Tithe Map as the dwelling house of Thomas Hughes and Samuel Lewes is retained within the property beside the newly straightened road.

In 1877 Edward Holt Glegg died leaving Backford Hall and all his estates to his eldest son Birkenhead Glegg and his nephew Edward Townshend (son of his sister Emma Glegg), or survivor of him, in a will dated 10th May 1869.[19] The 1881 census records that Birkenhead Clegg, his mother, brother and a number of servants were in residence.[20] Some of the servants may be those in a photograph (Photo 2) at the south east door of the hall, ca.1888.[21] Birkenhead Glegg died 18th November 1914, and his brother Edward Maxwell Glegg died at Backford 6th February 1927. As neither of them had produced heirs[22] the property was inherited by Lettice Valentine Lee Townshend, daughter of Edward Townshend Logan who had been killed in action in France 19th February 1915 (Edward Townsend's eldest son, Edward Lee Venable had predeceased him, dying at Gorstage Hall 13th February 1915, age 14).[23]

Lettice Townshend was legally granted the property on 10th January 1928. Her inheritance comprised

'Backford Hall estate 923.439 acres, of which land in hand comprised:
Hall, grounds and 3 cottages 27.736 acres
Plantations 35.461 acres
(The rest of the land was all tenanted.)
Irby Hall estate 276.168 acres', all tenanted'.[24]

Lettice Townshend never lived at Backford but placed the estate in the hands of Gandy and Sons, surveyors of Northwich. Prospective tenants included a boys school, Mr and Mrs Jacobs (Jacobs biscuits), and a Salvatorian Order who occupied the hall for 3 months. After a period as a country club the hall was finally sold to a shipping company in 1941. Lettice Townshend married John Robert Collie in London on 22nd November 1934.[25] Gandy's letter books provide a record of the property during Miss Townshend's ownership.[26]

Fig. 3 1910 Ordnance Survey

5th June 1927 Road to be widened and estate to be paid £55 for land, £2 for trees[27]

12th Sept 1927 – enquiry for land at Backford Hall to be used as a golf course[28]

10th Oct 1927 – reference to summer house purchased in Backford House sale that is no longer wanted by purchaser and is still on site[29]

17th Oct 1927 – Mr T Humphreys of Backford Hall Lodge and his family to take over kitchen gardens as market gardens[30]

1st Nov 1927 – 6 elm trees down in hall grounds due to gale[31]

21st Dec 1927 – 'Everywhere is beginning to look very much tidier and less overgrown'[32]

30th June 1928 – to Mr Humphreys –'I have given permission for Mr Douglas Jones to come over probably Monday pm to try his luck fishing in the pool'[33]

3rd Dec 1928 – to G E Ashford, the Castle, Chester – will remove dangerous trees overhanging road[34]

14th Jan 1929– Mr and Mrs Jacobs would like to take a lease on the Hall[35]

11th March 1929 – re proposed greenhouses, central heating and independent hot water supply by Foster and Pearson. Greenhouse plans meet with Mrs Jacob's approval[36]

15th March 1929 – to Messrs Dickson and Son, Chester re list of shrubs which Capt Jacob has asked the owner to plant[37]

5th April 1929 – negotiations with Jacobs fall through[38]

10th August 1934 – letter to Rev Father Enderlie, Wylde Green House Birmingham (Salvatorian Order) who is interested in a lease of 7 years

22nd August 1934 – letter confirming verbal agreement to lease

8th October 1934 – negotiations with priests have fallen through and they vacate the Hall[39]

7th Feb 1935 – Mr F W Woodhall had applied for tenancy of Hall as a country club

20th March 1935 – lease refers to pool as a fish pond
24th April 1935 – Mrs Collie objects to the pool being used for bathing
24th June 1935 – lease signed[40]

On 25th July 1941 a Conveyance to 'Alan Heathcote Williams of Craigbet Liverpool Road in the City of Chester Engineer (thereafter called the purchaser) of the third part of Dock Services Limited of 18 Chapel Chambers North, 28 Chapel Street Liverpool – the Company', records the sale of the property to a shipping company. The schedule includes 'lodge outbuildings conservatory glass houses gardens grounds and appurtances'.[41]

In December 1945 Backford Hall was advertised for sale by private treaty, 'with extensive gardens and grounds extending to 25 acres'.[42] On 9th January 1946 a Cheshire County Council note entitled, Staff Sub-Committee – Office Accommodation records:

> Backford Hall. I have been told privately that this property has not yet been sold and that the owners are likely to accept £12,500 instead of the original figure of about £15,000. The hall includes an area of 25 acres. There is a lodge from which an income could be derived. The accommodation at the Hall is the same as that at Watergate House, so that we should only have to move the two huts from the grounds of Watergate House.[43]

The Hall and surrounding land were acquired for £10,000.[44] By 29th March 1946 the Conveyance had been signed and ex army huts were transported from Linenhall stables to provide the additional accommodation required by the County Surveyor's Department.[45]

About 1971 the Chester–Birkenhead Road was widened to create a central reservation. This resulted in the closing of the entrance by the lodge[46] and creation of the principal access from Gordon Lane. In 1972 a new purpose designed building was completed (see Fig. 3) for the department of Trading Standards[47] replacing some lean-to garages by the wall of the kitchen garden.[48] Also in 1972 a pair of semi-detached houses was erected in the area of the former walled gardens to provide accommodation for caretakers.[49] During the 1970s over 100 trees on the roadside frontage of the hall and grounds to the north succumbed to Dutch elm disease and had to be felled. A storm in 1976 resulted in the loss of a Redwood near the car park.

In around 1980 construction of the M56 over the A41 involved emptying a couple of ponds. The fish, including pike, tench, rudd, perch and roach, were removed and taken to the pond at Backford Hall. About 1985 the pond was covered in blanket weed and duck weed. The groundsman used a chemical to treat the weed which resulted in the death of all the fish and there have been no fish since. In ca.1991 the pond was de-silted and pumped out to a wagon situated beside the A41. The pond depth varied between 0–4ft suggesting that it did not originate as a marl pit, marl pits tending to be of greater depth. About 1992 the path around the pond was improved as part of a staff project. Work included cutting back vegetation, creating steps (using railway sleepers,) installing edgings and laying gravel surfacing. Prior to this it was not possible to walk around the lake due to vegetation on the west side. (The path was subsequently refurbished by the groundsman who installed new board edgings). A timber balustrade was erected around a stone paved viewing point on the southern edge of the lake. It replaced an earlier stone balustrade. It is understood that the roof drainage from the rear of the hall drains to the pond and that an old shed near the lake, erected in 1946, accommodated a pump in case of fire.[50]

Photo 1a Main entrance 1970s

Photo 1b

Photo 2 Staff outside the Hall 1888

Photo 3 Boundary wall by A41, former Turnpike

Photo 4 Gateway from church to hall 1774

Since 1990, various mature trees have been lost due to age, storm or disease. These include a large oak near the car park c.1996, a large beech tree at the front of the hall in a storm, 1998, and a mature oak west of the hall due to honey fungus 2003/4.[51] Some replacement planting has been undertaken. A tree survey report was produced in 2001/2.[52]

There was a nine-hole putting green in the grass area (roundabout) at the front of the hall. In about 2000 this was removed and the 9 holes added to the existing 9 holes at the back of hall. The putting green was used by staff.

Backford Primary School used a small field north of the hall as a playing field until the school closed in 1996. Since then the field has been let to a local farmer, together with the adjacent field.

In 2001 a small area of woodland south of the lake was sold to the church for a car park. Until about 2005 the lodge was occupied by staff on short term lets. The grounds were maintained by site-based groundsmen until 2009 when Backford Hall was transferred from Cheshire County Council to Cheshire West and Chester Council, since which time the site has been maintained by contractors.[53]

Photo 5 Walled garden wall

Photo 6 Lodge dated 1863, now closed

A description of the site prior to sale in 2011

Boundaries and entrances

The western boundary adjacent to the A41 is defined by a coursed sandstone wall with rustic sandstone coping (Photo 3) backed by a tree belt and extending both sides of the former main entrance flanked by the lodge (Photo 6) of 1863, listed Grade II.[54] This entrance is now barred by a locked timber gate with a pedestrian gate to the side. The wall has been partially rebuilt beside the pleasure grounds, probably in association with road improvements. There is more sandstone walling to the southern boundary a section of which was replaced by a close-boarded timber fence when the car park was built, extending to the current site entrance on Gordon Lane. Beyond the entrance the boundary is formed by the rear wall of a historic building constructed of sandstone and brick (that shown as the dwelling of Thomas Hughes and Samuel Lewes on the Tithe map, and continued by a high free-standing sandstone boundary wall up to another entrance, now closed. This entrance appears to have been an earlier service entrance to the property and was still in use in the 1970s by Sid Hawes and others.

North of the service entrance a small field formed by the earlier straightening of the road, is bounded by trees and an informal hedge on Gordon Lane. The northern boundary is defined by a tree belt and

Photo 7 Drive with banks each side and Irish yews.

a deep ditch at the eastern end. The ditch becomes shallower as it turns in a southerly direction across the enclosed meadow. The tree belts and meadow are overlooked by the hall. The meadow is enclosed on the northern and southern boundaries by iron hurdles in varying states of repair, and within the trees is evidence of the informal path shown on the historic maps. The western tree belt bounding the meadow includes some large tree stumps and much elm regeneration.

Pleasure grounds

The main approach to the hall from the lodge, now closed, curves up a slight incline between banks planted to the north with Irish yew (Photo 7). The route appears to have been reconfigured in association with the 19th C. rebuilding of the hall. This approach leads to an impressive view of the main facade (Photos 1a and 1b) of Backford Hall, Grade II[55] and the main entrance. Twentieth century council buildings have been constructed within the pleasure grounds which formerly extended all around the hall except on the north eastern side where there were service areas. The path network shown on the 1910 Ordnance Survey appears to have been lost, but many mature trees remain including some large open grown oaks, sweet chestnut and cedar, thought to be 18th century or earlier, and araucaria, wellingtonia and yew, considered part of the 19th century planting. Plantings of laurel, cherry laurel and rhododendron combined with natural regeneration have created a dense understorey so that the area has the character of ornamental woodland rather than of a pleasure ground.

A flagged path leads through a treed area to an arched gateway (Photo 3) into the churchyard. The keystone on the arch is dated 1774. Another flagged path leads to the staff car park which has been developed on open ground outside the pleasure grounds. A mound with mature trees separates the car park from a lawn within the pleasure grounds. The lawn, at the rear of the hall, is consistent with that shown on a photograph of the hall c.1900 and was used as a putting green until 2008. It contains a mature weeping ash for which a replacement weeping ash has been planted alongside. To the north east is an area of raised ground with scattered trees including an old pear tree, one of four pear trees remembered by Sid Hawes, remnants of an orchard indicated by regular tree planting on the 1875 Ordnance Survey. No conservatories or glasshouses survive.

Photo 8 The pond

The pond

The pond (Photo 8) is screened by pleasure ground planting and circumscribed by a gravel path. The path has railway sleeper steps in two locations, a stone-flagged viewing area with modern timber balustrade, and passes by the old pump house and a couple of seats. The location of the former boathouse is indicated by brick edging. It is understood from Sid Hawes that the bricks form a curved base. The pond has an overflow to an outlet passing beneath the A41.

Working areas

East of the hall the 19th century stables and carriage shed remain around a cobbled courtyard , but the structure of other working areas associated with the hall has been altered since the war. The walled kitchen garden has been perforated in two places by the late 20th century access drive (Photo 4), and although considerable lengths of the wall survive in good condition, these are partially obscured by the late 20th century building of offices and caretakers' houses and by planting. An original entrance in one of the walls is consistent with the central access indicated on the First Edition Ordnance Survey.

Conclusion

Despite neglect and under tenancy for several years in the first half of the 20th century, and the changes undertaken by Cheshire County Council post 1946, substantial elements of the historic landscape associated with the 19th century gentleman's residence survive. These include the lodge, carriage house and stables, sections of kitchen garden wall, a framework of mature pleasure ground planting and open views across an enclosed meadow from the principal elevation of the hall. It is to be hoped that the historic layout and remaining features are respected by Backford Hall's new owners.

Endnote abbreviations

CALS – Cheshire Archives and Local Studies
CHER – Cheshire Historic Environment Record

References

1. Ekwall, E. 1991. *The Concise Oxford Dictionary of Place-names* Oxford: Clarendon Press, 21.
2. Ormerod G. 1882. The History of the County Palatine and City of Chester. V.2, 362.
3. Ormerod G. 1882. The History of the County Palatine and City of Chester. V.2, 364.
4. Ormerod G. 1882. The History of the County Palatine and City of Chester. V.2, 366.
5. Ormerod G. 1882. The History of the County Palatine and City of Chester. V.2, 366.
6. Handwritten note in *Box of information collected by Des Carroll,* former employee at Backford Hall. Box now in the possession of John Hess (2011).
7. Ormerod G. 1882. The History of the County Palatine and City of Chester. V.2, 366.
8. Ormerod G. 1882. The History of the County Palatine and City of Chester. V.2, 366.
9. The plan of improvements to the Chester to Birkenhead Turnpike 1832, CALS QDP 109, records nothing of the grounds of Backford Hall around this time.

10. http://maps.cheshire.gov.uk/tithemaps.
11. *Box of information collected by Des Carroll.*
12. www.ancestry.co.uk.
13. The contract is understood to be in the E. Gandy and Sons Collection, CALS DGN, but has not been seen. This information is taken from a document in CALS Local Studies a print-out from a now defunct Backford Hall website derived from a 2006 publication 'CCC at Backford Hall' (not seen).
14. www.ancestry.co.uk.
15. John Cunningham's obituary in the Builder 18th October 1872 does not mention Backford Hall but does say that he was the engineer for several water works.
16. Figueiredo, P, and Treuherz, J.1988. *Cheshire Country Houses.* Chichester: Phillemore, 214.
17. Ormerod G. 1882. The History of the County Palatine and City of Chester. V.2, Appendix 898.
18. Sid Hawes, caretaker at Backford since 1976.
19. *Box of information collected by Des Carroll,* Order of High Court dated 10th March 1941 with documents attached.
20. www.ancestry.co.uk.
21. *Box of information collected by Des Carroll,* photograph
22. *Box of information collected by Des Carroll,* Order of High Court dated 10th March 1941 with documents attached.
23. CALS DGN – E. Gandy and Sons, letter books, book 1, p189.
24. *Box of information collected by Des Carroll,* Order of High Court dated 10th March 1941 with documents attached.
25. *Box of information collected by Des Carroll,* Order of High Court dated 10th March 1941 with documents attached.
26. CALS DGN – E. Gandy and Sons, letter books.
27. CALS DGN – E. Gandy and Sons, letter books, book 1, p59.
28. CALS DGN – E. Gandy and Sons, letter books, book 1, p109.
29. CALS DGN – E. Gandy and Sons, letter books, book 1, p141.
30. CALS DGN – E. Gandy and Sons, letter books, book 1, p153.
31. CALS DGN – E. Gandy and Sons, letter books, book 1, p161.
32. CALS DGN – E. Gandy and Sons, letter books, book 1, p200.
33. CALS DGN – E. Gandy and Sons, letter books, book 1, p343.
34. CALS DGN – E. Gandy and Sons, letter books, book 1, p461.
35. CALS DGN – E. Gandy and Sons, letter books, book 1, p484.
36. CALS DGN – E. Gandy and Sons, letter books, book 2, p44.
37. CALS DGN – E. Gandy and Sons, letter books, book 2, p47.
38. CALS DGN – E. Gandy and Sons, letter books, book 2, p61.

39. CALS DGN – E. Gandy and Sons, letter books, book 3, p364, 367, 448.
40. CALS DGN – E. Gandy and Sons, letter books, book 3, p525, 564, 594, 630.
41. *Box of information collected by Des Carroll,* copy of Conveyance.
42. Chester Chronicle.
43. *Box of information collected by Des Carroll.*
44. Backford Hall history on front desk of hall, researched and compiled by Alistair Haydock.
45. *Box of information collected by Des Carroll,* 24th April letter from County Surveyor to Chief Inspector Lloyd, Chester City police, confirming a telephone conversation.
46. Sid Hawes.
47. Backford Hall history on front desk of hall, researched and compiled by Alistair Haydock.
48. CALS Local Studies collection, a print out from a now defunct Backford Hall website derived from a 2006 publication 'CCC at Backford Hall'(not seen).
49. Sid Hawes.
50. Sid Hawes.
51. Sid Hawes.
52. By J P Hess and R Burlingham.
53. Sid Hawes.
54. Listed 20.12.1983, CHER.
55. Listed 20.12.1983, CHER.

The History of Backford (Written in 1953)

by John B Davies

(This is John Davies' own personal view of the history of Backford Parish and was written in the early 1950s. Two versions of his work exist: the original manuscript and a transcription typed by Ruth Shone in 2003, to prepare it for publication. The version below is based largely on the typed document but where paragraphs or sentences were obviously incomplete, these have been completed from the manuscript version. Editor.)

The word "parish" can have one of two meanings. It may be used to indicate a district under the supervision of one clergyman (or minister) or it may mean the smallest area in local government. For the purpose of the present paper, "parish" will be taken in its ecclesiastical sense, namely, the district served by one clergyman, while the "manor" and "township" will be used to mean an area of local government.

Exactly when the Parish of Backford was delineated one cannot say. About the year 669 the Papacy sent to England a Greek named Theodore to be Archbishop and to organise the Church. For twenty-one years Theodore vigorously pursued this object. He increased the number of bishops from six to fourteen. Undoubtedly, each diocese in its turn gradually became divided into parishes, owing to increases in population. Whether or not it may be claimed that the Parish of Backford dates from these days it is impossible to say, but the dedication of the Church to Saint Oswald would seem to indicate that we have an ancient parish dating from early English days. Moreover it is one of the few Wirral parishes which has never been divided.

Geographically, the Parish is situated at the southern boundary of the Wirral Peninsula. Its importance as a site lies in the fact that it controlled the crossing places (or fords) over the valley which separates the Peninsula from the rest of Cheshire. The valley, usually known as the Broxton Valley, runs from the Gowy marshes on the Mersey side to the marshes which bordered on Blacon Point on the Dee side. A little more detail about this valley may be of use here. At the northern end, where the valley joins the Gowy marshes, stands Stoak, perched on higher ground. Moving southward along the valley one comes to Croughton, opposite the settlement of Wervin on the opposite bank, on a cross road. This was probably the lowest point at which the valley could be forded in winter on the Mersey side. Little Mollington was possibly the lowest bad-weather ford at the Dee side. Backford, on sandy soil, was presumably the middle ford, and the one most generally in use, as it offered an easy landing in all weathers on a sandy shore. It is necessary to remember that until the eighteenth century the tidal waters of the Dee in the west and those of the Mersey on the east flooded this valley probably as far as the ridge at Backford, thus making the crossing place at Backford one of considerable importance. In 1732, however, the mayor and citizens of Chester obtained an act of Parliament which empowered them to construct a new channel for the river Dee, in order to make a navigable way for ships up to Chester. Work was begun in 1735 and continued for many years until by 1826 nearly four thousand acres had been recovered – land which we now know as Sealand. Since that time tidal waters have not approached Backford. It is because of the importance of these fords as a means of communication that there are to be found in this neighbourhood so many sites of ancient manor houses which have been semi-fortified, having had moats round them.

As has already been pointed out, the Parish of Backford lies on the southern border of the Wirral Peninsular. To the north it is joined by the ancient parishes of Eastham and Stoak. On the west it adjoins the parish of Shotwick while on the south it shares boundaries with the parishes of Holy Trinity and Saint Oswald, in Chester. Its eastern boundary is shared with the ancient parishes of St.Mary-on-the-hill, Chester, and Stoak. Since mediaeval days several of these ancient parishes have been sub-divided, the consequence being that the new parishes of Ellesmere Port, Great Sutton and Capenhurst lie to the north, the parish of Saughall to the west and that, of Upton-by-Chester to the south.

BACKFORD. "The ford by the ridge" (Ekwall)

The name suggests the proximity of a ford. As has already been shown, the ford was most probably the only one passable in all kinds of weather, and this fact determined the original settlement of the place. The manor is situated on glacial sands and its average height above sea level is 100 feet. A bridge existed here in early times, as a charter of the late 13th century speaks of "the bridge of Backford over the water of the river".

Backford is not mentioned in Domesday Book but it seems fairly certain that the manor was given either at the Conquest or soon afterwards to the Barons of Dunham. Hamon, the third Baron of Dunham, gave the manor and church of Backford to the Benedictine Priory which he had founded at Birkenhead. During the life of the sixth Baron of Dunham the manor of Backford passed to the Masseys of Timperley. It continued in the possession of this family until 1424, when it became, by marriage, the property of Richard de Chatterton. His only daughter married Richard de Radcliffe, in whose family and that of the Parres, the estates remained until 1570, when Robart Parre sold them to Thomas Aldersey, a citizen and haberdasher of London and he, shortly afterwards, sold them to Henry Birkenhead, gentleman. The Birkenhead family held Backford until 1724 when, on the death of Thomas Birkenhead, the family became extinct in heirs male and two nieces of Thomas Birkenhead became co-heiresses. The elder, Frances, married John Glegg Esq. of Irby. In 1816 the estates were held by Major-General Birkenhead Glegg and they are still held by a representative of the Glegg family, with the exception of two-thirds of a small estate near the Church, which has been supposed to be the estate possessed by the abbeys of Stanlow and Whalley, under the name of Roches Croft.

Backford Hall appears to have become the residence of the Birkenheads in 1605, in which year the entries of their baptisms begin there and cease at Waverton, the parish church of their other residence at Huxley. The ancient mansion was taken down during the eighteenth century and a handsome brick mansion built on the site by John Glegg, son of John and Frances Glegg already named. During the nineteenth century the house was again removed by Lieutenant-colonel Edward Holt Glegg and the present Elizabethan-style mansion built.

The School at Backford was erected in 1843, on a site given by Lieutenant-Colonel Edward Holt Glegg.

It was during the rebuilding of the Hall in the eighteenth century that the line of the highway from Chester to Birkenhead was altered at Backford. In order to make a plantation between the mansion and the road, the latter was moved further towards the west. The result of this alteration can be seen by observing the direction of the line of Church Farm House and comparing it with the present line of the road. The two are not parallel, the reason for this being that formerly the highway ran in the same direction as the line of the farm house and passed close to the door of the Church Tower.

In common with most English villages which adjoin main roads, Backford had its turn-pike after the passing of the Turn-pike Act of 1751. The toll-gate here was at the Cottage, near the canal bridge.

Among other changes which have taken place within the last two centuries may be mentioned the following: the footpath which leads from opposite the Hope Farm to the Whitby Road is marked on old maps as a lane. The lane leading up from Backford Brook towards the Garage used to pass directly up to the highway behind the Post Office. The alteration here, I think, explains the name "Merciful Hill", the more gradual slope being more "merciful" in the days of horse traction.

> During mediaeval times the Hundred Moot or Court for the Hundred of Wirral was held usually at Backford and sometimes at Willaston. In 1307 the ...

(Editorial note: The following sentences, in parenthesis, were omitted from this typed version but are present in the handwritten version:)

> (... Prior of Birkenhead applied to the Justices of Chester, sitting at Backford, that he might be copies [*sic*] of the lists of individual persons. In 1408 Edward the cooper of Eastham was charged at the Hundred Court, sitting at Backford with having taken from the Prior of Birkenhead 3d. a day for his labour. In 1534, at the same court, the tithe barn, the tithes and a piece of land for a ...)

> ... riksted were leased to one Thomas Poole (heir of Sir William Poole) in the sum of £12.13s. 4d. for a period of 36 years.

On the Dissolution of the Monasteries the Commissioners appointed to enquire into the affairs of Birkenhead Priory, were Sir William Stanley, of Hooton, John Birkenhead and Ottiwell Worsley. Their findings shewed a Temporal Revenue (rents etc.) of £19.19s.3d, and spiritualities (tithes) amounting to £82.17s. 6½d (Bowden £45.7s. 6d, Wallasey £14.3s.8½d., Bidston £10.19s.8d, Backford £12.6s.8d). From this there was an annual deductible payment of 20/- to the vicar of Backford. The Rectory of Backford also paid £12.13s.4d. to the Priory together with a small rent from Richard Newton of Backford.

The township of Backford contains 764 acres of land and at the census of 1841 its population was 200. At the census in 1931 the number of people was 124. The boundary of the Manor is formed on the west by the Backford Brook; which rises a little south of the site of the ancient manor house at Capenhurst and flows southwards, finally joining the stream which runs along the Broxton valley to the River Dee. Backford boundary is along this stream from where it flows under Powey Lane to the point at which it joins the stream in the Broxton Valley. The northern boundary of Backford passes along the old Powey Lane, much of which is now incorporated in the Shotwick–Frodsham road, to the point where the old pack-horse road branches off just to the south-west of Whitby Roundabout. Then the boundary line follows the old lane past the Mount Farm, leaving the latter in Chorlton, until, having passed, the lane leading to Chorlton Hall, it finally leaves the lane and wanders along field fences until it reaches the canal bridge. From here it turns southwards and follows the stream to the point at which Backford Brook joins it.

Until the early nineteenth century the first week in August, was always "wakes week" in Backford. The dedication of the Parish Church is to Saint Oswald and the Feast of St. Oswald falls on 5th August. Hence the reason for the festival week then.

Formerly the Church Farm House was a Public House, but by what sign the house was known I have failed to ascertain. The Birkenhead Arms perhaps? (*The 1861 census for England and Wales confirms the name at that time as "The Birkenhead Arms" – Editor*).

CAUGHALL: "Cockhill" i.e. hill frequented by fowls

The little township of Caughall, although situated in the Hundred of Broxton, forms part of the ecclesiastical parish of Backford. It covers an area of 348 acres and in 1841 had 16 inhabitants. At the census of 1931 its population numbered 13. The manor is not mentioned in Domesday. It was probably retained by the Earls of Chester for a considerable period. During the reign of Edward I, Ralph (or Roger) de Ceghull occurs as lord. His grandson Roger de Ceghull was one of the 43 Cheshire gentlemen who were summoned by Edward the Black Prince to do homage for lands which they held as tenants-in-capite. In the reign of Richard II Roger de Ceghull was appointed keeper of the Castle of Flint, for which service he received £20 year. Later, he was appointed Sheriff of Flint for life. He seems to have been the last in direct male line of his family. The estate then passed to co-heiresses, one of whom was the wife of Sir John Osbaldesten of Chadlington. The Massey part of the manor passed, with Puddington estates, to Sir Thomas Stanley Massey Stanley of Hooten (1815) who sold 170 acres of it to William Hope Esquire of Bebington.

The township contains only two houses and is let in two farms. The farm house on Sir Thomas Stanley's estates, though mostly rebuilt, contains portions of an old timber house, which in the reign of Elizabeth, was the residence of John Massay, esq., who succeeded, on the death of his brother in 1600, to the Puddington Estates. For many generations this farm was held under the Masseys said Stanleys by a family of the name of Amery. Now, however, the family is entirely unknown. The other part of the estate was purchased from the Osbaldeten family by the trustees of Whitchurch Grammar School in whom it is now vested.

A steep sandy hill in this township has the name of the Butter Hill, from a tradition that the Wirral market people deposited their butter and other commodities here, when the plague at Chester prevented their entering the city.

CHORLTON: Tun of the Villeins (Caeorlaten); Tun of the Free Peasants

The Township of Chorlton lies to the east of Backford and is immediately contiguous to it. For the most part it stands about 100 feet above sea level and the ground which slopes from this part to the canal is reputed to be some of the richest land in the county. It is a settlement on glacial clay and has an area of 545 acres. In 1801 it contained 12 houses, occupied by 68 persons. At the census of 1841 the population had increased to 85 while the number of people shown by the census (1931) was 82.

On the west, Chorlton shares the boundary with Backford, on the north the boundary leaves the old lane (Goldsworth Lane) passes along a field fence south of Stanney Wood and near to the old quarry, from where it runs, across the lane leading to Rake Hall, along further field fences to the east of the Grove Farn until it reaches the lane which leads to Croughton at a point about opposite to the Chapel House in Wervin. After another short distance along this lane southwards, the boundary line turns east to meet the canal towing path which it follows in a southerly direction until it meets the Backford boundary again a little to the west of Caughall Bridge.

It is probable that the Barons of Dunhan were Lords of Chorlton soon after the Conquest, although the manor is not mentioned in Domesday. In all likelihood it was included in the village of Backford. In the time of Richard I (12th Century), Hamon de Mascy, Baron of Dunham granted a part of the manor to Chester Abbey. At any rate the connection between the Abbey of Saint Werburgh and this township began at an early period. Robert de Hastings, abbot 1186–1194, granted lands in Chorlton to William Fitz Warner, and several grants of estates in the township given to that monastery during the time of Edward I & II are still preserved. By the time of King Edward III, nearly the whole of the manor seemed to be vested in the Abbot and Monks of Saint Werburgh.

At the dissolution of the Abbey, these estates formed part of the endowment of the Dean and Chapter of Chester. They were obtained from them by Sir Richard Cotton, a portion thereof held under him in fee form, by Richard Ashton, Margaret Forshaw, Thomas Trafford, John King, Thomas Whitfield and Robert Cook for the annual rent of £10. 4s. 2d. By a charter in the reign of Elisabeth, the fee farm rent was directed to be paid to the Dean and Chapter of Chester Cathedral and the lands declared to be held by the fee farmers and their heirs.

From then various changes in ownership of land have occurred in Chorlton. About 1796 Chorlton Hall and the larger portion of the land was purchased by Richard Wicksted, Esq. of Nantwich. Another portion of the estate descended to the Stanleys of Hooton and in 1791 Sir William Stanley sold his Chorlton estate to William Pownall, esquire of Chester. In 1799 Mr Pownall conveyed his lands to William Nicholls Esq. F.S.A., deputy registrar of the Archdeaconry of Chester and in 1811 the widow of William Nicholls sold the Chorlton Estates to George Ormerod, Esq. This Mr. Ormerod is the famous Historian of Cheshire and he lived in Chorlton during the summers and autumns of six years. During the winters and springs he lived in London.

In 1823 Mr. Omerod disposed of all his estates in this manor to Mr Wicksted for the sum of £8000. Thus Mr. Wicksted, of Chorlton Hall, added the Ormerod estate to his possessions. He died in 1835, leaving a daughter and heiress, Martha wife of Mr. Swan, of Olive Mount, Wavertree near Liverpool. The estate descended to her son and heir James Wicksted Swan. He died without issue leaving his Chorlton estates to his sister's son Rev. Perkins of Bradford, Yorks. In 1876 this gentleman disposed of the whole in parcels. The principal purchaser was Carruthers Charles Johnston M.P. of Chester. The other purchasers were Mr. Minshull, Mr. Price and Mr. Denson.

LEA. Ley or Les

Originally a woodland clearing but the meaning seems to have broadened to mean also open land or meadow.

Lea (Domesday Book – Wisdelea)

Lea (1230) "la Lea juxta Backford" 1275 leah – an open space in a wood, (glade).

The township of Lea lies immediately west of Backford. It has an area of 697 acres and at the census of 1841 it had a population of 115 occupying 16 houses. At the census of 1931 the number of people was 165.

On the north the boundary line follows the line of Powey Lane (now Shotwick–Frodsham road) from a point to the north-west of the Dunkirk Wood (now felled) at which a stream runs under the roadway to the point at which the stream – which forms Backford Brook – flows under the road. The eastern boundary of the township is shared with Backford i.e. Backford Brook. On the western side the boundary follows the line of the water-course to the point at which the stream flows beneath Grove Road, near The Chalet. From here the boundary turns along the ditch along the northern side of Grove Road and follows it until Mollington School playing field is reached. Then it follows the hollow in the field to join the water-course again opposite Mollington Post Office and continues to follow that water-course till it reaches the stream to the south of the canal.

The manor of Lea is mentioned in Domesday Book under the name Wisdelea. The entry is as follows: "The same Church (i.e. Abbey of S. Werburgh) hold and held Wisdelea. There is 1 hide (120 acres = unit of assessment) that pays geld. There is land for 3 ploughs. In the demesne is 1 plough and 2 serfs and there are 2 villeins and 2 borders with 1 plough and there is 1 acre of meadow. It was worth 10/- T.R.E. Now the same." The Manor was part of the original endowment of the monastery of St. Werburgh and its inhabitants did service to the Abbots in their court at Upton. In the thirteenth century, much of the land in the township was appropriated as part of the official estate of the master or chief cook of the Abbot. This office was hereditary, and by virtue of it, the cook was entitled to certain perquisites of and in the kitchen; together with eight bovates of land in Huntingdon, which, during the Abbacy of William de Marmien (1226–1228) were exchanged for an equal quantity in Lea and Newton. The duties of the office were divided between the two daughters and co-heiresses of the cook, Geoffrey the Chief Gunware. These perquisites and estates were assured to the representatives of Geoffrey by Thomas de Capenhurst abbot from 1249 to 1265. At first it is probable that only about one fourth of the Manor was controlled by the Abbey as the greater part seems to have been held by one Adam de Bacford and the family of Lees who were descended from him. This may account for the fact that in this township there appears to have been a manor, within the manor. The name Demage belonged originally to one of the farms, a name derived from the word demesne.

(Editorial Note: The following paragraph does not appear in the typed version of this article and is taken from the manuscript version:)

"In the agrarian rising of 1381 (Wat Tyler), the abbot's serfs and others rose under arms and assembled at Lea-by-Backford. Many of the men were imprisoned in the gaol at Chester Castle. The rising was quelled."

In or about the 16th century Chester Abbey most probably acquired the mesne manor by purchase from the Lees, subject to an agreement for a demise to that family for a long term of years. The Lees were still in possession as late as the reign of Elizabeth.

After the dissolution of the Monastery the manor and the whole township were granted, along with Whitby and Overpoole to William Glaseaur, Esq. and John Glasier, gent, subject to a fee farm rent of £10. 11s. 4d. (1541). In 1709 it passed by the foreclosure of a mortgage from Thomas Glasier to George Hayler, of Sussex, by whose successor it was sold to Thomas Bootle, of the Inner Temple. His descendants sold the manor to John Feilden Esquire of Mollington. In the early years of the present century, the estate was sold by the Feilden family.

Lea Hall is a house of much interest. It was last rebuilt in 1907. Previous to that the house was the one which Ormerod states was "built a few years ago", that is prior to 1819. This house succeeded an older building "composed of timber framework, the interstices of which were filled up with brick, resting on a stone foundation". The house "was approached by a stone gateway and stood within the present garden". Sulley, in his work published in 1889, remarks that the moat which formerly surrounded the old hall, could still be traced. In his itinerary of Cheshire, written in the 17th century, William Webb describes the Lea as "a fair house and fine demesne, so called, and hath been the mansion for some descendants of the Glasiers, esquires, of special note and good account". The hall was the country residence of William Glasier, vice-chamberlaine of Chester and alderman of the city. His will is dated 1588 and in it he mentions his chief or manor house in Lea otherwise Ley near Backford which the testator devised to his wife for life and, for the better maintenance of her husbandry, and good usage of the house of Lea, he gave his wife ten of the best draught oxen, two horses or mares used to draw with them, twelve of the best milch kine, etc.

The inventory enclosed with the will gives a list of the rooms and farm buildings and their contents. The hall consisted of a parlour, a chamber over it, and an inner chamber; a gallery, with a middle, a foremost and a third chamber under it; a maid's chamber; a kitchen, two ox houses, and a milk-house. It is noticeable that there were bedsteads in all the rooms except the gallery, the kitchen and the milk-house – there were even two bedsteads in the ox-houses.

The Hearth Tax was introduced in 1662 and in the returns for the two succeeding years Lea Hall appears with 5 or 6 hearths respectively.

As late as the year 1730 there were Glaseours who are described as of Lea, but probably from about that time the hall was let to tenant farmers including the following:

1840 and 1865	Richard Woodfine
1880	Peter Robinson
1889	Samuel Carter
1902	Wilfred Carter.

We still have in Lea the ancient tithe barn – the very large building on the opposite side of the road to the Hall. The east end of the barn has been adapted to form two cottages. This was the barn to which the inhabitants of Lea brought their tithes of produce in the days when the township was under the control of the abbey.

Formerly the road-way which now passes Lea Hall towards the Demage Farm and is now enclosed by fences, passed through the farmyard which was known to the inhabitants as the fold.

A question which appears to hold some interest when answered is "Why is the field adjoining the Tithe-barn so known as the "Jimmie-George"? Has it any connection with James, the Old Pretender and the accession of King George I (1714)?

MOLLINGTON: The tun of Moll's People

The last township of our Parish to be considered will be Mollington. There are of course two Mollingtons, Great Mollington and Little Mollington. The former is in Backford while the latter is now in the Parish of Upton-by-Chester and was originally in the Parish of St. Mary-on-the-Hill, Chester.

Great Mollington has an area of 824 acres and its population in 1841 was 140. Little Mollington has an area of 259 acres and in 1841 it had 25 inhabitants. At the census of 1931 the two townships together had a population of 336.

About these townships Domesday Book (1086) says:

> Robert de Rodelent, Baron of Rhuddlan holds Molintone Banastre of Earl Hugh. Godwine held it and was a freeman. There are 1½ hides that pay geld. There is land enough for 3 ploughs. In the demesne there is one and 3 serfs. There are 3 villeins and 3 bordars, 2 acres of meadow and 2 acres of woodland. It was waste T.R.E. when Robert received it, it was worth 20/-; now 15/-.
>
> The same Robert hold Molintone Torront and Lambert holds it of him. Gunner and Ulf held it as 2 maners and were freemen. There is one hide that pays geld. There is land enough for 2 ploughs. In the demesne there is one plough with 2 serfs and there are 2 acres of meadow. It is worth 14/-. It was waste and he found it waste.
>
> (virgate = 120 acres hide = 4 virgates)

This Robert de Rodelent was slain by the Welshmen on 3rd July, 1088 and as he had no legitimate heir, his barony was split up into numerous subdivisions. In the first year of the reign of Edward II Molintone Torrant was possessed by the family whose name was Terrant, Torrant or Torrold. By this name it is distinguished from the adjacent township of Mollingtan Banastre (another family name). In that year William Terrand obtained from James, son of Roger de Coghull lands in Mollington and early in the reign of Edward III he obtained other lands, with the manor of Molintone from William de Backford, then chaplain. In the reign of Henry V the manor was inherited by Katherine de Eulowe and she married Roger Booth, brother of Sir Robert Booth, founder of the house of Dunham Massey. It remained in the family of their descendants until the reign of Elizabeth I when it passed by marriage to the Mordaunts of Bedfordshire; soon after this they alienated their Cheshire estates and the Manor of Mollington came into the possession of the Gleggs of Gayton and in 1758 it passed by marriage to John Baskervyle Esquire of Old Withington. By him it was sold to Thomas Hunt and in 1797 his granddaughter sold it and all their estates to John Feilden, Esquire of Blackburne in the county of Lancaster. The Feilden Family sold the last of their Mollington Estates in 1907.

There are no vestiges remaining of the ancient hall of Mollington Torrant, but its site is supposed to have been near a pool in the centre of the village. Since we still have the name Torrant preserved in that of the Tarrant Farm, one might suggest that the site of the ancient mansion was at the Tarrant Farm. Certainly, by observing the line of ancient trees, it would appear that the original entrance to that house was from the Parkgate Road nearby opposite to the present entrance to the Paddock.

The Feilden mansion, which was handsome and spacious building in the Georgian style, was erected in 1756. It was dismantled and token down in 1937. This house was built on the site of an ancient manor house.

The northern boundary of Mollington follows the line of old Powey Lane from a point about 400yd. from its junction with the Parkgate Road to the point at which the western boundary of Lea joins the lane. From this point the boundary of Mollington is shared with that of Lea. On the west side the Mollington boundary line follows a water coarse from Powey Lane and passes under Coalpit Lane at the foot of the slight, rise just to the west of Coalpit Lane Farm (now known as Hill Farm). The boundary continues to follow the stream, passing under the Chester–Parkgate Road just south of the Wheatsheaf Inn and continuing after leaving the stream in a direction almost parallel to the main road, passing behind Mollington Paddock and joining the south side of the road by the entrance gate of that residence. From here the boundary line follows the road to the entrance gate to Crabwell, where the boundary of Great Mollington separates from that of Little Mollington, crosses the road and passes south of the Elms Farm and along a field fence to Dodd's Wood from where it crosses the canal and joins the stream to the south of the canal.

COMMUNICATIONS

(This Communications chapter was omitted from the typed version and has been transcribed and added from the handwritten script. Editor)

Some recent research has been taking place regarding any possible Roman development in the Wirral peninsula. It is a well known fact that Deva Castra (Chester) was an important Roman military centre. Also it has been practically ascertained that the Romans had a small outpost at Meols in North Wirral. As communication between the two in the form of a road would be very probable, it is well to establish, if possible, the line which this road took. Recent observers have found it highly likely that the Roman way left Chester along what is now Parkgate Road and followed it to the Mollington finger-post corner, whence it took the line of Townfield Lane to the point where that lane turns eastward near to the residence called 'The Grey House'. From there it is thought that the ancient road followed the green lane across the fields towards Coalpit Lane Farm from where it followed the present footpath leading to Capenhurst and so on to North Wirral. These statements, it must be remembered, are not yet established facts and much research remains to be done.

Powey Lane, which passes along our northern boundary, through Backford Cross, and much of which has been incorporated in the new Shotwick–Frodsham road, was the medieval Pack-horse road leading from the Deeside into the South Lancashire country. From earliest times till the 16th and 17th centuries the River Dee was the great western highway for shipping and Chester was the most important sea-port of this part of the west coast. Indeed, so important was Chester deemed to be that King Henry VIII raised it to the rank of a County (the County of the City of Chester). This is the reason why Chester has a Sheriff (Shire-reeve) as well as a Mayor. As the Dee gradually silted up its channel, however, the landing quays were moved further down the estuary so that the creeks at Saughall and Shotwick became centres of business. The two parallel lanes of Shotwick and Woodbank led directly from the riverside and strings of pack-horses loaded with goods wended their way to the Chester road, thence into Powey Lane, along via the old lane through Chorlton and on through Upton to the Manchester road.

The Dee and Mersey Canal passes along the southern part of our parish. The Canal is about nine miles long and was constructed under the supervision of Thomas Telford between the years 1793 and 1806. In the early part of the 19th century there was a regular goods and passenger traffic between Liverpool and Chester through the canal, a steam packet on the canal connecting with a daily packet on the Mersey from Liverpool at Whitby Locks (since called Ellesmere Port).

In September 1840, the Chester to Birkenhead railway was formally opened. The route of the railway line was surveyed in 1824–5 by George Stephenson and his scheme received Parliamentary sanction in 1837. Originally it was estimated to cost £250,000 but the actual expenditure was more than double this sum. When the line was first opened the Birkenhead terminus was what was then known as the Grange Lane Station, now called Town Station. The Chester terminus was what is now the Station Master's house (Brook Cottage) in Brook Street and the railway lines running into the wagon repair yard formed part of the line. The first sod was cut in 1838 and the line took only two years to complete. The speed of its construction was chiefly due to the fact that there were no serious engineering difficulties to surmount, the deepest cutting being between Rock Ferry and Bebington, and the only bridge of any size being the one over the canal at Mollington. For many years there was a single track only with loops here and there for trains to pass. Only three stations were built between Chester and Birkenhead – Mollington, Sutton (now called Ledsham) and Hooton. The Booking Office at Mollington bears the crest of the Feilden family and the date 1844. The Feilden crest also was carved in the wall of the bridge which carries the road over the railway, but that has become almost obliterated. It was from the Feilden family that the land was purchased for the construction of the part of the railway which passes through Lea.

A contemporary account of the formal opening of this railway is rather interesting:

> The Chester Courant 29th September 1840
>
> The Chester and Birkenhead railway was formally opened by the running of a special train in the afternoon (22nd Sept.) from Birkenhead by the directors, who were accompanied by the Mayor of Liverpool, the Mayor of Chester and a number of other gentlemen. The line was opened to the public on the following day. The inaugural train, made up of first class carriages, was of great length and hauled by two engines bearing the names Touchstone and Zillah. It received an enthusiastic send-off by a multitude of cheering spectators and the firing of a cannon. The journey to Chester was made in exactly one hour. This, of course, was nearly double the time that will be occupied by the transit on ordinary occasions, the train being not only very lengthy but excessively loaded. The bridges and banks were crowded with anxious and curious spectators who evinced their interest in the undertaking by the cheers with which they greeted the train.

BACKFORD PARISH CHURCH

At the time of the Norman Conquest of England, the part of the country which now comprises Cheshire was given special treatment by the King. It was created a County Palatine. Owing to its position on the border of Wales, William saw that it was very necessary to place a strong military power in this part of England, to protect his newly-won kingdom from invasion from the west. So he bestowed the county upon his nephew Hugh d'Avranches, surnamed Lupus or "the Wolf", and his heirs, giving him the title Earl of Chester. Royal rights were granted to him over all land within the earldom, which was held by him "as freely by the sword as the king held England by the Crown". Hence Cheshire became a County Palatine that is a county whose ruler exercises all the powers of an independent prince, save only that he owes allegiance to his overlord the King.

Hugh Lupus, in his turn, appointed Norman barons to be overlords of the various districts of the County Palatine and the baron appointed to supervise the Wirral seems to have been Hamon de Masci of Dunham.

It was Hamon, the third Baron of Dunham who founded, in 1150, the Benedictine Priory for sixteen monks at Birkenhead. This Hamon was one of the Massey family who owned, in later years, Puddington Hall and one of the endowments which he bestowed on the new priory was the Manor of Backford.

This is the earliest known reference in any document to Backford. While Mollington and Lea are mentioned in Domesday Book (1087), no reference is made therein to Backford. Whether or not there ever was a Norman church at Backford, we do not know. It appears that there was a tendency among the Norman manor-lords, when they newly came into their properties, to build places of worship on their estates if a church did not already exist there. At any rate, this was a practice forbidden by the Synod of Westminster in 1102. Nevertheless, the dedication of our church to Saint Oswald (essentially an English dedication) may indicate the existence of a church in pre-Norman times. Unfortunately, we have no remains of buildings earlier than the 13th century and no records of the parish during the Norman age.

The Church is sited on one of the highest points in the Parish (about 100 ft above sea level) and almost at the centre of the parish. This may seem an exaggeration to those parishioners who live at furthest part of Mollington. Yet the distance there to the Church is very little greater than the distance from the Church to Backford Cross or to the outer boundary of the township of Caughall. The Church stands close to the main road from Chester to Birkenhead but is now sheltered from much of the noise and bustle of the highway by a plantation of trees. It was during the rebuilding of the Hall in the late eighteenth century that the line of the highway was altered at Backford. In order to make the plantation between the mansion and the road, the latter was moved further towards the west. The result of this alteration can be seen by observing the direction of the line of the Church Farm House and comparing it with the present line of the road. The two are not parallel, the reason for this being that formerly the highway ran in the same direction as the line of the farm house and passed close to the door of the Church Tower.

The present building of the Church shows three different stages.

The Chancel – the oldest part. (13th Century).

The Nave – wholly restored 1879.

The Tower – late 15th century.

The Chancel

The Chancel of our Church as it is at present can be said to date from the 13th century, say some time between 1250 and 1300. The east Window and the smaller window on the north side of the sanctuary are Early English in style (1190–1270). The east window is a rather good (rural) example of the direct development from the three-lancet type of window. The three narrow lancets were built in one window. The ancient oak beams which support the roof of the chancel are, as far as is known, original work. They have been shaped out of tree trunks with the adze. When the chancel roof was re-decorated after the nave restoration of 1879 the original decorations were adhered to as far as possible and the letters S.O. which appear between the rafters indicate the Church dedication to Saint Oswald. On the south wall of the Chancel are two indentations or niches. The one nearer to the west is thought to be an ancient aumbry – the only one in Wirral. An aumbry was a cupboard in the wall near the altar and was used for various purposes. One of those was the reservation of the Sacrament. The aumbry was also a convenient place for the priests' vestments, or for the storage of the altar vessels. In the example at Backford there are evident signs of the place where hinges were affixed for the door. Further to the East and nearer the altar there is in our Parish Church the ancient piscina, but the bowl has been replaced by a stone ledge. The piscina consisted of a bowl from which a drain lead out through the wall, so that the water used for various ablutions at the altar passed into consecrated ground. The best example of a piscina in Wirral is to be seen in West Kirby Parish Church. Although there is no documentary evidence of alteration to the floor of the Chancel, it seems to be very probable that at some time in the past (probably 1879) the level of the floor has been raised considerably. In ancient days Chancel and Nave were built on the same level, whereas at Backford now the Chancel floor is several feet higher than that of the Nave.

The Nave

The Nave of the Church was wholly restored in 1879 and thus contains no ancient stone work. Practically the whole of the walls was rebuilt, the old windows removed and the present pseudo-gothic ones put in. The old roof was taken off and the present roof built on. The old pillars were entirely removed and the present pillars put in. Thus the style of the present Nave may be described as Victorian.

Before the restoration of 1879, the Nave had a flat roof and the windows had semi-circular arches. The south entrance had a doorway also having a semi-circular arch and the porch was surmounted by three ornamental stone vases. A triangular piece of yellow sandstone was built into the south porch above the outer entrance, bearing the inscription – "this church was builded in the year 1728 – Robert Denson, Vicar". Thus an earlier restoration took place in 1728, during the Vicarate of Rev. Robert Denson. On this occasion the Nave was rebuilt in what may be called the "Queen Anne" style of architecture. In connection with this restoration, it is interesting to note that in a list of briefs dating from 1685 to 1735 in the Church of Saint Lawrence at Reading, there occurs an entry which says that on 29th January, 1727, St. Lawrence's Church, Reading contributed 11s. 3d. towards the rebuilding of Backford Church in Cheshire which was to cost £1,532. The triangular piece of stone to which reference has been made, was, probably in 1879, built into the wall of the shed on the north side of the Church and may still be seen there.

The Tower

The Tower dates from the late 15th century probably some time between 1450 and 1500. It is rather a good rural example of the change in building styles which took place about the period from the Decorated to the Perpendicular. The window in the west wall of the Tower is almost decorated in style, yet it shows the addition of a transom, while the doorway beneath the window is purely Perpendicular in style. On the other hand, the arch which divides the Tower from the Nave is purely Gothic. The pinnacles were put on the Tower in 1879. As far as can be ascertained, there had been no pinnacles before that date, although the building appeared as though it had been the intention to add pinnacles.

In the days when our Tower was built, small details of design or ornament were left to the ingenuity of the individual craftsmen. Thus, among various forms of rosettes, faces and flower carvings, we have carved on our Tower a hen followed by her four chicks, a goose, a dog chasing a rabbit and a fox on the prowl. Such things would naturally come to the minds of rural masons. No doubt if such liberty of detail was allowed to modern masons we should find the latest jet aircraft figuring in their work.

CHURCH FURNITURE

The earliest reference to seats in Backford Church is the seating plan dated 15th April, 1636 when the Vicar was Rev. William Bagaley. This was probably the first time there had been seats for the congregation in the Church. In Mediaeval times the worshippers either stood or knelt during service. The only seat provided was one round the wall of the Nave and it was intended for the use of those who were unable to stand – "the weak go to the wall". Apparently there have always been three "isles" in our Church, from 1636. The plan is authorised by Bishop John Bridgman of Chester.

These seats had to be taken out during the Vicarate of Rev. Robert Denson, when the Nave was restored in 1728. We have entries in an ancient minute book of the dimensions of some of these old pews "The Dimensions of certain Pews in Backford Church which were taken April 16th 1728 when the Church began to be taken down in order to be rebuilt.

Mr. Hunt's pew in length 7 ft. 3 in., in breadth 6 ft.

Mr. Birkenhead's pew in length 6 ft. 3 in., in breadth 6 ft.

Mr. Booth's pew in length 6 ft., in breadth 5ft. 6 in.

Numbers of the seats or pews.

In the North Isle	12 pews.
In the Middle Isle	14 pews
In the South Isle	10 pews"

Following the restoration of 1728 the seating remained unchanged until 1840 when a gallery was erected along the north side of the Church. This gallery contained sixty-two free sitting places and cost £50.

The next change in the seating of the Nave was in 1879, when the last restoration took place. All the old oak pews, with the ancient doors, were taken out and the present pitch-pine pews put in.

The present pulpit and font in Backford were installed in memory of Rev. Francis Bryans, who died in 1877, after being Vicar for 39 years. We have no record of the ancient pulpit but there was an ancient English font here until the present font was put in. The old font was loaned to Saint Thomas's Church Whitby but whether or not it is still there one cannot say.

In our Nave we have two old Church Chests. The older one is, of course, our original Church Chest dated 1636 when Thomas Pierson and William Davies were churchwardens.

The other chest bears the date 1702 and was bequeathed to the Church by the late Mrs. Thornton, a member of the Denson Family. The chest originally belonged to the mother of Vicar Robert Denson and the initials A. A. indicate the name Ann Arbridge, which was the lady's name before her marriage.

FURNITURE OF THE CHANCEL

The present Reredos and altar were put in the Church in 1892 to the memory of Mrs. May Taylor who died in 1891. She lived at the Willows, Mollington. The two chairs in the sanctuary are said to have been made from old altar rails. They are Jacobean in style but it is doubtful whether they date from the 17th century or not. In a list of items of expenditure on Improvements in Backford Church in the year 1840 there is one entry which says that two large chairs were provided for the communion chancel. The original Jacobean Communion Table is now in the Church vestry. As far as can be ascertained, the present Choir Stalls were put in at the restoration of 1879.

The remaining piece of furniture in the Chancel is, of course, the Organ. The present instrument was built by the late E. Franklin Lloyd, an organ builder from Liverpool, and it was "opened" on 25th October 1883. The opening recital was played by the late Canon Hylton Stewart, M.A., who at that time was Precentor of Chester Cathedral.

For a short time before the installing of this new organ, the church services were led by an instrument of the American Organ type. The organist's seat at this instrument is now used by the Head Schoolmistress at Mollington as the seat at her desk. (*Margin Note*: "Since disappeared").

In the list of Improvements in Backford Church in the year 1840 (to which reference has already been made) the following items are found:

Messrs, Gray & Son. Organ, including erecting in Church and packing,	£78. 16s. 7d.
Erection of Gallery for Organ	£11

G. Sherwin, instructing the Choir £4. 10s.

J. Podmore, Gilding Pipes £1. 10s.

These items probably refer to the installing of what was known as a "barrel" organ. This was an instrument which worked on the same principle as one of the old-fashioned "musical boxes". "Winch" organs as the barrel organs were called, were in vogue for many years. They were furnished with separate barrels, each pricked with ten or twelve tunes. It fell to the village clerk to turn the handle. He was the only person who understood the mechanism and how to change the barrels.

Parts of the ancient "winch" organ used at Backford are still lying in one of the outbuildings of the Vicarage but, of course, it would not be possible to have the instrument rebuilt because several pieces are missing.

Whether or not string and wood-wind instruments were ever in use at Backford for leading the Church Services one cannot say. It is very probable that they were, but there is no documentary evidence of this.

Another object of interest in the Church is, of course, the ancient chained Bible. It is now to be seen at the west end of the north aisle of the Nave. It is the second oldest Bible in Wirral and is an early edition of King James I's Authorised Version. Our copy was printed by Robert Barker of London and bears the data 1617. It will be remembered that during the reign of King Henry VIII, it was ordered that "one boke of the holy Bible shall be sett up in some convenient place within the churche where as your parishioners may most commodiously resorte to the same and reade it". This was in 1539 and it is probable that when the copy placed in Backford became too much worn for use. The present chained Bible was put in its place in 1617 or thereabouts and has been in the church ever since that time. It became necessary to keep the book in a glass case because souvenir hunters have been known to remove pages.

THE INCUMBENTS OF BACKFORD

As has already been stated the first patrons of the living at Backford were the priors of Birkenhead Priory and thus until the Dissolution of the monasteries in the 16th century, the Vicars of Backford were monks from the Priory.

The earliest name given as Vicar is that of William de Aston who seems to have been appointed to the living in October 1305. Thence there is a succession of appointments down to the time of the dissolution of the monasteries:

	Dominus Gilbertus
May 1349	Henry de Molynton (local name)
Sept. 1396	John Spencer
Apr. 1427	Thomas Calf
Jun. 1450	Gilbert Hesketh
Jul. 1452	Thomas de Coghull (local name)
Mar. 1457	Henry Ball
Jan. 1461	William Forschagh
Jul. 1471	William Mason
Dec. 1482	Hugh Zurdeslay or Yardsley,
1524	William Ashton
Dec. 1539	Ricard Garratt.

After this date the dissolution of the monasteries took place. The new bishopric of Chester was founded in 1541 and much of the monastic wealth was given as an endowment to the new Diocese. Thus the Bishop of Chester was henceforth Patron of the living of Backford.

Richard Garratt seems to have retained the living under the new Patron, since he was still vicar in 1557.

The next appointment was that of Hugh Morrey about 1579. He was followed in 1582 by Thomas Lawson. In the same year a second appointment seems to have been made, namely, that of Robert Hutton. Hutton was followed in 1591 (May 23) by William Denson (a member of the Denson family who lived at the Chapel House, Wervin from 1422 to 1879).

From 1630 to 1632 the Vicarage of Backford seems to have been unsupplied.

In January 1632, however, William Bagaley became the Vicar, appointed by the Bishop of Chester. His signature occurs in our own parish registers. It was during his vicarate that the Church was furnished with seats in 1636. The plan of this seating arrangement is still extant.

About 1644 John Willson M.A. became Vicar. He was of Brasenose College, Oxford and a man of learning. He died in Chester in 1672.

From this time till after the restoration of King Charles II to the throne, things are rather uncertain. About 1646 a Mr. Frecketon seems to have been the minister at Backford. It was, of course, the time of the Civil War in England and Frecketon was resident in Chester when it was taken by the Parliamentary forces. He had his goods sequestered by the committee of sequestration for delinquency. He was, however, placed in the living of Backford pro tempere by the Deputy Lieutenant of the County, and on 10 June, 1646 he had £50 awarded to him by way of augmentation by an order from committee of plundered ministers.

Following the restoration of the King to the throne, about 1664 Rev. John Haughten became Vicar. He has a monument in the Chancel and died in 1685.

Haughten was followed by Robert Cottrell and in 1691, on the death of Cottrell, William Barratt became Vicar. He, however, died in the same year and on 18th Aug. 1691 John Turner was Vicar. Turner was followed on 9th Nov. 1720, by Rev. Robert Denson, the second member of the Wervin family to hold the living. It was during this Vicarate that the Nave of the Church was completely rebuilt and refurnished with seats. The seats seem to have been numbered and paid for.

Robert Denson died in 1750 and was followed by Thomas Broadhurst B.A. He was a minor canon of Chester Cathedral and vicar of St. Oswald's. He died in 1803 aged 84 years and his grave is under the east window of the Church (outside).

In 1803 Thomas Armitstead B.D. became vicar and he was followed in 1827 by Charles Butler Stevenson M.A., who exchanged livings with George Stevenson M.A., in 1831.

The Rev. Francis Bryans M.A. became Vicar in 1838 and held the living for 39 years. He was followed in 1877 by Rev. Richard John Fairclough M.A. It was during his vicarate that the last restoration of the Church was carried out (1879).

Vicar Fairclough was succeeded to 1904 by Rev. Canon James Marr New, M.A., and the latter was followed in 1931 by the present vicar Rev. Canon A.H. Blencowe, M.A.

THE CHURCH REGISTERS

It has not always been compulsory for a parish to keep a register of its baptisms, weddings and burials. It was on 5th Sept. 1538, that Thomas Cromwell, Chancellor of King Henry VIII issued a mandate by which every parson, vicar or curate must enter in a book every wedding, baptism and burial in his parish, with the names of the parties. The parish also was to provide a "sure coffer" with two locks, the parson having the custody of one key, the wardens that of the other. The entries were to be made each Sunday after service, in the presence of one of the wardens. These entries were generally made on paper, sometimes on loose sheets.

On 25th Oct. 1597, a provincial constitution from Canterbury, approved by the Queen (Elizabeth I) in 1598, ordered that parchment registers should be purchased by each parish and that all names from the older (usually paper) registers should be copied therein from the beginning, "but especially since the first year of Her Majesty's reign". It is for this reason that so many registers begin in 1558, the transcriber indolently complying with the last part of the injunction only, and omitting to copy the first twenty years of the original register. This time it was ordered that entries should be made as before, on Sundays, but in the presence of both wardens. Every page was to be subscribed by them as well as by the Minister and it was ordered that the coffer should have a third lock, the minister and each warden to have a key. The entries of the past week were to be read out each Sunday after service. Finally, it was provided that the churchwardens of each parish should, within a month after Easter each year, transit to the diocesan registry a transcript of the register entries for the preceding year.

In our own parish the earliest Register begins in 1562. It is probably a copy of an earlier writing made after the Elizabethan order.

The Church Chest (dated 1636) still has an iron plate on it which has three key holes, from the time when the Minister and each church warden had a Key and chest could not be opened unless the three persons were present.

By Act of Parliament of 1666 and 1675, it was ordered that "no corpse of any person (except those who die of the plague) shall be buried in any shirt, shift, sheet or shroud, or anything whatsoever made or mingled with flax, hemp, silk, hair, gold or silver, or in any stuff or thing, other than what is made of sheep's wool only – or be put into any coffin lined or faced with any other material but sheep's wool only".

The Act was ordered to be given in charge at the sessions and assizes and heavy penalties were ordered upon those neglecting to comply with it. Sometimes a new volume of the burial register begins in 1678. The Act provided that within eight days of the funeral, affidavit must be made that the law had been complied with.

At Backford a new Register was begun in 1678 by Vicar John Haughton. These are some typical entries:

> 20th day of October 1678 Samuel Fisher buried in Woollon only.
>
> (b) 17th January 1678 Ralph Morgell of Heston, Esq., buried in the Chancel at Backford with an affidavit.
>
> (c) Joan Ryder was buried in the Churchyard of Backford the second day of September, Anns. Dom., 1879, being wound up and lapt in woollen only, as appears by affidavit.

The Inscriptions and Memorials in Backford Church

1. The painted panels (in the Chancel).

> On north wall.

Inscription on above:

> Margareta nux Radulp Morgell gen
>
> vxor et Edward Glegge de Geton ar. filia

The Morgells were of Moston Hall, formerly in Backford Parish, but now in the parish of St. Mary-on-the-hill. John Morgell was Principal Registrar for the Diocese of Chester, and died on the 27th November, 1636. His son and heir Ralph married Margaret, daughter of Edward Glegg of Gayton. Elizabeth, sister and heiress of William Morgell, sold the property in 1718.

Below this

Inscription on above:

> Her lyeth ye Body's of Rafe Morgall gen and Eliz: his wife, who had Issue Rafe William and Elisabeth Morgall. He died Nov. ye

27 1683 she died may ye 9th 1683: They gave five pounds to ye Parish of Backford ye use of it to be given to ye Poore on good friday in money for ever.

Ralph Morgell, of Moston, co. Chester, gent, made his Will 24th Nov. 1682, and it was proved at Chester 1683. He mentions his wife Elizabeth, his son William and an unborn child. He also mentions his aunt Anne Morgell, his uncle Peter Hurlesten, his brother Richard Morgell, his sister Mary Morgell, and his brother (in law) Thomas Glaseour. His wife was Elizabeth, daughter of William Glasier, of Lee, co. Chester. (Ormerod, History of Cheshire, Vol II)

To the east of the two panels, on the north wall, is a grey stone inscribed:

Underneath lieth Interred the Body of Robert Denson,

Vicar. Who died Feb. 1st 1750.

The Rev. Robert Denson was of Brasenose College, Oxford B.A. 1717. Instituted Vicar on 9th Nov.1720. By his will dated 29th Nov. 1747, he gave, among other bequests, to his daughter Anna a small cabinet with all the things in it except a gold ring, which he gave to his daughter Mary. Catherine and Mary were minors. He devised to his son Robert his house and lands at Childer Thornton with the residue of his estate, after making provision for his daughters. To his nephew Thomas Denson he gave £5 or its value in books out of his study. This Thomas Denson was of St. John's College, Cambridge, B.A. in 1746, and was the son of Richard Denson of Wervin. He was bred at Backford under his uncle and was admitted to St. John's College on 6th May, 1643. He became curate of Dodleston, Cheshire in 1748.

Below this there is a white marble tablet inscribed:

Richard Denson Ch. Warden at Stoak 1686.

In memory of George Denson, second son of Samuel and Martha Denson of The Chapel House, Wervin, which farm the family occupied from A.D. 1422 to February, 1849 when George Denson removed to Picton Hall, in this county, where he died 6th Nov. 1875, aged 64, and was interred near the chancel door. His father and mother were interred in a vault inside the church, the Church and Churchyard of Backford having been the burial place of the Densons of Wervin from time immemorial.

To the east of this tablet is a marble tablet inscribed:

To the memory of Rev. Samuel Griffith, D.D. Rector of Avington in the County of Berks. Who died 29th April, 1796, Aged 64.

The Rev. Samuel Griffith was of St. John's College, Cambridge. Deacon 1757. B. A. 1757.

Priest 1758. M.A. 1790. Son of John Griffith of Backford, husbandman. Educated by Rev. Robert Denson. Instituted Vicar of Halesowen in Worcestershire, 1784 and Rector of

Avington 1788.

To east of last monument is another painted panel.

Inscription on above:

Here lyeth interred the Bodies of Lenox sone & heire of Sr. George Beverley late of Huntingtcn Knt. who died the 5th day of Aprill 1660, he married Elizabeth daugh: to Henry Birkenhead of Backford esq: by whom he had issue 8 sones & 4 daugh: she died the 19th day of January 1656 .

Sir George Beverley was knighted at Leixlip in Ireland 8th May, 1604. He was of Huntingdon, in Broxton hundred, co. Chester. The issue of Lenox Beverley were: George, Henry (died young), Birkenhead, Thomas, Anthony, Lenox, Alice, Frances, Elizabeth, Elinor.

On the south wall a painted panel.

Inscription on above:

Here lyeth ye Bodyes of Iohn Houghton

who died 15 Aug: 1682. Robert Houghto:-

5th son who died 19th Sept: 1681. Mary Hough

ton 2d. dau: she died 23rd Apr. 1672 they

were sones & dau: of Iohn Houghton:

vicar of Backford by Iane his wife dau:

to hugh Hopkin of Chomley gen.

The Rev. John Haughton was instituted Vicar of Backford about 1665, and died about 1685. He was born 1633 and was a son of William Haughton, of Haughton, in the parish of Bunbury, by his first wife Dorothea, daughter of George Davenport of Calveley, Esq.

Two other painted panels on south wall of the Chancel:

Over priest's door.

Inscription on above:

> Margaret Birkenhead eldest dau
> hgter of Henry Birkenhead esqr.
> dyed ye xth day of August Ao.

Beneath the arms is the date J 6 24

Margaret Birkenhead was a younger sister of Mrs. Beverley, whose monument is on the north side of the Chancel.

(Editorial Note: The following four epitaphs from the Backford Churchyard do not occur in the typed version of this document but do occur in the hand written version.)

1. Samuel Lewis died 1835 – aged 19 years.

> Sing and pray without delay,
> You do not know the time:
> For I was one that was soon gone,
> And cut off in my prime.

2. Thomas Jones of Backford died 1769.

> Stop here your foot and cast an eye;
> As you are now so once was I;
> As I am now so you must be,
> Prepare yourself to follow me.

3. Jane, wife of William Maddock of Backford, died 1875

> Long days and nights I bore great pain,
> To wait for cure was all in vain;
> Till God above saw what was best,
> He took me hence and gave me rest.

4. John Baxter of Sealand who died in 1811

> A faithful friend, a husband dear,
> A tender father lieth here;
> Great is the loss as we sustain,
> We hope in Christ it is his gain.

SUNDIAL

Plate date 1772
Stone base John Hancock }Churchwardens
Joseph Waring }
1832.
Door into hall grounds date 1774.

BELLS

1. A.M.D.G. et in Piam Memoriam Reverendissimi in Xto Patris Gul. Jacobson Cestr. Nuper Episc. D.D. R.J. Fairclough
2. R.J. Fairclough, M.A. Vicar. W.Taylor and R. Davies, Churchwardens. The above were cast in 1887.
3. Let none be in anger. We were cast by Richard Saunders 1714.
4. J. T. 1714. (These are the initials of John Turner, the Vicar.)
5. John Birkened Esqre, 1714.
6. John Welesbe, William Hatton, Ch. Wardens. 1714.

John Davies – History of Backford, 1953

John Davies was organist and choirmaster at St. Oswald's, Backford, for 42 years, retiring in 1963. His tenure coincided with the long incumbency of Alan Blencowe (1931–1964), and these two made a strong team, even allowing for the arguments every week over the hymns. John is remembered as reliable and conscientious, and both were active in organising the regular choir outings.

John was also known as Backford's local historian, and used to lecture in the Village Hall. His research was carried out at a time when facilities were few, but, according to Derek Venables, "his work touched on the core of village knowledge, revealing horizons beyond for young and old". No one was better qualified to write a history of the area.

John Peter Hess

BENNETT FAMILY TREE

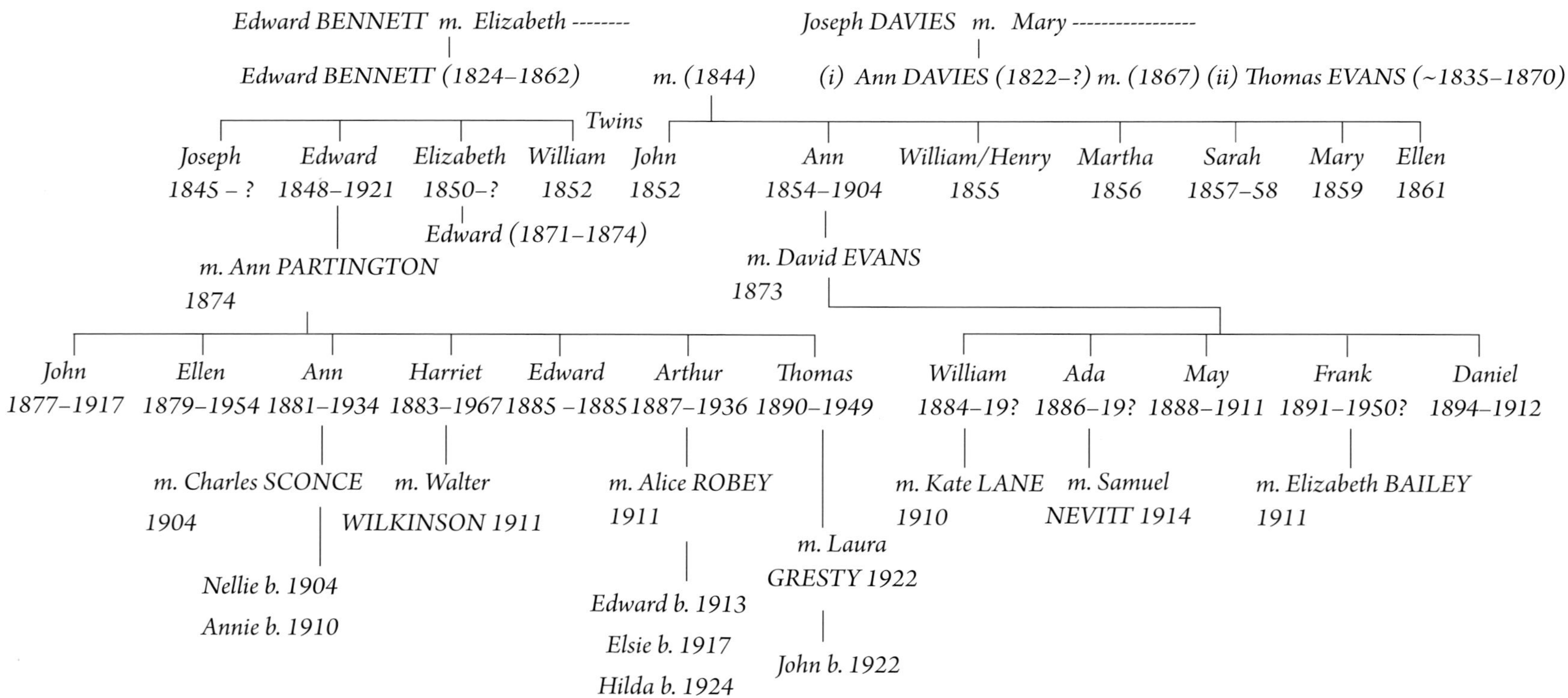

The story of the Bennett family of Backford and Chester

by Michael Richardson

As part of work in 2008 to develop new toilet and storage facilities on the north side of St Oswald's church in Backford one of the old gravestones, which had been leaning and partly hidden, was re-erected and can now be seen and read by all who use those facilities (figure 1). The inscription is brief and, even by Victorian standards, suggests a family history touched by sadness; it reads "*In memory of William, John, Henry, Martha, Mary, Sarah, Ellen, who died infants. Edward Bennett, father of the above, died Feby 5th 1862, aged 38*". Although we are told that the father died young, there is no clue about when or where the children died, nor how old they were and there is no mention of their mother. Some preliminary research into the story of the Bennett family was published in the Backford parish magazine for March 2009 and further work has now shown that the family had to endure more tragedies up to the 1870s although two members of the family did flourish and indeed have descendants living locally today.

Figure 1 – Bennett gravestone on North side of Backford church.

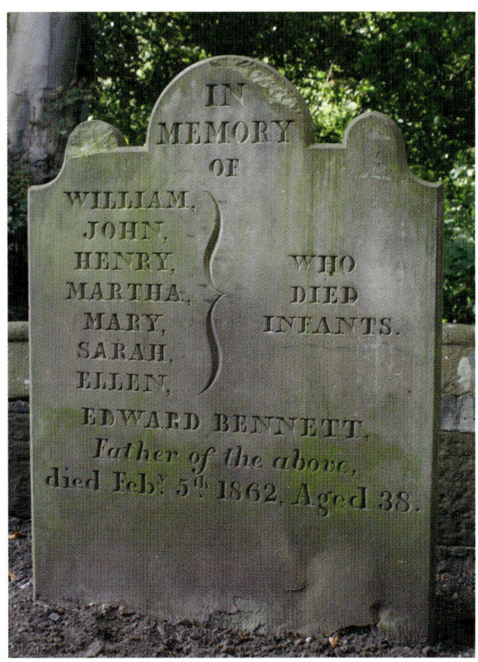

Details of their deaths can be found in the burial register for St Oswald's church.[1] From this we learn that Edward Bennett of Chester, age 40 (although the gravestone correctly gives his age as 38) was buried at Backford on 9th February 1862; as we will see later he was a toll-gate keeper. The register also give the dates of burial of six of the children named, but there is no record of Henry (nor could his birth be traced); it seems that the first two children (William and John) were twins, baptised at Backford on 24th March 1852, who died within a week of each other in May 1852. A second William was buried in November 1855 (he may have been recorded on the gravestone as Henry to avoid confusion) and his residence was given as Pulford, although he had been baptised at

Figure 2 – Toll gate shown on Backford Tithe map.

Backford on 21st September 1855, so it seems that the family must have moved to Pulford about that time, where Edward continued to work as a toll collector. They had a further four daughters, born at Lavister between 1856 and 1861 and all died young – Martha (December 1856, an infant), Sarah (March 1858 aged 4 months), Mary (May 1859 aged 11 weeks) and Ellen (July 1861 aged 7 weeks). Although infant mortality rates in the nineteenth century were high it certainly appears that the Bennetts were particularly unlucky.

From the census for 1851 we know that Edward Bennett was the toll-gate keeper at Backford. The toll-house was situated on the west side of the main road just to the north of the canal bridge and is shown on the tithe map for Backford[2] (figure 2); despite the widening and improvement of the A41 trunk road the remains of the building can still be seen there (figure 3). In the 1841 census the toll-gate keeper was recorded as William Gooch and we know (from the 1851 census) that he had moved with his family to Daubhill Bar near Bolton some time after the birth of their seventh child in 1847, which must be when Edward took over the toll-gate at Backford. A notice in the *Chester Chronicle* on 12th November 1847 (figure 4) announced that the tolls, including that at Moston gate (i.e. Backford) on the Chester to Woodside Turnpike road would be let by auction to be held in Chester on 2nd December.[3]

Figure 3 – Remains of the old Toll House beside A41 at Backford Bridge.

The 1851 census also tells us that Edward had been born in Tranmere and the parish registers for Bebington, St Andrew record the baptism of Edward Bennett on 13th June 1824; his parents were Edward and Elizabeth. The Eastham parish registers record the marriage on 30th December 1844 of Edward Bennett (age 20), a servant living at Brimstage whose father was Edward Bennett, a labourer, to Ann Davies (age 22), a servant living at Eastham whose father was Joseph Davies, a labourer. The Eastham registers also record Ann's baptism on 14th November 1822 and give her parents' names as Joseph and Mary. In the 1841 census we find Ann living with her parents and four brothers and from the tithe map and apportionments we can see that they were living in a cottage near St Mary's church.[2] Edward's father died in 1832 and was buried at Bebington and the 1841 census records his mother living in Tranmere, aged 65, with another son, William aged 25; from the tithe map it appears that they were probably living on what is now Prenton Road. Edward was also living in Tranmere but appears to have been living on what is now Church Road and working for a farmer named John Carter.

Figure 4 – Turnpike Notice in Chester Chronicle, 12 Nov. 1847.

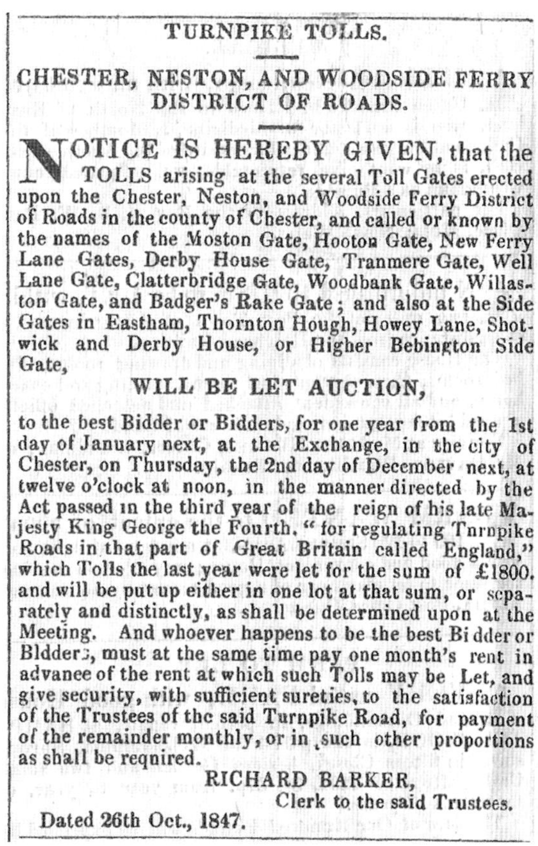

TURNPIKE TOLLS.

CHESTER, NESTON, AND WOODSIDE FERRY DISTRICT OF ROADS.

NOTICE IS HEREBY GIVEN, that the TOLLS arising at the several Toll Gates erected upon the Chester, Neston, and Woodside Ferry District of Roads in the county of Chester, and called or known by the names of the Moston Gate, Hooton Gate, New Ferry Lane Gates, Derby House Gate, Tranmere Gate, Well Lane Gate, Clatterbridge Gate, Woodbank Gate, Willaston Gate, and Badger's Rake Gate; and also at the Side Gates in Eastham, Thornton Hough, Howey Lane, Shotwick and Derby House, or Higher Bebington Side Gate,

WILL BE LET AUCTION,

to the best Bidder or Bidders, for one year from the 1st day of January next, at the Exchange, in the city of Chester, on Thursday, the 2nd day of December next, at twelve o'clock at noon, in the manner directed by the Act passed in the third year of the reign of his late Majesty King George the Fourth, "for regulating Tnrnpike Roads in that part of Great Britain called England," which Tolls the last year were let for the sum of £1800, and will be put up either in one lot at that sum, or separately and distinctly, as shall be determined upon at the Meeting. And whoever happens to be the best Bi dder or Bldders, must at the same time pay one month's rent in advance of the rent at which such Tolls may be Let, and give security, with sufficient sureties, to the satisfaction of the Trustees of the said Turnpike Road, for payment of the remainder monthly, or in such other proportions as shall be reqnired.

RICHARD BARKER,
Clerk to the said Trustees.

Dated 26th Oct., 1847.

Edward and Ann's first child was Joseph, baptised at St Catherine's, Tranmere, on 2nd August 1846. The next born was Edward, who was baptised at Eastham on 23th July 1848, and in both cases their father was described as a labourer. He must have taken up the post of toll-gate keeper at Backford soon afterwards as their first daughter Elizabeth was baptised there on 31st March 1850. Their sixth child Ann was baptised at Backford on 15th February 1854 and as already mentioned the family probably moved to Pulford soon afterwards as that was given as their address at the time of the children's burials from 1855 to 1861; the toll-gate on the Chester to Wrexham Turnpike road appears to have been on the Welsh side of the border at Lavister, although it is not marked on the Old Series one-inch Ordnance Survey map.

There was no sign of the Bennetts in the 1861 census for Pulford and a search eventually revealed that by then Edward had moved to be the toll-gate proprietor at Saltney (Flintshire) where his sons Joseph and Edward were described as toll-gate keepers and the daughters Elizabeth (age 11) and Ann (age 7) were both listed as scholars.

From the census returns for 1851 and 1861, together with entries in the Backford baptismal register and online records of births, marriages and deaths (BMD) we know that Edward and Ann had a total of eleven children, the seven named on the gravestone together with four who survived until at least early adulthood – Joseph, Edward, Elizabeth and Ann.

In order to see if there was any common factor in the deaths, certificates were obtained for two of them.[4] John Bennett, one of the twins, died on 26th May 1852 at Backford at the age of 9 weeks and the cause of death was recorded as "marasmus, from birth". Marasmus is a term for extreme emaciation in infancy and is now taken to mean wasting as a result of gross malnutrition so the likelihood is that the mother was unable to provide sufficient nourishment for two children and unfortunately it seems that neither survived. Sarah Bennett, who was tenth in the family, died on 2nd March 1858 at Lavister, aged 4 months and the cause of death was recorded as "inflammation of the chest". Without checking all of the death certificates we can't be sure but it appears that the children were probably undernourished and may have been prone to infection as a result. It must have been quite a challenge trying to rear nine children over as many years, but there seems to be no evidence that they succumbed to any of the infectious diseases which were prevalent at the time such as typhoid and cholera.

After Edward's death in 1862, it seems that Ann moved to Chester with the four remaining children; she re-married (in Q3 1867) a man called Thomas Evans[5] and in the 1871 census we find the family living at 4 Kitchen Street – off Crane St near the railway bridge – but by then Ann's second husband had already died, as she is recorded as a widow; BMD records include the death of a 35 year old Thomas Evans in Chester in Q4 1870.[5] Her sons Joseph and Edward are described as labourers, Elizabeth as "servant (out of place)" and Ann as "servant (visiting)", so both appear to have been visiting their mother at the time. Also living with them was Edward Bennett (grandson) aged 2 months, although all four of the Bennett children are listed as "unmarried". It seems probable that one of the girls had returned to the family home to have a child and this is confirmed by an entry in the parish registers for Holy Trinity, Chester which records the baptism of Edward Bennett on 4th March 1871, mother Elizabeth Bennett; there was no entry for the father and her address was given as Kitchen Street. A few years later, Elizabeth's son Edward died on 7th February 1874, aged 3, in Chester Infirmary as a result of accidental burns[4] – yet one more tragedy in the story of this unfortunate family. An inquest was held by the Chester Coroner John Tatlock two days later and was reported in the *Chester Chronicle* on 14th February.[6] Young Edward was living with his grandmother and it seems that she had left him alone in the house while she went to a nearby shop; his night shirt had caught fire as he played on the hearth and on hearing his screams his grandmother rushed home. With help from a neighbour the boy was taken to the Infirmary where he died later that day. The inquest jury returned a verdict of accidental death and this tragedy must have left the child's mother and grandmother distraught.

There appears to be no record of Ann Evans nor of her daughter Elizabeth or son Joseph in the 1881 census and the only Edward Bennett in the area was listed as having been born in Yorkshire, but on further investigation turned out to be the right person! He was living in Catherine Street with his wife Ann and two children, John (aged 4) and Ellen (aged 1). In 1891 they were still living at 8 Catherine St and this time his place of birth is correctly given as Eastham; by now they had four more children. The parish registers for St John, Chester record the marriage on 26th December 1874 of Edward Bennett, a labourer, to Ann Partington whose father was John Partington, a labourer. The couple had seven children, John, Ellen, Annie, Harriet, Edward, Arthur and Thomas, whose baptisms are recorded in the parish registers for St Oswald, Chester from 1877 to 1890. As already mentioned, six of them are listed in the 1891 census but it appears that Edward, baptised on 23rd March 1885, had died as an infant a few months later.

The family continued to live in Catherine St and in 1901 Edward is recorded as a builder's labourer, while John, aged 24, was a carter for a furniture company, Ellen, aged 21, a domestic servant and Arthur, aged 14, was a cellar boy for a wine merchant; Thomas was aged 11. By 1911 three of the children remained at home, John was a labourer, Ellen still a domestic servant while Thomas was now working as a black-smith's striker. Of the others it appears that Ann had married Charles Sconce in 1904[5] and in 1911 they were living at 23 Catherine St with

Figure 5 – Grave of Edward and Ann Bennett, Overleigh.

two daughters, Charles was listed as a clerk with the City Council. There were two family weddings in 1911,[5] with Harriet marrying Walter Wilkinson whilst Arthur married Alice Robey. Harriet and Walter do not appear to have had any children but Arthur and Alice had three children, Edward (born 1913), Elsie (born 1917) and Hilda (born 1924). The 1918 Electoral register records Edward and Anne Bennett living at number 8, while their son Arthur (but not his wife Alice) was at number 4 and Charles and Ann Sconce were at number 23. The youngest of Edward and Ann's children, Thomas, married Laura Gresty in 1922 and they had one son, John, born in 1922.[5]

Edward Bennett died in 1921 aged 73 and his widow Ann in 1937 aged 87, two of the very few members of the family to reach 'three score years and ten'! They are buried in Overleigh Cemetery (figure 5) as are other members of the family, including five of their children and their spouses.[7] Arthur must have moved to number 15 at some stage as we find his widow Alice living there in 1938, whilst her daughter Elsie (who had married George Crimes in 1935) was at number 4. Arthur and Alice's son Edward had married Margaret Joinson in 1937 and they lived at number 2, so the 1945 electoral register shows five houses at the southwestern end of Catherine St occupied by various members of the family! It seems that they had recovered from the misfortunes of the mid-nineteenth century and prospered to become quite a 'colony' in that part of Chester; in fact members of the family continued to live in Catherine St until very recently.

After much searching, the eldest Bennett daughter, Elizabeth, was found in the 1891 census, lodging with a family in Jackson's Court, off Duke St in Chester and working as a charwoman; in 1901 she is recorded, aged 52, a pauper, in the Chester Union Workhouse in Hoole (which was later to become the Chester City Hospital). The Workhouse register records her admission on 19 April 1900[8] and her discharge just a year later, soon after the 1901 census; her brother Edward was recorded as next of kin. However, it is not known what happened to her after that as there is no sign of her in the 1911 census and no record of her death has been traced.

The eldest of the surviving Bennett children was Joseph (born in 1845) but it has not been possible to trace him after the 1871 census when he was living in Kitchen St with his mother and three siblings. Searches of later census returns and death registers have failed to find him, so it is not known what became of him and his sister Elizabeth.

The younger daughter, Ann, married David Evans (an engine fitter) on 18 February 1873 at St Nicholas, Liverpool when they were both minors.[9] The address given for both of them was Boundary St and one of the witnesses was her sister Elizabeth. In the 1881 census they are listed living at Jones' Terrace, Sandicroft where David was working as a metal turner, probably at one of the nearby engineering works. By 1891 they had moved back to Chester and were living at 28 Gloucester St. which is where Arthur and Alice Bennett were living 20 years later! Their eldest two children were baptised at St Oswald's, Chester – William in 1884 and Ada in 1888; by that time the family were living in Catherine Street. The next two children, May (born 1889) and Frank (born 1891) were baptised at Christ Church, Newtown on 7 August 1891. The family moved to Cefn-Mawr soon afterwards where another son Daniel was born in 1894. From the 1901 census we know that David continued to work as a metal turner, as did his eldest son William, now aged 17. In fact, most of their neighbours were working as metal turners or steam engine fitters, possibly at the former British Iron Co. factory in Acrefair, which had been taken over by Hughes & Lancaster of Chester in the 1890s.

Ann Evans died in 1904 and was buried at Ruabon and David then married Elizabeth Wright, a widow, on 29th October 1905. In 1911 they were living at Rosa Cottages, Acrefair with his younger two sons but Daniel died in April 1912 and was buried at Ruabon. Of the remaining Evans children, William married Kate Maria Lane at Ruabon church on 26th Dec 1910 while Frank married Elizabeth Bailey, also at Ruabon church, on 14th May 1911; in the 1911 census May was recorded as a housemaid with George Millet and his family at Llyndir Hall, Rossett (now a hotel) but it appears that she died later that year and was buried at Ruabon on 8th July. There was an Ada Evans of the right age working as a waitress for the Powell family at Oakbank in Hoole village in 1911;

it appears that she married Samuel Nevett in Chester in 1914 and they had two children.

Starting with the limited information given on the gravestone in Backford churchyard, it has been possible to follow the fortunes of the Bennett family through several generations and despite a succession of early deaths the family line has continued and descendants of two of Edward Bennett's children have been identified, some of whom are still living in this area.

References and Sources

1. Backford burial registers, Cheshire Register Office microfilm 99/2.
2. Cheshire Tithe maps, searchable online at http://maps.cheshire.gov.uk/tithemaps/.
3. Copy held in the Local History Society Archives.
4. Death certifcates from General Register Office, Southport.
5. Births, marriages and deaths searchable online at http://www.freebmd.org.uk/.
6. Chester Chronicle, on microfilm at Cheshire Record Office.
7. Overleigh Cemetery Burial records, searchable online at http://archivedatabases.cheshire.gov.uk/cms/LacOverleighCemetery/home.aspx.
8. Chester Poor Law Union, Creed Register 1899–1901, Cheshire Record Office ZTRU20.
9. Liverpool marriages, 1813–1921, searchable at ancestry.co.uk.

Other information came from the following sources

Census returns 1841–1911, searchable online at ancestry.co.uk or http://www.findmypast.co.uk

Cheshire Parish Registers (baptisms and marriages), searchable online at http://www.findmypast.co.uk

Denbighshire Parish Registers (baptisms, marriages and burials), searchable online at http://www.findmypast.co.uk

The Origin of Field Names – Survey of Backford Parish 2010–11

By John Peter Hess

A version of this essay appeared in the Newsletter of Chester Society for Landscape History, number 49, September 2011

In February 2010 the Chester Society for Landscape History decided to carry out a survey of field names and their origin. This was to be over a wide area around Chester, including adjacent parts of North Wales. As an interested member, I was invited to take part and became part of the team – I concentrated on the Parish of Backford. Why do fields have names, anyway? I think they must originate in the desire of one person to define a piece of land for another person's understanding – probably in the same way country roads are named. The name chosen will reflect obvious characteristics or the name of a previous owner known to both parties, and in the difficulty of such description, will perhaps use terms already employed locally and therefore familiar to both.

When did field names come into use? I have, of course, mid 19th century tithe maps for all Backford Parish's townships, for which fields and their names are listed separately – described as apportionments. I have made those the starting point for analysis. Before that, only a 1796 Chorlton estate map exists, though even from that limited evidence I can say that the same names were being used then. Thinking more generally, most names can only have come after enclosure, which probably means a 17th or 18th century start. That ties up with the discovery that some names of people associated with fields are of known 17th or 18th century churchwardens. Even so, land must have been named earlier still, because many of the names have an old English origin and refer to land division before fences or hedges.

Are the same names in use today? Many must have been lost, as uses changed and fields were built over by houses and roads. In fact, it may only be on legal documents for land sale that a name is found necessary, and even that may not be the same. Our history society has a sale catalogue of 1907, which covers the break-up of the Mollington Hall estate and although many are the same as on the tithe map, not all names are. In other words, change occurs as need for identification changes.

The tithe maps for Backford's townships, Caughall, Chorlton, Lea, Mollington and Backford itself show 612 tithe apportionment field names in all. 450 of these contain name elements occurring more than once and, as an appendix to this report, I have produced a summary of those elements. The remainder are fields with unusual, isolated names, gardens to the many houses and cottages, or woodland plantations. In order to find probable name origins, I have consulted J. Dodgson, 'The Place Names of Cheshire', 1972; Margaret Gelling, 'Place Names in the Landscape', 1984; and A.D. Mills, 'Dictionary of English Place Names', 1991.

Most field names contain two or three elements. One can be a personal name, which may be an owner or tenant closely associated with the field. I mentioned churchwardens above, who would fit the personal category, and there are certainly others. Thus we have 'John Lees upper field' in Backford, or Eaton Hays' in Mollington. Alternatively, a connection with the church might produce 'Glebe', meaning land previously worked for the benefit of a clergyman: for instance 'St. Bridget's Glebe' and 'Stoak Glebe' in Mollngton.

Dam Hay, Caughall.

Chester Croft, Lea by Backford.

A second element might describe an old use. 'Croft' is a word of old English origin, meaning a small enclosure, and is very commonly used. 'Hay' is another old word, this time meaning a fenced enclosure. Three names older than enclosure itself are 'feld', modern field, 'aecer', modern acre, and 'maed', modern meadow, which are also common in the tithe apportionments. 'Looms' or 'Loons' derives from land and describes a well worked area divided into strips in pre-enclosure days, while 'Townfield' indicates land originally held for the benefit of the whole community. 'Smithy' applies to land connected with the village smithy and there are two fields in the parish with that name element, one, as expected, in Lea, but one also in Mollington. 'Brick Kiln Pits' is again an obvious reference and, indeed, the two Chorlton fields of that name are well placed for the purpose.

A third element could describe a peculiarity or individual characteristic of land. Thus recently recovered land might be 'Inclosure' or 'Nines', while 'Heath' might be applied to a field recently rough and unused land. 'Backside' is land behind a building or premises. 'Hooks' is land at the corner of a specific area or at the junction of two roads. 'Gorsty' is recovered from gorse. 'Cleys' implies the presence of heavy clay soil, an interesting point, because much of the parish has clay soil. It may be that in Chorlton, which has extensive areas of sandy loam, the presence of clay would be worth remarking. 'Hanging ground' is a field on a steep slope. 'Rake' means connection with or on a country lane.

'Hill' or 'Knowl' refers to raised ground and 'Overwood', a field next to woodland.

Most names encountered are compositions of two of these elements. Thus, there is 'Heath Field' in Backford, in which an old use and a characteristic are combined. Also in Backford is 'Gladwin Hay', an example of old use and personal name combination.

Here are some other interesting name elements encountered in the survey. 'Brans' describes an area cleared by burning. 'Dam' or 'Damage' or 'Demmage' refers to the damming up of a stream, whose purpose may have been to supply drinking water for farm animals. It is possible to examine good examples in Backford and Mollington, and especially with 'Dam Hay' in Caughall. 'Benty Parts' describes grass often bending in the wind, while 'Whitland' and 'Weat Reans' are connected with wet or marshy ground. The name element 'Cross' occurs in a group of three fields and may indicate where a cross was once raised for services to take place in the days before a parish church had been built. The name 'Butt' may be the irregularly shaped end-piece of the common field, according to one authority, or land worked out, as in 'Sour Butts'. However, it may also, but more rarely, refer to an archery practice area.

All the name elements mentioned so far are quite easy to identify, but there are a few much more difficult ones in the survey: 'Nugwith', for instance, which supplies the names of two fields in Mollington. Various

Hanging Ground, Mollington.

Backsides, Mollington.

suggestions have been made, including: a) woodland, depending on the old Norse 'vior', a wood, which can be changed to 'with'; b) a group of willow trees, from 'withig', OE for willow; c) a dowry, where 'with' is altered to 'wydd', from the Welsh gwyddw, a single person and; d) a profitable plot of land, derived from 'nug', a 17th century term of affection. However, it all remains a mystery, and the present farmer doesn't know or use the name.

'Hungrel' is probably a word for poor, infertile land, although that could hardly be applied now. 'Gredo' could have a religious connection, if the G is changed to C – perhaps glebe land. 'Goothills' may be a dialect version of good but high land.

I have looked for a pattern in all this: something which might indicate a policy or logic of naming. The name element 'Heath' occurs in 26 fields concentrated in the north of Backford township, which had indeed been heath for a long time – so these fields had all been recovered from heath. Other groups of names close together may suggest a tendency to copy – the six marled fields in Lea make up such a group, of which there must surely have been more. 'Hooks', the term for fields on the edge of an area, are found mainly in Mollington, but there must have been similar fields elsewhere.

How should this survey be summarised? I think the naming of fields started as an unwritten practice, necessary for identification, but not made by any ordered or scientific method. It has been what has immediately occurred to the namer, whether a use coming to mind, or the special position of the field, or a person thought to be important in its past, or a combination of all three. The resulting names give an impression of being quickly chosen, almost at the time of asking. They have only stuck because of a need to put something on a legal or other document: their casual origin is given away by today's landowners not always knowing or using the old names.

I conclude with another curiosity, which can illustrate how names come about. In John Davies' History of Backford, 1953, he mentions that the field adjoining the tithe barn in Lea is known as 'Jimmie-George' (the actual tithe apportionment name is 'Hall Croft'), and asks; "Has this any connection with James, the Old Pretender and accession of King George 1st in 1714 ?". What do you think?

Appendix: Field Survey 2010 – Summary

Names or parts of names occurring more than once – but not including 'garden' or personal names

	Total	Backford	Lea	Mollington	Chorlton	Caughall
'Croft'	88	27	20	27	8	6
'Heath'	33	26	2	-	2	3
'Field'	93	32	26	17	18	-
'Hays'	28	6	4	4	2	12
'Looms'	13	3	-	7	3	-
'Backsides'	17	11	1	4	1	-
'Meadow'	22	10	3	4	5	-
'Acres'	24	8	13	2	1	-
'Glebe'	10	-	-	10	-	-
'Hooks'	9	-	-	8	1	-
'Gorsty'	9	1	4	3	1	-
'Hill'	8	-	3	-	5	-
'Townfield'	10	-	2	4	-	4
'Damage'	9	-	2	6	-	1
'Cleys'	4	-	-	-	4	-
'Collinge'	4	4	-	-	-	-
'Brans'	4	-	-	4	-	-
'Cross'	3	3	-	-	-	-
'Overwood'	3	-	-	3	-	-

'Knowl'	2	-	2	-	-	-
'Rake'	2	2	-	-	-	-
'Benty Parts'	2	2	-	-	-	-
'Weat Reans'	2	2	-	-	-	-
'Marl'	8	-	6	2	-	-
'Hanging'	2	2	-	-	-	-
'Ground'	6	6	-	-	-	-
'Nines'	2	-	-	2	-	-
'Pingo'	2	1	-	1	-	-
'Flat'	4	-	1	1	2	-
'Inclosure'	5	1	2	2	-	-
'Brick Kiln'	2	-	-	-	2	-
'Longcorns'	2	-	-	-	2	-
'Whitland'	4	-	-	-	4	-
'Close'	2	-	-	-	2	-
'Orchard'	4	2	-	1	1	-
'Butt'	2	1	-	1	-	-
'Goothills'	2	2	-	-	-	-
'Smithy'	2	-	1	1	-	-
'Nugwith'	2	-	-	2	-	-
Total	450					

Field Survey – List of single occurrences

Backford	Ox pasture		
	Waste		
	Browyard		
	Churchyard		
	The Gredo		
Caughall	Hungrel		
Chorlton	Stone quarry		
	Old Hall		
Lea	Fox Covert		
Mollington	Horsestone		
	Lilly	Total	11

Field Survey – others

Plantation	Backford	13		
	Chorlton	2		
	Lea	1		
	Mollington	7	Total	23
Garden/house (or cottage)	Backford	34		
	Caughall	4		
	Chorlton	18		
	Lea	7		
	Mollington	20	Total	83
		Grand	Total	117

Road Names in Backford Parish

by John Peter Hess

These may have some relevance to nearby fields, but, being in everyday use, are much better known. Like fields, they can originate in a personal name, an old need or a special characteristic, and may also derive from or give direction towards a building or settlement. Our parish contains a good variety of names and their number is small enough to permit examination by township.

Abbreviations: OE old English, ON old Norse, ME middle English, OS ordnance survey.

The M56 runs E/W across the parish and cuts off N/S lanes 'Coalpit Lane' in Lea and 'Cobler Lane' in Chorlton.

Backford

A41 Liverpool Road: this was made a turnpike in 1787 and was then the main road from Chester to Liverpool – via a ferry. On the 1970s Police map it is called Birkenhead Road and in other sources New Chester Road.

A5117: roughly E/W across north of parish. On 1970s Police map is called Shotwick–Frodsham Road and in guides Shotwick–Helsby By-pass.

A5032: leads north from Backford to Ellesmere Port. Called either Whitby Road or Whitby Lane.

The Channel: runs from Church Lane to Rake Lane, but was actually part of Church Lane as recently as 1913 (OS). Name probably derives from OE 'cannel', a water course, which was no doubt present before the road's existence.

Church Lane: associated with St. Oswald's Church.

Gordon Lane, Backford.

Gordon Lane: In the census of 1881 this was known as Church Road, running from Church Lane to Rake Lane. Renamed probably in the 1890s, perhaps after General Gordon of Khartoum. No other person of that name had lived in any of the houses along it.

The Nook: in ME means 'a triangular plot of land', or 'having corners', but is in fact a side road off Gordon Lane.

Rake Lane: OE 'lane', Rake Lane can therefore mean Lane lane, but also applies to a sunken lane through raised ground. May also be a track used by cattle. Modern use may derive from 'the lane leading to Rake Hall'.

Stanney Lane: track from Rake Lane to Collinge Farm is marked as Stanney Lane on modern map.

Caughall

Caughall Road: origin is probably OE 'Cog's Hill', referring to a person of that name. Runs from Caughall Bridge to Long Lane, Upton, but 1970s police map shows it as 'Croughton Cottage Road'. On the 1881 census, however, it was 'Chester Road'.

Flag Lane: a track passing through Chester zoo down to Caughall

Bridge. May derive from ON 'fleag', a place where turf is cut, or 'flagge', a reedy lane.

Fox Covert Lane: forms boundary between Caughall and Wervin. On Bryant's map 1831 was called 'Green Lane' and was probably a grass track then. By OS 1913 was a road Fox Covert Lane, a name which may be taken from a nearby wood.

Wervin Road: from junction with Caughall Road, it leads to Wervin and Croughton. On 1970s police map is 'Wervin Road' in Caughall and 'Croughton Road' in Wervin.

Chorlton

Chorlton Lane: origin is OE 'Ceorl's Tun, a peasant's farm. On 1970s police map is called 'Chorlton Hall Road'.

Cobley or Cobler Lane: used to run from Strawberry Farm on Whitby Road to Poplar Hall Lane, until cut off by M56. Now it is an overgrown track.

Croughton Lane: 1970s police map calls it 'Croughton Cottage Road'.

Poplar Hall Lane: from Rake Lane, branching west to Thomas' Farm, east to Poplar Hall. On census 1881 the west branch was called 'Heath

Wood Lane, Chorlton

Lane' and the stretch past Mount Farm was 'Black Lane'. On 1970s police map the whole length was 'Poplar Hall Road'. The name may come from poplar trees in that area. The road continues after Poplar Hall as a track.

Little Rake Lane: name created recently for road from Chorlton to Grove Farm, which used to be 'Grove Cottage Road' on 1970s police map. Also known incorrectly then as 'Rake Lane' and hence the recent change.

Wood Lane: from Chorlton to Croughton Lane on Bryant's map 1831. Now just a line of trees. Was a private road even in 1796.

Lea-by-Backford

Demage Lane: associated with a dam, which may have been collecting water for cattle from the brook near Lea Manor Farm. Also called 'Damage' or 'Demmage Lane'.

Grove Road: was called 'Damage Lane' in 1831, before that name was switched to present road (which was then a driveway for Lea Hall). A grove is a small wood, often surrounded by a ditch or bank, and there may have been one at Grove Farm.

Station Road: leads to the railway station in Mollington.

Demage Lane, Lea-by-Backford

Powey Lane

Mollington

A540: Hoylake Road, a turnpike in 1787. On 1970s police map is called 'Parkgate Road' and the small stretch cut out when the road was straightened near southern end of Townfield Lane was called 'Old Parkgate Road'.

Austin Lane: on Bryant's map 1831 it extended from Townfield Lane to Coalpit Lane, cutting out the present less direct route. Probably derived from a personal name. Now part of fields and is a public footpath.

Coalpit Lane: NE/SW across township and originally swung north to A5117. Name derives from 'Coalpit Farm' (by 1842 OS was Carter Farm but now Hill Farm) at which charcoal was prepared. In 1830 the eastern portion of the lane was known as 'Hook Pit Lane' because the 'pit' or place of charcoal making was in a corner of the parish.

Gypsy Lane: unadopted and off Grove Road. Perhaps once a stopping place for gypsies.

Meadow Court: originally the back entrance to Mollington Hall and preserves the old cobbles from that time.

Overwood Lane: a field derivation, being next to a wood. 'Over' implies the wood is on the crest of a summit.

Powey Lane: parallel to A5117. Origin possibly 'port-weg', OE a road to a market, in which case probably part of the medieval packhorse trail from Deeside to South Lancashire.

Strawberry Lane: north from Coalpit Lane, is a dead end. Connection with growing of strawberries ?

Townfield Lane: a field connection, it refers to the old community land 'Mollington Torrold Fyeld', 1583, and passes the area where the four fields of that name in Mollington are situated.

Well Lane: origin a direction to a natural spring (not a well).

The Bradley Family at Chorlton Hall – Memoirs of a Cheshire family in the 1920s

by John Peter Hess

Chorlton Hall, near Chester, originated as a farmhouse, but by the late 18th century was already Chorlton House, a gentleman's residence.[1] It is probably best known from that time for Cheshire's early historian, George Ormerod, who lived there from 1811 to 1817. Later again, it was extended in a Scottish Baronial style by the Wicksted Swans, from whom it obtained the title Hall. By the 1850s it was the centre of a considerable estate, comprising nearly all the land in the Township of Chorlton.

However, the Wicksted Swans could never establish a long lasting family home, since they had no children. After their deaths the estate was broken up and the house sold to a businessman, whose Liverpool based company became insolvent a few years later. By 1880 the Hall had become part of a property portfolio held by a local man, Samuel Davies, and was thereafter rented out.

All evidence available suggests that Chorlton Hall was well looked after,[2] especially by its tenants from 1900 to 1923, the Walker family – William Walker was a chartered accountant, with practices in Liverpool and the Isle of Man. He also took a full part in affairs locally. However, William died in 1923, and his family moved away. For a few months the house lay empty, until Eleanor Bradley saw the property during a trip through Wirral.

Up to then Eleanor had lived at 22 Grove Park, Liverpool, with her husband Percy and step-children. But they liked what they saw at Chorlton, especially the size of the house, and soon it was rented by them with some surrounding land. Percy had six children by his first marriage, and all these moved in, together with Percy's brother, Harry, three of Eleanor's sisters (Doris, Rita and Gwen) and brother Jim.

There were also five servants, including a cook, housemaid and nursery maid, and with old Bill Firth, kept on for general maintenance, it was quite a substantial household.

The Bradleys were indeed a large family, as can be seen from the family tree below. Percy was one of sixteen children, and had lived as a boy at Thornton Hall, Childer Thornton. His father had an engineering business with interests in Liverpool. Percy was born in 1879 and married Dora Young, a Liverpool girl, in 1904. By then he had become a cotton broker, and with a brilliant mathematical mind and ability in languages, rose quickly in his company. Inevitably the couple were never far from the city. Their home was in Southport for a few years, then Meols, and after 1916, 22 Grove Park, Liverpool. Six children were born in the meantime, but, were left very young when Dora died in the influenza epidemic of 1918. By this time, too, Percy's business connections were in jeopardy, in spite of his becoming a senior partner. His company, Reiss Bros, was owned by Germans, and the First World War created some difficult problems for them. From then on until the company finally ceased in 1939, and although he was always exceptionally generous with the family, Percy was hardly ever free from money worries.

However, he was now lucky enough in Liverpool to meet Eleanor Hart, who was Northern Irish and only twenty years old. Percy and Eleanor were married in the Anglican cathedral in 1922, and at first lived in his old home. But, as mentioned, some of Eleanor's family were invited to live with them, and more space was needed. How fortunate for them all, then, that Eleanor possessed financial capability as well as beauty. Indeed, she had previously been employed by a fashion house in Liverpool as an accountant. She would need all that ability when they came to Chorlton with so many dependants: a big responsibility for one so young.

For memories of the Bradleys at Chorlton Hall, there are eyewitness accounts from one son, Howard[3] and one of Eleanor's sisters, Rita (Ramsay).[4] Information has also come from John Bradley, second son of Percy and Eleanor, who was born at the Hall, and from Norah Hart,[5] daughter of Eleanor's brother Jim. Their descriptions, either first or second hand, have given some interesting perspectives of life in Chorlton from 1923 to 1930. It should be said at once that the young people had a pretty free hand at Chorlton – seemingly quite a 'free zone' for the boys. Percy, who was a Colonel in the T.A., a Freemason, lay reader and preacher, never tried to preach to his family, but instead set a dignified and good example, and was highly respected by all of them. He did manage to send all the children to boarding school, too: Howard, George, Raymond and Osman to St. Lawrence's in Ramsgate, Dick to Ruthin School, North Wales, and Nora to Belvedere School in Liverpool.

Chorlton Hall is quite large, of course, with twenty-seven rooms on three floors, including nine bedrooms and the servants' quarters on the third floor. Rooms are well proportioned, with high ceilings to match. Maintaining a house of its size in the 1920s would require much effort by many – servants if available, otherwise members of the family, because many activities were labour-intensive then. Howard's comment about how scarce house servants were becoming perhaps reflects conditions in the 1920s, and meant that he and the other boys would have to offer some support. Turnover was apparently high even among the help they could hire. Sometimes he would come home to find none at all.

There were, fortunately, a permanent gardener and a chauffeur, who lived in cottages nearby. Together with Bill Firth, there was always someone to call upon.

Considerable effort must have gone into keeping warm in those large rooms. Virtually every one has a fireplace, and many would have been required for use, if labour permitted. Fortunately coal-fired central heating was also available on the two lower floors, with its boiler in the cellar. Howard remembers that brother Dick had the job of stoking and raking regularly – no servant allotted to that task – and he had to flee from the fumes every day. However, the system worked, even though circulation was by convection alone. Coal came from Mollington Station by truck delivery or collection – £10 bought ten tons at a time – and was stored in the cellar.

Cutting the grass, including two tennis courts and a croquet lawn, was another labour intensive task, this time performed by a gardener. A gang mower was pulled along by a horse, suitably shod in wellington boots to avoid spoiling the surface. No horse being available meant the use of a scythe. By 1930, a new Atco 14" mower was bought, but cutting the big lawn would have involved a twenty-five mile walk for someone!

If heating was a problem, so also was lighting. Electricity was not yet generally available, so some houses made their own. At Chorlton, Howard remembered, there was a cell house of batteries in one of the outbuildings, providing just enough power to bring light to some of the rooms. A generator ran on petrol and paraffin to top the batteries up.

Piped water supply had recently been installed locally, but it was inconsistent, with the pressure very low at times. It seems to have been the chauffeur's job to pump water from the yard well, and carry it upstairs. Interestingly, there was even a tank in the yard, kept full, and heated by the generator. Buckets of hot water were taken for baths upstairs, because the hot-water system indoors was poor.

Cooking in the absence of electricity, gas and oil had to be over a coal fire and grate, but they certainly ate well, as described by Howard. Roasts were done in a large 'hastener' standing in front of the grate. It had a clockwork motor, which turned the hanging spit slowly but regularly. An ample and regular supply of vegetables came from the kitchen garden, looked after by the permanent gardener, with additional assistance from one labourer.

Memories of the house do tend to concentrate on the unusual; the front hall, into which an Austin Seven was introduced one Christmas as a surprise present; the ancient upstairs lavatory, which could be flushed from the floor above while an unsuspecting victim was sitting below; the stairwell with a huge painting of Napoleon's Retreat from Moscow; the full size billiard table; and the baize door between kitchen area and main house, through which the only telephone, a hand wound instrument, could be reached. Rita Ramsay and Howard Bradley both remember the house interior to be much as now, given differences in decoration, and both emphasise its spaciousness. There was plenty of room, even with their numbers, for everyone to have comfortable privacy.

Both, again, remember the garden clearly; climbing ivy on the house, the rose bushes, the peaches growing against a wall, the huge greenhouse, the fine old copper beech, which still dominates the far end of the lawn, flanked by magnificent beds of rhododendron. Beyond was a gravel path flanked by herbaceous borders, an area of demanding and continuous maintenance. That was Percy's own special task, and he spent many hours on his hands and knees at it.

Near the copper beech was a summer house, which could be swivelled to catch all available sun. No doubt it was well used, even if one memory is of its windows being used for target practice from the house, using Jim Hart's shotgun (usually reserved for rabbits).

Perhaps leisure activities are the best remembered. Howard talks of bicycle hockey on the front gravel; of the family layout of Basset Lowke and Hornby gauge two model trains in the old carriage shed – the whole length of the upstairs floor; and of the four eldest brothers, George, Osman, Raymond and Howard making up a regular four at tennis.

In the yard the family built and kept a caravan, timber butted and clad in plywood, on an old Chevrolet back axle (eventually John Bradley knew it as the 'hen-pen', and recognised it as beginning his interest in caravans generally). This contraption was towed by their Austin Twenty motor car, and used for many tours of England and Wales. Unfortunately, the caravan suffered many punctures, as the tyres were too small for the weight they had to carry. Apparently, in 1938[6] it was abandoned on a farm behind Old Colwyn, and genuinely became a 'hen pen'.

The Bradleys moved to The Firs, Newton, only a few miles away, in 1930, later to Hoylake and finally to Oxton, Birkenhead. Percy's business failed to improve and was closed in 1939. When he died in 1946, Eleanor and the family left to go their own ways, and to make individual and very different careers. However, it's plain from Howard and Rita's notes now, that Chorlton Hall had always remained for them a contented and memorably happy time. Even John was just old enough to have one special memory of when they were leaving. The family rocking horse was strapped to the roof of Coleman's removal van, and as the van moved off, the horse was about to be swept off by a low branch of the beech tree near the gate. Just in time the driver was alerted. The horse afterwards remained in their nursery, a precious souvenir of that house-moving day. The offending branch remains still, a trap for the unwary.

Chorlton Hall was let again in the 1930s, but was eventually sold as a family home – which it still is.

References

1. 'Chorlton Hall', J.P. Hess, 1979, page 1
2. 'Perambulation of the Hundred of Wirral', H.G. Young, 1909
3. Letters from Howard Bradley to the author 1994 to 2000, and visit 1998.
4. Visit of Rita Ramsay to Chorlton Hall 1974, and letters 1997.
5. Visit of Norah Hart 1996.
6. Visit of John and Tina Bradley 1st January 2009.

The Bradley Family at Chorlton

Dora Young = Percy Bradley = Eleanor Hart

1881–1918 1879–1946 1902–1986

Children of Dora Young and Percy Bradley:

George	*Raymond*	*Osman*	*Howard*	*Nora*	*Dick*
b.1905	*1906*	*1908*	*1910*	*1912*	*1916*
d.1946	*1933*	*2007*	*2004*	*1998*	

Children of Percy Bradley and Eleanor Hart:

Jim	*John*
1923	*1928*
2012	

The Hart Family Connection

William Hart = Elizabeth Williamson

b.1836 b.1836

John *= Metha* — *James* *= Georgina*

Gladys	*Eleanor*	*James*	*Dorothy*	*Rita*	*Gwen*
b.1900	*Florence*	*'Jim'*	*b.1909*	*b.after*	*b.after*
	b.1902	*b.1905*		*1911*	*1911*
	m.Percy	*m.Irene*		*m.Ramsay*	
	Bradley				
	1922				

Norah (child of James 'Jim' and Irene)

A Short History of Lea-by-Backford in the early 20th Century

by Michael Richardson

Introduction

In our first volume of local history, I wrote about the township of Lea, which had remained largely unchanged during the 19th century. The only new buildings to appear between the time of the Tithe map of 1839 and the census of 1901 were the Station House and Station cottage, erected at the time of the opening of the Chester & Birkenhead Railway in 1840, the arrival of which must have been the most significant event in the area since the Civil War two hundred years earlier. In many cases properties had been occupied by the same family throughout the 19th century and in general the township had seen very little change during more than sixty years. Then, in June 1907, the sale of the Mollington estate which had belonged to the Feilden family heralded an era of change in Lea – with some properties seeing a change in ownership and a growing number of new houses being built. One of those professionally involved in the sale was the surveyor Arthur Hughson (who produced the estate maps in the sale catalogue) and he bought a plot of land and built a new house. The publication of the 1911 census has revealed the start of this development within the township, with the Bluegate Wood cottages appearing close to the railway bridge on Demage Lane, a new house on Demage Lane and two bungalows under construction by Backford Brook (near the present Village Hall).

A few years later the outbreak of war in 1914 was to have a significant impact on the area, with many of the young men enlisting and some giving their lives for King and Country. After the end of the Great War housing development in Lea continued and a number of houses were built along Grove Road, so that by the time of the 1920 Electoral Register the number of properties in the township had grown to 32, more than double the number at the turn of the century. To put this rate of growth in context, it was to take another 80 years for the number of properties to double again so that by the 2001 census there were 73 houses in Lea.

Map of Lea by Backford showing principle buildings

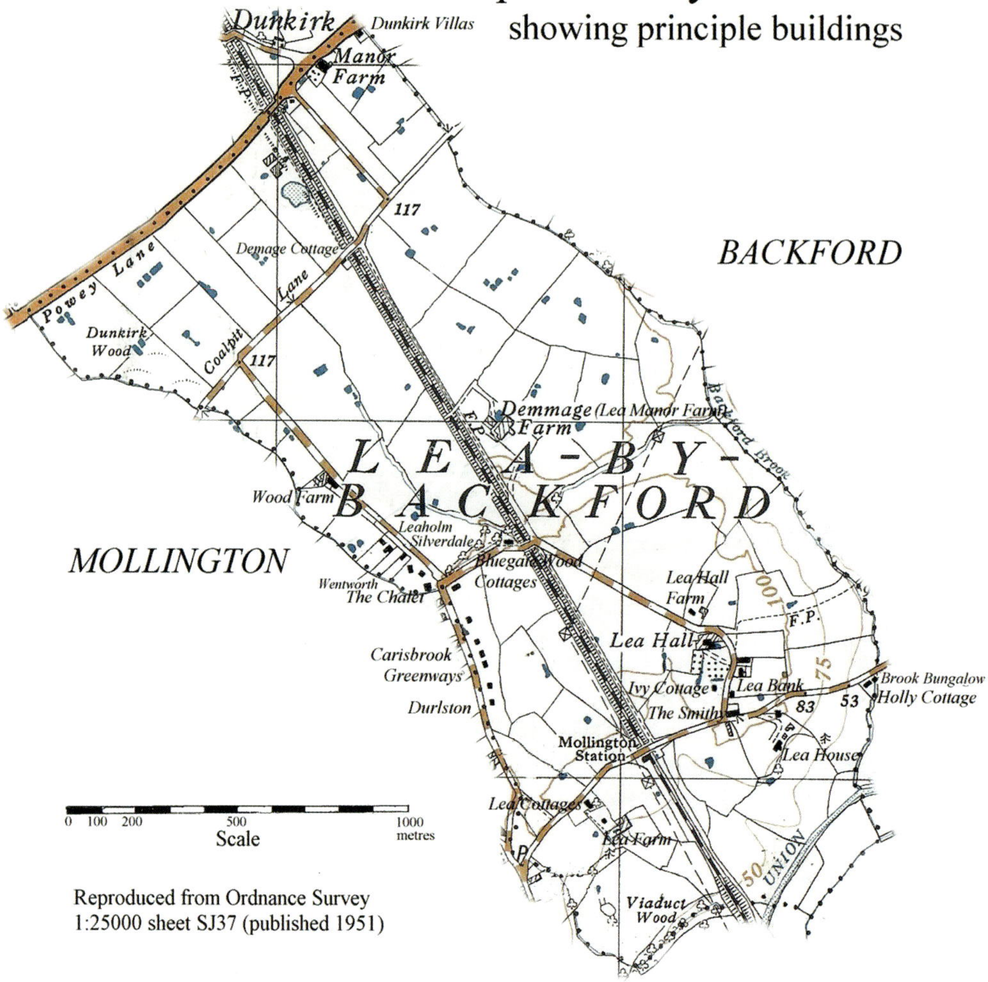

Reproduced from Ordnance Survey 1:25000 sheet SJ37 (published 1951)

The 1911 census has 23 entries for Lea but this total includes a signalbox (near the Coalpit Lane railway bridge) and two bothies for farm workers at Lea Hall Farm and Manor Farm; also listed in the summary (but not counted in the total) are a pavilion at the bowling green on Station Road (where Leamoll stands today), a 'maisonette' (uninhabited) which seems to have been part of what is now Wood Farm on Grove Road and the two bungalows being built by Backford Brook. Details of individual properties follow, starting with those included in the 1901 census, followed by newer buildings in chronological order.

Lea Hall

Lea Hall was occupied by the Carter family from some time in the 1880s and in 1901 Wilfred Carter, aged 27, was recorded as head of the household at Lea Hall Farm; he was the great-grandson of the John Carter who had lived at "Carter's Farm" on Coalpit Lane in Mollington in the early 19th century. Living with him were his younger brother Samuel and their widowed mother Susannah. Wilfred had married Edith Jane Hughes in 1900 and by the time of the 1911 census they had four children and three servants living with them, also two farm workers separately listed living in a bothy (possibly at the tithe barn?). Some time after this, Wilfred and Edith moved with their family to farm near Stafford.

In the 1907 sale, Lea Hall had been bought for £9000 by James Edward Hughes, a Liverpool cotton dealer, who had been living at Childer Thornton. The auctioneer congratulated him on having become, by virtue of his purchase, "Lord of the Manor of the Township of Lea". James was the elder brother of Edith, who had married Wilfred Carter so it seems that Lea Hall and farm was very much a family affair at that time. Although there are two separate entries in the 1911 census the location of Lea Hall Farm is not known; the census form tells us that it had 9 rooms (whilst Lea Hall itself had 16). It is believed that the house now known as 'Haresfinch' was built as the farmhouse but it is thought to have been built in 1912; perhaps it was completed earlier and was the building included in the census?

James Hughes had married Margaret Emily Shone in 1886 and in the 1911 census return for Lea Hall, she was listed as head of the household; living with her were her youngest child Edward, aged 8, and two servants. Margaret died on 28th July 1913 and James then married Ellen Gertrude, daughter of Robert Read, a ship's chandler, of Childer Thornton in 1914. Ellen died on 15th Jan 1947 and James on 31st March 1949, they are buried in Overleigh Cemetery, Chester.

Lea Hall Cottages

This pair of semi-detached cottages probably dates from the 18th century and they are on Demage Lane near Lea Hall. One of these cottages was occupied by the Hughson family throughout the period

1839 to 1901 (in our first volume it was incorrectly reported that the family had not been living there at the time of the 1851 census but this arose from an error in reading the census returns). William Hughson had been a gamekeeper and after his death in 1905 it was occupied by the Donnelly family; Thomas Donnelly was a signalman at Mollington station, and had married Fannie Chaloner from Lea Cottages at Backford church on 12th September 1895. They had two daughters, Annie Isabel (born 31st August 1899) and Gladys (born Q1 1910). Kelly's Directory for 1923 lists Mrs Frances Donnelly as a farmer and they appear to have lived there until at least 1933 when Thomas died, Fanny's address was given as 'Greenacres' at the time of her death in 1947.

The other cottage had been occupied by the Crofts family from the 1870s and in 1911 William and Sarah were still there, with their daughter Bessie and son-in-law George Hackney who had married at Backford on 27 December 1909; they had a son Samuel who was aged 7 months. Bessie's younger sister Fanny had married John Reynolds just two days earlier and they were to be found living at one of the cottages on Station Road near Lea Farm (Hough's). As for other members of the Crofts family, both George and John had married and were living in Ellesmere Port and Upton respectively. George Hackney's nephew Thomas was one of those men from the parish to serve during the First World War and he was killed at the battle of Passchendaele in July 1917.

Lea Smithy

Our first volume of local history included a chapter on the history of the smithy and in 1901 the blacksmith was Joseph Dean, who was living there with his wife Sarah, son William and daughter Annie, also John Roberts, aged 15, an assistant blacksmith. In the 1907 estate sale the smithy was bought by Joseph Dean for £560 and this was greeted with loud applause at the auction in the Grosvenor Hotel. The 1911 census returns available online are the original forms completed by each householder and that for Lea Smithy is in Joseph Dean's very elegant copperplate handwriting, an art inherited by his son William, as evidenced by an invoice reproduced in our first volume. Joseph continued to work at the smithy until his death in 1930.

Mollington Station House

Of all the houses in the township this one has seen most changes of occupancy, as the Station Masters rarely stayed for more than a few years. In 1901 Alfred Pinches held the post and during their time at the station he and his wife had four children. In 1911 the Station Master was Thomas Leathley Roberts, aged 30, from Orford, near Warrington; his wife Emmie was from Dunedin, New Zealand and they had a daughter Marion, born in 1909. In 1918 the Station Master was George Parry and he was still there in 1920 with his wife Frances; in 1911 he had been a railway company clerk living in Hoole. By 1926 the Station Master was Charles Dorricott who had earlier been a signalman, probably based at Chester station as he and his wife Annie were living in Hoole in 1901. They had three daughters, two of whom became teachers in Liverpool; Dorothy Carline recounts several stories about the family in her memoirs, published in our first volume of local history. Charles had been born in Shropshire where his father, also Charles, had been a station master before moving to Heswall. It was very much a railway family as his younger brother John married Ethel Clarke (daughter of George Clarke who lived on Grove Road) and in 1901 was the station master at Bebington, and later Bromborough.

Station Cottage

The Townley family had moved into this cottage in the late 1890s and in the 1911 census we find William and Fanny Townley (but now known as Tunley!) and their four children still living there. William was a railway platelayer, their son William (19) was a gardener, Andrew (18) a railway clerk, Florence (15) an apprentice dressmaker and Edith (13) was still at school. Florence died in 1915 aged just 20, while Andrew served during WW1 as a sapper with the Royal Engineers, was married in 1918 (to Florence Adams in Salford) but then died in 1923 aged only 30. William and Fanny died within a few weeks of each other in January 1939 and are buried in Backford churchyard as are their children Florence and Andrew.

Lea Cottages

These three cottages, also referred to as Hough's cottages, used to stand on the south side of Station Road just before it enters Mollington village. A pair of semi-detached houses stands on the site now.

In 1901 one of the cottages was occupied by Thomas and Elizabeth Smith and their infant daughter Mary; they had another four children while living in Lea, one of whom was James (born in 1903) who joined the RAF in WW2 and was killed in March 1945 while serving in Morocco. The family moved to live on Parkgate Road around 1906 or '07 where they had a further two children. In 1901 the other cottages were occupied by the Coppack family and by Thomas and Fanny Donnelly, who later moved to one of the Lea Hall Cottages.

By 1911 all three of the cottages had changed hands, the first was occupied by Alfred Thompson, a gardener, with his wife Annie and three sons. By 1918 they had been replaced by Joseph and Martha Griffiths and son Percy James. The second cottage was occupied by Samuel Morris (a platelayer with LNW Railway) with his wife Mary, two sons and a daughter; their elder son William was still at school in 1911 but later worked as a gardener for T. Gibbons Frost at Mollington Hall. At the outbreak of war he joined up and was killed in 1916 towards the end of the battle of the Somme. The family was still living there in 1920.

The third cottage was occupied by John Reynolds, his wife Fanny (née Crofts) and daughter but by 1918 they had been replaced by Arthur and Martha Ottershead but they stayed only a short time and in 1920 Samuel and May Louise Pritchard were living at this cottage.

Lea Farm

The Hough family had been at this farm since the 1850s, working as wheelwrights in addition to running the farm. By 1901 only John, a 52 year old bachelor, remained; however on 4th February 1909 he married Eva Jones, 25 years his junior, who we know from the 1901 census had been a domestic servant there and they had a daughter Emily, born on 6th April 1909. The farm was not included in the 1907 sale as it was in that part of the estate retained by Thomas Gibbons Frost. The Houghs were still at the farm at the time of the 1911 census but by 1918 it was occupied by William Jones who had been brought up at Powey Lane Farm in Capenhurst. William built a new farmhouse and in 1915 married Charlotte Farrall of Warren Farm in Mollington. Their grandson is still farming at Lea and other members of the Jones family have been prominent members of the local farming community for many years.

Lea Manor Farm (Demage Farm)

The early history of this old farm, from the 14th century onwards, was described in detail in our first book, and in the 1907 sale of the Feilden estate the property was bought by Edward Littler of Hapsford for £8200. In 1911 Edward and his wife Florence née Bower were there, together with their three children, Edward (20), Fred (18) and Maragret (sic) (16). Edward (jnr) served in the Royal Navy as a stoker during WW1, being based at Devonport from July 1918 and then serving on board HMS *Benbow* from the end of the war until being demobbed early in 1919. Edward Littler (snr) died in 1928, aged 61, and the family continued to farm there.

Demage Lane Cottage ('Wood Farm')

This property had been the home of the Williams family for several generations up to 1901 when the widowed Sarah Williams and her daughter Martha and son Edward were there. It was Lot 19 in the 1907 sale of the Mollington estate, described as 'House, Buildings and Land, a desirable farm of 60 acres or thereabouts. The House is small but the Buildings are quite new.' It was bought by William Chaloner of Holt for £2680 and the 1911 census lists him with his wife Fanny (Hannah), brother George and two children, Hannah (2) and William Thomas (1). They were still living there in 1926, William died in 1948 age 64 and Hannah in 1970 aged 91.

The 1911 census records a 'maisonette' but it is unclear whether this was part of Demage Lane Cottage or a separate building on Grove Road or Demage Lane; the occupier was given as H. R. West but it was listed as 'unoccupied' at the time of the census in April. Henry Rock West was also listed in the census living at 15 Raymond Street in Chester with his wife Sarah and five children; he was a retired LNWR agent and later lived at Dee Fords Avenue in Chester.

Demage Cottage, Coalpit Lane

In 1901 Charles and Catherine Bithell were living there and after Charles' death in 1905 Catherine remained there until her death in December 1912 aged 89; they were buried in Backford churchyard. After this the cottage was occupied by George and Margaret Foster who had previously lived in Ellesmere Port, where George was listed in the 1911 census as a 'restaurant keeper' in Whitby. He died on 26 Jan 1921 when his address was given as Fernlea Cottage, Lea.

Manor Farm (Dunkirk)

In 1901 John and Catherine Davies were living at the farm with their two children and John's widowed father Henry. In the 1907 Mollington Estate sale catalogue, Lot 17 was listed as "The Dunkirk Farm, a Very Excellent Milk Farm, with house ... recently restored". Bidding reached £4475 in the auction at which point it was withdrawn and was later sold to William James Jones (born in Rose Farm, Mollington). In the 1911 census he is living there with his wife Sarah May (née Hughes) and their son William born in 1904; William Bowker was working as a cowman on the farm at that time and he was one of those from the parish to be killed during the Great War while serving with the Cheshire Regiment. William Jones and his family remained at the farm until at least the mid-1920s.

Dunkirk Cottage

This cottage had been occupied by the same family throughout the second half of the 19th century, first by John and Margaret Lewis and then, following the marriage of their daughter Mary to James Lee on Christmas Day 1861, by the Lee family until at least the 1920s. James was a railway platelayer and he and Mary had nine children, of whom just the youngest two, Peter (aged 35) and Alice (33) were living at home at the time of the 1911 census. Mary died in December 1916 aged 78, James in May 1917 aged 83 and Peter and Alice were still living there in 1920.

The 1911 Census

By the time of this census five new houses had been built and three of these were occupied.

Ivy Cottage

Although not named as such in the 1911 census this house, near Lea Hall, was originally known as Ivy Cottage and is now named 'Roselea'; it does not appear on the maps included with the 1907 sale catalogue so must have been built between then and 1911, possibly about 1908. In 1911 it was occupied by Jonah Beattie, a farm bailiff aged 45, with his wife Jane, also 45, and their six children: John (18) and William (17), both described as 'horseman on farm', George (16) a railway store assistant and Annie (13), Mary (11) and Jonah (8), all at school. Every member of the family is recorded as born in Cumberland.

They were followed by the Williams family; Peter Williams (who had been a gardener at Backford Hall – see the photograph on page 94) married Sarah Wynne in 1913 and their son Allen was born there in 1915 and was to live in the parish all his life, apart from military service during WW2. At that time it appears to have been the gardener's cottage for Lea Hall.

Bluegate Wood Cottages

These two cottages, by the railway bridge on Demage Lane, do not feature on the 1907 map and may have been completed not long before the 1911 census as there were young children listed in both who had been born elsewhere. One cottage was occupied by Fred Jones, a farm labourer from Shropshire and his wife Louise; they had been married for 3 years and had a one year old son Arthur. There are two F. Jones listed on the WW1 Roll of Honour and it seems likely that one of these could have been this Fred. The other cottage was occupied by the Birchall family – William, a cowman born in Crewe and his wife Martha together with five children and Martha's mother Mary Peers. The Birchalls had obviously moved residence quite often as each of their children had been born in a different place!

It seems that these cottages were probably occupied by workers on Littler's farm as subsequent electoral registers list them as Manor Cottages. In 1918 John and Mary Jones were listed at one of the cottages – could this be the family who were listed living at Home Farm Cottages in Backford in the 1911 census (and later lived at Willow Cottage in Mollington)? The other appears to have been occupied by a number of farm workers, Samuel Burgess, Stephen Tiffin and George Frederick Powell; Samuel is listed on the WW1 Roll of Honour as having served with the Cheshire Regiment. Two years later both cottages had new occupants, with Joseph and Sarah Brown, Alfred Lawson and Walter Lockett recorded living at Manor Cottages. Walter Lockett was formerly a game keeper and farmer living at Dunham on the Hill and his wife had died in 1916, so he had probably taken up a new post in this area, but nothing is known about the others listed.

By 1926 one of the cottages was occupied by Louis Edward Horsfall and his wife Gertrude; Louis was born near Halifax and at the time of his marriage in 1908 he was a butcher but in the 1911 census he is recorded as a farmer near Mytholmroyd in West Yorkshire.

Bungalows by Backford Brook

In the 1911 census these were recorded as "building" and later electoral registers recorded the first occupants. However, information from the current occupants suggests that they may have been completed before this date as the deeds date from 1907.

Brook Bungalow (now Brookside)

In 1918 this was occupied by Charles and Elizabeth Formston. Charles was born in 1858 at Carden and at the time of the 1911 census had been working as a farm labourer near Colwyn Bay. Elizabeth died in 1922 aged 68 and Charles was still living in the bungalow in 1926.

Holly Cottage

The second bungalow by Backford Brook was occupied by John and Helène Duff. John had been born in Liverpool in 1844 and in 1901 was working as foreman in a timber yard in Liverpool. After the death of his first wife Margaret in 1902 he married Sarah Ellen Culshaw in 1910 and at the time of the 1911 census they were living at Chalet Cottage, Gwernymynydd with their young son John, aged 8 months. They must have moved to live in Lea soon afterwards; John died on 31st July 1921, aged 79 and Helène in 1927 aged 37.

A later occupant was a retired naval officer, Capt John Roberts OBE, DSO, RD.

Development from 1911 to 1918

Following the break-up of the Mollington estate in 1907 a number of new houses were built in Lea and by the time of the 1918 Electoral Roll there were eight new properties listed.

Lea House

The catalogue for the 1907 Mollington Estate sale offered Lots 21, 22 and 23 (approx 53 acres) as "one of the few remaining Sites in Wirral where a Mansion can be built in its own Park on lands which can never be built out, and with a nice Sporting Estate adjoining". Lot 21 was bought by John Minshull for £1950 whilst the other two lots were withdrawn. They were later bought by William Hutchinson, a Liverpool cotton broker, who lived at Bebington where the 1911 census records him with his wife Asta Carlotta and two sons John (age 7) and William (age 5), and about 1913 he built Lea House (now re-named Friar's Park). The family lived there until moving to Berkshire in 1931, although their son Ben continued to live in the area. John joined the RAF and was killed in a flying accident in 1940 (see page 197). Next to live at Lea House was Donald Buckley King and he is listed in Kelly's Directory for 1934.

Lea Bank

This house is dated 1915 and was built for William Harding, who had been butler to Birkenhead Glegg at Backford Hall. The next chapter in the book, by Alan Whitham, tells the story of this house and of the Harding family.

On Grove Road a number of houses were built on the western side north of its junction with Demage Lane, on land which had formed Lot 25 in the Mollington Estate sale – three fields totalling just over 5 acres which was bought by Joseph Dean for £365 in the 1907 auction.

Leaholm (Lea Holme)

This house was built for John Carline, the recently retired Chief Clerk of Chester Post Office, who had previously lived in Hoole. In our first volume, his grand-daughter Dorothy, who was born there in 1912, recounts memories of her childhood and mentions several of the families who lived on Grove Road in the 1920s and 1930s. John lived there until his death in 1938; his son, also John, worked for Cheshire county council (Roads Department).

The Chalet

This bungalow faces the western end of Demage Lane and was first occupied by Robert and Amelia Randall Roberts; he was a pharmacist with a shop on Eastgate St., Chester. In her memoirs (published in our first book of local history) Dorothy Carline records that she knew Mr & Mrs Roberts well and that Mrs Roberts used to take her out for trips in her pony and trap. Robert Randall Roberts later lived in Upton and he died in 1957.

The Bungalow

This house, at the junction of Demage Lane and Grove Road, first appeared in the Electoral Registers for 1918 and 1920 record Frances Beal living here. Her husband William, who had served in the Royal Navy as a Chief Engine Room Artificer, had died in January 1917 aged 77 and she died in August 1923. They are buried in Backford churchyard, in the section to the east of the church, together with their daughter Jessie Murray who died in 1944.

The Elm Trees

It has not been possible to identify which house this is but we know that in 1918 it was occupied by William and Alice Crowe and two years later the 1920 Electoral Register lists Lt Col Franklin Smith and his wife Helen. By 1926 Wallace Tristram and his wife Gertrude were living there.

In the north of the township a pair of semi-detached houses were built on what was then Powey Lane (now the A5117 By-Pass Road).

Dunkirk Villas

Dunkirk Villas appear for the first time in the 1918 electoral register and one of them was occupied by William Hughes and Elizabeth Thomas – they were living at Heath Farm, on Liverpool Road, in 1911, from which we learn that Elizabeth was William's daughter. William's wife Sarah had died in 1914 and he died in 1922, they are buried in Backford churchyard.

Living at the other house in 1918 was Richard Cleaver (there was no sign of anyone of that name in the 1911 census in Cheshire so we don't know where he came from) and then in 1920 we find Samuel Massey Woodcock. He had been living in Runcorn in 1911 and working as a grocer's assistant for the Co-Op. He married Eva Hewitt in Chester in 1916 and they had a son Norman who was killed in a flying accident in 1943 while serving with the RAF; they are all buried in Whitchurch.

Post-1918 development

By the time of the 1920 Electoral Register a further four houses had been built in Lea.

Tenby Mount

This house, on Grove Road, was first occupied for a few years by Bartholomew and Catherine Hobson; he was a retired master mason and contractor and they had previously lived in Waverton; they died in 1916 and 1918 respectively and are buried in Backford churchyard. Then, in the 1920 Electoral Register, we find Owen and Ellen Southcott living there, and according to Dorothy Carline he was the general manager of the Grosvenor Garage in Foregate Street, although in Kelly's Directory for 1923 he was listed as a farmer – possibly a spare time activity? Certainly at the time of his marriage in 1918 in Leeds he was recorded as an engineer with an address in Eastgate St. in Chester.

St Eloi

The 1918 Electoral Register lists Arthur Hughson as qualified by owning land in Lea and two years later we find him living at this house, together with his wife Isabella Elizabeth (née Ackland). As mentioned in the introduction, Arthur was a surveyor; he had been brought up in one of the Lea Hall Cottages and after his marriage in 1888 had lived at Crosslooms Villa in Mollington. In 1911 he was living at Eastgate Row North in Chester and was listed as a Registrar of Births, Marriages and Deaths, a post he held for 15 years up to his death in 1925; his widow died in 1938. It has not been possible to identify the location of their house – the name "St Eloi" suggests that it may have been named for the Belgian village which was the site of the largest deep mine explosion during the Battle of Messines Ridge in 1917 (perhaps one of the Hughson sons had served there?). The name must have been changed when new owners moved in.

Arthur and Isabella had two sons, Leonard and Cecil, and at the time of the 1911 census Leonard was working in London as a clerk/typist whilst the 18 year old Cecil was the census enumerator for Lea, Chorlton and Backford. They both served in the Royal Field Artillery in WW1 and Cecil later kept a shop and garage on Liverpool Road; in Kelly's Directory for 1923 he is listed as "Grocer, teas and refreshments" and in 1934 his entry read "Grocer, teas & refreshments & garage", by then he had a telephone – Mollington 59. His mother was still living at "St Eloi", his father Arthur having died in 1925.

Lea House Cottages

These two cottages first appear in the 1920 electoral roll when they were known as Hutchinson's Cottages and later, after the re-naming of

Lea House as Friar's Park they became Friar's Park Cottages.

The first occupants were the Dodd family in one and George Frederick Powell in the other. John Henry Dodd had been born in Blacon in 1878 and married Elizabeth Thelwell at Bickley in June 1900; in 1911 they had been living in Cholmondeley where John was working as a gardener. They had a daughter Olive (born 1902) and son Peter (born 1904). George Frederick Powell (1893–1965) had previously lived at Manor Cottages and he was probably the eldest son of George and Ada Powell of Backford; the 1911 records his occupation as "groom" and his father was the coachman at Backford Hall.

During the early 1920s there was further development along Grove Road, both on the west side north of the junction with Demage Lane and also on the east side south of that junction and by 1926 the following houses had been built:

"Greenways", John and Fanny Barber

"Silverdale", Frederick and Mabel Barratt

"Norstanholme", Stanley Dean Clarke

"Wayside", William, Gwylym and Elizabeth Davies

"Carisbrooke", George and Catherine Howell

"Durlstone", Geoffrey and Kathleen Pritchard.

Sources

Census returns for 1901 and 1911
Electoral Registers for 1918, 1920 and 1926
Cheshire Parish Registers on findmypast.com
Probate records on ancestry.com
Kelly's Directories for 1923 and 1931 (Chester History and Heritage
Overleigh Cemetery records (Cheshire Record Office website)
Catalogue for sale of Mollington Estate in 1907
Chester Chronicle 29 June 1907 (report of Mollington estate auction).

Memories of Lea Bank

by Alan Whitham

This house was built in Lea by Backford in 1915, and the date can be seen on the gable front in the photograph (figure 1) taken in the 1920s. Mr William Renfree Harding acquired the land on Demage Lane, adjacent to the smithy, in 1914 as the result of a gift from the estate of Birkenhead Glegg which enabled him to build Lea Bank and where he developed an extensive garden including an orchard containing apple, pear, cherry, damson, greengage, and plum trees, some of which remain today. Accompanying him in the photograph is his second wife Mary Elizabeth Shorthose, who had been the housekeeper at Backford Hall and was born at Lache-in-Saltney in 1865; she married William in 1915, following the death of his first wife, Jessie Augusta Dawson in April 1913 aged 56.

William Renfree Harding was born in 1861, the son of John Renfree Harding, shoemaker, of Overton, Flintshire. William married Jessie Dawson, born in 1858, at Stand, Lancashire, in 1888. He held a number of positions in service before becoming butler to Birkenhead Glegg of Backford Hall in the 1880s.

Figure 1

The Hardings had three children, Robert Stuart born 1889 in Derbyshire, Jessie Helena born 1890 in Chester and Evelyn Overton born 1895 in Backford. Backford School records show that Evelyn was a pupil there from 1899 to 1909. It is also recorded that on 15th February, 1911 the head teacher attended the funeral of Miss J.H.Harding, aged 21, certificated teacher, who was an ex-scholar of Backford School and the winner of a County Council Scholarship in 1903.

The family lived at The Nook, Backford until after the death of their mother, Jessie, in 1913. After their marriage in 1915, William and Mary moved to Lea Bank; a photograph of William in costume (figure 2) may have been taken at the time of the 1910 Chester Pageant, although the programme for that event, which was held at Eaton Park, doesn't tell us what role he played. He died in March 1938 aged 76, followed by Mary in the following month, aged 74; both were buried at Backford Church.

Figure 2

William's son, Robert, married Elsie Violet Lockett, from Gateshead, in 1929, and they, together with three daughters, Audrey, born 1931, Doris, 1935 and Violet, 1940, lived at Lea Bank at the same time. On the death of his father, Robert became owner of the house. In 1942 twin boys were born to Robert and Elsie, and they were named after their father and grandfather, Robert and William.

It was through Violet that some background information about the family has been recorded. Robert Harding, it turns out, used to work at Backford Hall, as did his father before him, both for the Gleggs. Robert drove a horse and cart in the course of this work and was well known for his rose growing, for which he won prizes.

After leaving Backford Hall, Robert went to work for the Royal London Insurance Company and served in 10th Battn. South Lancashire regiment during WW1.

On Christmas Eve 1953 Robert went out on his bicycle, leaving the car at home. Unfortunately when crossing the road (now A41) he was involved in an accident and killed. Robert, who had lived to be 63, was buried in Backford Churchyard, as was his wife Elsie, who died, aged 65, in 1965. Both are commemorated on a gravestone there.

According to Violet, the Hardings' children attended Mollington School, when the head teacher was Miss Bowcock, though Violet was actually taught by Miss Penrith. William has since died and is also commemorated on the family gravestone, as is a nephew, Terence, whose age was only 6 months. Violet's married name is Burling (sadly her husband has also died) and after her marriage lived at Lea Bank. She had three children, Deborah, Gaynor and Darren. Violet now lives in Chester. Audrey Stevenson is also a widow, now living in Crewe.

In 1965 Lea Bank was conveyed to Mr and Mrs Cowper where they lived until 1977. They were followed by Derek and Marion Hillaby and their two daughters Kathryn and Caroline. The Whitham family then bought Lea Bank in 1985 and extended it, bringing up their three children, who all attended Mollington School.

Audrey and Violet returned to their old home in 2010 with their families to recall their childhood days and to show their own children where they had enjoyed many happy times.

St Oswald's Church
Memorial Window

The War Memorials in St Oswald's Church, Backford

by Michael Richardson

Introduction

In the years following the end of the Great War (1914–18), many memorials to those who had fought and died in the conflict were erected, both in the various theatres of war and in the home communities of those who had served in the forces. War memorials were erected in towns and villages, Rolls of Honour put up in workplaces, railway stations etc. and church windows designed and dedicated to military units and individuals. Then, following the end of the Second World War (1939–45), details of those killed in this conflict were often added to existing memorials and in some cases separate plaques or memorials were erected.

In St Oswald's Church, Backford the Great War memorial is a brass plaque giving the names of those local men who "at the call of duty and in defence of the Empire gave their lives for their King and Country". The cost of this, and a similar memorial placed in the non-Conformist chapel on Townfield Lane, was met by public subscription which raised just over £855. The two memorial plaques cost £142 and the Book of Remembrance a further £25. The balance, together with interest, amounted to £724 and this was invested with the income being used to provide one or more Scholarships for children from the parish going into secondary or higher education. Appropriately, the first recipient of a Backford War Memorial Scholarship was Dorothy Carline, whose uncle had been one of those to give his life in the service of his country during the Great War.

The first suggestion that a memorial should be erected to those who gave their lives in the Second World War came from the bellringers of St Oswald's, two of whose number had been killed during the conflict; unfortunately there are no records of who these were. At that time, major work was needed on the bells and from donations received it was decided that a memorial to all those from the parish who had given their lives should be erected.[1] This was erected in 1950 and is a Hopton Wood (limestone) wall tablet inscribed "In proud & honoured memory of the men of this parish who fell in the World War 1939–1945 ... Their name liveth for evermore". It lists eleven names without giving details of their service units.

There are also two memorial windows – the first, which is adjacent to the two memorial plaques, also dates from 1950 and was organised and paid for by the Royal British Legion; it was designed and made by G. Maile & Son of London.[1] The other window, in the south aisle, commemorates Wing Commander John Harvey Hutchinson who was killed in 1940 and his uncle Ambrose who had been killed while flying with the RFC during the First World War.

Great War memorial

Details of the twelve servicemen named on the WW1 memorial plaque in Backford church have been researched, and most appear to have lived in the parish or had other local connections; however, Henry Higgins has no obvious connection with the parish and Leonard Blurton remains a complete mystery as the details of the two men of that name found do not match those on the memorial. The plaque gives only initials and abbreviations of service units but full details are recorded in the Book of Remembrance kept in the church and the names listed below are as recorded in that book. It has been discovered that, in addition to those named on the memorial, three former pupils of Backford School were killed whilst serving during the war and all are named on the Ellesmere Port war memorial, although they are not mentioned on the memorial in Backford church. They were William Bristor (at school 1899–1904) and his brother Frank (1904–1911) also Albert Nixon (1900–1907); some further details of their family background

World War I Memorial

and service records are given at the end of this section dealing with casualties of the Great War.

Pvt. Leonard Blurton, Royal Field Artillery

This remains a mystery as there is no record of anyone of this name in the parish, and the only deaths listed on the Commonwealth War Graves Commission (CWGC) website are of a Private in the Grenadier Guards in 1918 and of a Rifleman in the Kings Royal Rifle Corps in 1915. They are the only two Leonard Blurtons in the 1911 census and lived in Staffordshire and Derbyshire respectively. The only Blurton family in Cheshire at that time was living in Stockport and while there were a few Blurtons serving in the Royal Field Artillery none was named Leonard and none of them was killed in the Great War!

Pvt. William Bowker, 5th Cheshire Regiment

William was born at Pipers Ash, Hoole, Chester on 27th February 1891, the fourth child and second son of Kendrick and Frances E. Bowker (née Millward). By 1901 the family was living at Abbot's Meads on Parkgate Road; William was educated at Guilden Sutton Primary School and the British School on Victoria Road, where he started on 15th January 1899. On leaving school he worked on William Jones' farm at Dunkirk, Lea by Backford, where the 1911 census lists him as a 'cowman'. The newspaper report of his death records that he was employed in farm work by Mr Davies of Mollington (*at Tarrant Farm, MTR*). He married Bessie Ellams at Chester Register Office in Q4 1913 and they had three children, Cyril (1914), Frances (1915) and William Ernest (1917) who was born just ten days after his father's death.[2] William joined the 4th Battn. Cheshire Regiment on 13th March 1917 and served in France and Flanders from May. He was killed on 7th June 1917 in the assault on Messines Ridge and was buried in Lindenhoek Road Military Cemetery, Wulverghem, 13 km. south of Ieper (Ypres), where he is recorded as being with the 13th Battn. which is more likely as neither the 4th nor the 5th Battalion fought in that battle.

William's widow emigrated to Canada in June 1919 where she married John Gorman and had a further five children. She left her eldest son Cyril in Cheshire with his grandparents, and his descendants still live locally.

2nd Lt. Thomas Carline, 18th Kings Liverpool Regiment

Thomas Carline was born on 17th December 1887 at 93 Francis St, Chester, the third son of John and Elizabeth (née Tulloch); his father was a Post Office clerk and later a superintendent. He was baptised at St John the Baptist church on 21st March 1888. The family moved to 19 Hamilton Street in Hoole and the 1911 census describes Thomas as a "clerk with a soap manufacturer". He worked for Lever Bros. at Port Sunlight and later at the Liver Building in Liverpool.[3] In 1911 his father had bought a plot of land on Grove Road and built 'Leaholm' where his niece Dorothy, whose obituary appears elsewhere in this volume, was born in 1912. Tom Carline joined the Liverpool 'Pals' when they were formed in September 1914 and served in France from September 1915, rising to be Company Quartermaster Sergeant in The Kings (Liverpool Regiment). After his marriage to Edith Marion Hallam at Christ Church, Port Sunlight[4] in Q4 1917 he was commissioned as temporary 2nd Lieutenant attached to the 15th Battn. Lancashire Fusiliers. Tom had been back in France for only a couple of weeks when he was killed on 30th September 1918 during the Battle of the St Quentin Canal, when the 46th (N. Midland) Division stormed the Hindenburg Line at Bellenglise and took 4000 prisoners and 700 guns. He is buried in the Uplands cemetery at Magny-la-Fosse, in the St Quentin district of Picardy and is also named on the Port Sunlight Memorial which commemorates Lever Bros employees and on the War Memorials in Chester Town Hall and on Hoole Road in Chester.

Cpl. William Cartmel, Denbighshire Hussars

William Edward Cartmel was born in Saughall in Q4 1893 and baptised in Shotwick church on 2nd February 1896, the second of four children of William Edwin and Elizabeth (née Bithell), who had been married in Shotwick church on 27th March 1890. His father, who worked as a traction engine driver, was killed in an accident in July 1899 and his mother then married John Griffith on 23rd January 1901 at Shotwick; the family continued to live in Saughall, although the CWGC website records his mother living in Ellesmere Port. In the 1911 census William was living at Factory Cottages in Saughall and working as a horseman on a farm. It is not known when he joined up but he served initially with the Denbighshire Yeomanry, transferred to the 1st Battn. King's Shropshire Light Infantry in October 1916 and sailed with them to

France in November. They were involved in raids and attacks on Hill 70 near Loos on 18th and 19th April 1917 and according to the Battalion history spent a week in billets in Philosophe before returning to the trenches on the front between Loos and Halluch.[5] It is possible that William was one of three soldiers who were killed in a daring raid by the Germans on 4th May.[6] He is buried in the Philosophe British Cemetery at Mazingarbe, between Bethune and Lens. In addition to the memorial in Backford Church, William is also listed on the War Memorial in Saughall, on the west base of the clock tower of the Vernon Institute.

His elder brother Ernest (born 1891) also served in France during the War, with the Royal Engineers.

Pvt William Dentith, Cheshire Yeomanry

William was born on 25th January 1898 and baptised in All Saints Church, Saughall on 24th April, the son of Thomas Dentith, a farm labourer, and his wife Mary (née Hopwood), who lived on Parkgate Road. William was their fifth child and youngest of three sons and was attending school at the time of the 1911 census. He joined the Cheshire Yeomanry on the outbreak of war and in a postcard sent to his sister in September 1914 wrote that "*We are not having it all … now. It is not very nice being woken (?) out of camp at 3 o'c in the morning. Love from Bill.*" In 1916 they went to Egypt and were involved in guard duties on the Suez Canal; after a spell at El Alamein they were amalgamated in March 1917 with the Shropshire Yeomanry to become the 10th Battn. King's Shropshire Light Infantry (KSLI).[5] The history of the Battalion records that they took part in the Third Battle of Gaza during October and November 1917; towards the end of the battle they came under heavy fire while occupying the village of El Tireh to the west of Jerusalem and it seems likely that William was one of the casualties.[6] His death was reported in the Chester Chronicle for 22nd December 1917 which reported that "*he was only 19 years of age and had served for 3 years in the Cheshire Yeomanry, being transferred to the KSLI when drafted out to Egypt*"

and the Wirral Parish Magazine for January 1918 reported "*The sad news of the death from wounds of Trooper William Dentith of the Cheshire Yeomanry, somewhere in the neighbourhood of Jerusalem. Dentith was a promising young man, bearing a thoroughly good character*". According to Army records he died of wounds in Egypt on 5th December 1917 and is buried in the Kantara War Memorial Cemetery on the east side of the Suez Canal. This had been the site of a major base and hospital centre.

William's elder brother Frederick (1896–1962) also served during the War, with the 5th Battn. Cheshire Regiment and with the Royal Engineers. Their parents are buried in Backford churchyard.

Stoker 1st class James Greenwood, HMS Good Hope

James was born at Port Carlisle on the Solway Firth on 12th November 1884[7] to Paul Greenwood, a fisherman and his wife Mary Jane (née Morton). After his father's death in 1887 his mother married Robert Dalton and the family then lived near Maryport where James is recorded as a scholar in the 1891 census. By 1901 Robert and Mary Jane had moved with their family to Wirral and lived at several locations before settling at Caughall Bridge; they died in 1927 and 1952 respectively and are buried in Backford churchyard. In 1901 James was a farm servant, lodging with William Smith, a farm bailiff living in Blacon. He became a railway fireman with GWR in November 1902 and left in December 1906 to join the Royal Navy as a stoker, he served in several ships during his five year service before transferring to the Royal Fleet Reserve on 1st January 1912. James married Annie Lee at Seacombe Congregational Church in Q1 1914 and was called up in July 1914 to serve in the armoured cruiser HMS *Good Hope* when she was taken out of reserve and became the flagship of Rear-Admiral Cradock in the South American Squadron. *Good Hope* and three other ships including the cruiser *Monmouth* were ambushed by Admiral Graf von Spee's cruiser squadron at Coronel, off the coast of central Chile, on 1st November and were outgunned, with *Good Hope* and *Monmouth* being lost with all hands. Greenwood was one of 280 stokers on board,

HMS Good Hope

almost one third of the crew of 900. The Battle of Coronel was the first defeat of British naval forces for over a century; more about this battle can be found on website www.coronel.org.uk.

James and Annie had a daughter Marjorie, born on 2nd December 1914, just a month after her father's death. Annie re-married, first to George Mollon in 1919 (he was a ship's engineer on the White Star Liner *Baltic*) and after his accidental death in Canada[4] in 1924 she married his brother William in 1936; they moved to N Ireland where she died in Co. Down in 1969.

Three of James' Dalton siblings served during the war; Richard (born 1891) was with the Army Service Corps in France, Robert (1899–1968) served in the 2nd Company, Machine Gun Corps whilst Edward (1900–1976) was in the 9th Battalion, Cheshire Regiment.

At least one other local family was affected by the huge loss of life in this first major naval battle of the war, as one of the officers on HMS *Monmouth* was Engineer Lieut. Lionel Wansbrough, whose uncle was Vicar of Shotwick from 1902 to 1936.

Pvt. Thomas Hackney, 10th Royal West Kent Regiment

Thomas Henry Hackney was born at Gresford, Flintshire in Q2 1898, the eldest of five children of Thomas and Annie Elizabeth (née Dutton);

Thomas senior had been born in Mollington and before that the family had lived in Capenhurst. The family then lived in Aston, near Runcorn and by 1901 they were back in Mollington living on Parkgate Road in one of the cottages near Mollington Grange. Thomas was a pupil at Mollington School from 1903 to 1912[8] and according to his service record he enlisted in the Lancers at the Curragh Camp in Ireland but transferred to the 10th Battn. Queen's Own (Royal West Kent Regiment). This had been formed in May 1915 and went to Aldershot in January 1916 before being sent to Flanders where they fought in the Third Battle of Ypres, better known as Passchendaele. This started on 31st July 1917 and Thomas must have been killed as they 'went over the top' on the opening day of the battle; his name is one of 54,000 on the Menin Gate memorial to soldiers whose graves are unknown.

Pvt. Henry Stafford Higgins, 6th South Staffs Regiment

Henry Stafford Higgins was born on 1st March 1900 and baptised at St Clare's RC church, Arundel Avenue, Sefton Park, Liverpool, the fourth child and eldest son of Henry and Emma (née Carruthers).[9]

Both of his parents died in 1910 and from Feb 1911 to May 1914 census he was a pupil at St Edward's School, Thingwall, a poor law school run by the Brothers of Charity. It is not known what he did on leaving the school but it appears that he enlisted in Chester in the Royal Army Service Corps and later transferred to the 1/6th South Staffs regiment. He was killed in action on 3rd October 1918 and his name is on the Vis-en-Artois memorial, which contains the names of more than 9,000 men who fell in the advance between the Somme and Loos between 8th August 1918 and the Armistice. It is not clear what his connection, if any, with Backford parish may have been.

2nd Lt. Ambrose Hutchinson, Royal Flying Corps

Ambrose was born at Rock Ferry in 1885 and baptised at Bebington on 31st January 1886, the youngest son of John Heap Hutchinson (a cotton broker) and his wife Fanny Elizabeth (née Forwood). He was educated at Sedbergh School from 1897 to 1903[10] and on leaving school spent a few years farming in New Zealand, returning to England in 1908. He then appears to have spent some time in Texas[11] before returning again to England and joining 6th Battn. The King's (Liverpool Regiment). He was promoted to Lieutenant and in late October 1917 was attached to 20 Squadron of the Royal Flying Corps where he flew with 2nd Lt. Baron Starfield (South African). They were credited with one combat victory for an Albatross scout plane shot down near Ypres on 8th November 1917 and they themselves were killed in action on 19th January 1918 while flying Bristol F2B A7193. They were last seen near the village of Wytschaete (SE of Ypres) and were shot down by Ob.Ltn. Bruno Loerzer of Jasta 26 (his 20th combat victory).[4] Ambrose was originally buried in the German Military Cemetery at Kortemark but was later moved to Larch Wood (Railway Cutting) Cemetery, 4 km southeast of Ieper (Ypres). His brother William later lived at Lea House and was one of the original Trustees of the Backford War Memorial Trust.

The Hutchinson memorial window is inscribed

> *To the Glory of God and in proud memory of Lieut. Ambrose Hutchinson R.F.C killed Jan 19th 1918 … Also of Wing Com. John Harvey Hutchinson R.A.F. killed Oct 8th 1940, aged 36, while flying in the service of their Country. Per Ardua ad Astra*

Pvt. John Morris, 4th Cheshire Regiment

William John Morris was born in Mollington in 1897, while his parents Samuel and Mary (née Jones) were living on Parkgate Road; his father was a platelayer with the LNWR and he had a younger brother Frederick Arthur and sister Linda. John was enrolled at Mollington School in 1902[8] and moved to Backford School for his final year from 1910 to 1911, after which he worked as a gardener for T Gibbons Frost at Mollington Hall. His service records survive[12] so we know that he enlisted on 7th December 1915 and when he was called up on 1st June 1916 was assigned to the 5th Battn. Cheshire Regiment and arrived at the Infantry Base Depot at Rouen on 25th October 1916. From there he was posted to the 9th Battn. Cheshire Regiment on 5th November and would have been involved in the later stages of the battles on the Somme. Just two weeks later John was killed, aged 19, on 19th November 1916, at the very end of that year's offensive, probably during the final battle to secure a crossing of the river Ancre. He was buried in the Connaught cemetery at the edge of Thiepval Wood, which had been the scene of fierce fighting earlier in the Somme offensive.

2nd Lt. Roger Bingham Turner, 3rd Cheshire Regiment

Roger Bingham Turner was born in Moffatt, Scotland on 8th August 1895, the elder son of Bingham Dixon Turner (later to be headmaster of Loughborough Grammar School) and his wife Dora, daughter of the late Major James Swetenham of Moston Hall, who had been married at Backford on 9th August 1893. He was educated at Sandroyd School (1906–09), Charterhouse (1909–1914) where he gained Junior and Senior Scholarships and Jesus College, Cambridge (1914–15), where he won an open Classical Scholarship.[2] He trained with the Cambridge OTC and was gazetted 2nd Lt. with the 3rd Battn. Cheshire Regiment on 12th April 1915.

Roger went with a draft to the Dardanelles on 1st September 1915, where he was attached to the 8th Battn. and was present at the evacuation of Suvla Bay and Cape Hellas. In January 1916 he moved with the Battalion to Egypt and the following month to Mesopotamia where he was killed in action at Sanna-i-Yat on 9th April, during an engagement which saw two Victoria Crosses awarded. His name is recorded with over 40,000 others on the Basra memorial in Iraq and there is also a memorial window to him in the cloister of Chester cathedral (at south-east corner).

The Roll of Honour in Backford church also lists his younger brother James, who was born in 1897. He served during the War as a Lieutenant, and later Captain, in the Royal Field Artillery and was awarded the

Military Cross in 1919. During the Second World War he was a Colonel in the Royal Regiment of Artillery, and later served in Burma in charge of 505 District of the British military administration, for which he was awarded the OBE in 1946. He died in 1963.

Chester Cathedral Memorial Window

2nd Lt. George Henderson Walker, Royal Air Force

George Henderson Walker was born on 14th January 1895 at Birkdale, Southport and baptised at St James, Birkdale on 3rd April, the second son (of four children) of William Henderson Walker and Agnes (née Woodhead), who lived at Chorlton Hall from the late 1890s. He was educated at Rugby School from 1908 to 1911 and then spent almost two years in Berlin and Paris before joining his father's accountancy business in January 1914 as an articled pupil. On the outbreak of war he enlisted in the 1st Public Schools Battalion of the Royal Fusiliers, and was later commissioned in 11 Battn. South Lancashire Regiment in February 1915. He was promoted to Lieutenant in June 1915 and went to France in October of that year, transferring to the RFC as an Observer in June 1916. He went on to qualify as a pilot with 45 Sqdn. Royal Flying Corps. On 28th July 1917, as pilot of Sopwith 1½ Strutter A1031, he was leading a flight of four planes over the German lines near Polygon Wood (just east of Ypres) and was reported missing, having been last seen following a German plane to the ground.

His observer was 2nd Lt. Benjamin George Beatty, originally from Blackrock near Dublin, and records indicate that their plane was shot down by Ltn. Ernst Hess of Jagdstaffel 28 and was the fifth of his eventual 17 victims. In February 1918 Walker was recorded as officially presumed dead and his name is recorded on the Arras Flying Services Memorial.

The Roll of Honour in Backford church also lists his brothers William (b. 1892) who served in France as a Lieutenant with the 3rd Battn. King's (Liverpool) Regiment and was awarded the MC; he became a barrister and died in Sussex in 1958; also Alexander (b.1897) who served during the War as a Lieutenant, and later Captain, in the 11th Battn. South Lancashire Regiment and then with the RFC and RAF. He later became a chartered accountant based in Liverpool and died in 1961. Their parents are buried in Backford churchyard.

Backford School former pupils

William and Frank Bristor were the sons of William and Emma Bristor of Rose Cottage, Woodland Road, Whitby Heath. William John Bristor was born in 1890, the first of five children in the family of two boys and three girls (two of whom were baptised at Backford church); at the time of the 1911 census he was working as a "flour mill labourer". He served with the 8th Battn. Cheshire Regiment in Mesopotamia and was killed in action on 14th April 1917, during the Battle of Nahr Kalis, not long after the fall of Baghdad and is commemorated on the Basra memorial. His younger brother Frank was born in 1897 and baptised at Stoak on 20th June; he was serving in France with the 2nd Battn., Manchester Regiment when he was killed in action on 19th August 1918 at the start of the "Hundred Days Offensive" and was buried in Heath Cemetery, Harbonnieres.

Albert Nixon was born in 1893 and baptised at Stoak on 30th April, the fourth of six children of Ralph and Elizabeth Nixon of Stanney House. In 1911 the family were living at Woodland Road, Whitby and Albert was working as a gardener. He served in the 8th Battn. South Lancashire Regiment and was wounded at Thiepval Ridge in the closing stages of the Battle of the Somme. He was moved to one of the military hospitals at Rouen where he died on 20th October 1916 and was buried in the St Sever Cemetery at Rouen.

WW2 Memorial

This memorial is a Hopton Wood stone wall tablet inscribed "In proud & honoured memory of the men of this parish who fell in the world war 1939–1945" and after the names "Their name liveth for evermore".

It lists eleven servicemen, many of whom served in the RAF and almost all appear to have lived locally or had other connections with the parish, although it has not so far been possible to identify John Pritchard. To this list I have added Wing Cdr. J. H. Hutchinson, commemorated by a window in the church; his family had lived in the parish and his father served as Churchwarden for some time. The names below are as given on the memorial plaque.

World War II Memorial

As mentioned in the introduction, two of those named on the plaque had been bellringers at Backford church but it has not been possible to identify which they were.

Joseph J Donnachie

Joseph James Donnachie was born on 1st Feb (?) 1913 in the West Derby district of Liverpool to Joseph and Catherine née Mallon. His father Joseph (born 1885) was a Scottish professional footballer who spent the bulk of his career with Oldham Athletic (1908–1914) and then became player-manager with Chester City from 1921;[13] he was also the licencee of the Mariner's Arms pub in New Crane St. Chester from 1934 to 1942.[14] Joseph jnr. was also a footballer, playing as a junior in the Chester and District League and then for Everton, Bolton Wanderers and Chester. He was educated at the College School and then worked in the office of Mr A. B. Dye, the City Coroner, and later with Mr R. A. Williams, the Deputy City Coroner.[15] After joining the RAF at Christmas 1941 he spent some time training in Canada and returned to England in February 1944. On 17th August 1942 he had married Margaruite Milligan of Mollington at St Francis's R.C. church in Chester.[16] On his return from training he was promoted to Sergeant and on 12th October 1944 was a bomb aimer in Short Stirling LK465 of 1657 HCU (Heavy Conversion Unit[#]) which took off from RAF Stradishall in Suffolk for a night cross-country exercise. After the failure of one of the four engines, the pilot attempted to land at RAF Chedburgh, a subsidiary base nearby, but lost control and crashed near the camp cinema.[16] Donnachie and another crew member were killed in the crash, the pilot and two others died the next day while

Donnachie grave, Overleigh Cemetery

the remaining two crew members survived. His funeral was held at St Francis RC church in Chester on 17th October 1944 and he was buried in Chester (Overleigh) cemetery.

Joseph's widow Margaruite continued to live in Mollington and she served as Secretary to Backford PCC from 1953 to 1969;[1] she died in 1991 and was buried with her husband in Overleigh Cemetery.

[#] The Heavy Conversion Units began forming in late 1941 to qualify crews trained on medium bombers to operate the heavy bombers prior to assignment to an Operational Training Unit to gain experience before final posting to the operational squadrons.

Rayleigh Haller

Elliott Philip Rayleigh Haller was born in London in 1898, the younger son of John George Haller, a chemical merchant and his wife Agnes Mary (née Watts); he was christened on 15th June 1898 at St Mark's Church, Regent's Park (by Rev. W. J. Sparrow-Simpson, who wrote the libretto for Stainer's oratorio *The Crucifixion*). Rayleigh worked as an electrical engineer with the Western Telegraph Company in Barbados and Brazil.[4] He married Muriel Deane Neild on 23rd July 1932 in Rio de Janeiro and after the birth of their first daughter the family returned to London where they had two more daughters. Some time later they moved to Mollington where they lived at Grove Farm. Rayleigh joined the Royal Naval Volunteer Supplementary Reserve when it was

Lady of the Isles.

established in 1936[18] and on the outbreak of war was commissioned as a temporary Lieutenant in the RNVR; in October 1940 he was in command of the former Scilly Islands steamer 'Lady of the Isles', which had retired from the islands service in 1904 and then served as a RN cable ship and later as a salvage vessel, until requisitioned by the Admiralty as an auxiliary vessel. She was under tow by a tug, with a crew of 15 (3 Royal Navy plus 12 Merchant Navy) when she struck a mine on 3rd October and sank off Killigerran Head, with the loss of all those on board. Rayleigh is commemorated on the Portsmouth Naval Memorial.

Rayleigh's elder brother John Henry Lyle Haller was born in 1894 and was planning to follow his father into the chemical industry, but having been commissioned in the 3rd Battn. East Surrey Regiment for a period after leaving Lancing College he rejoined on the outbreak of war in 1914 and was with the 2nd Battn. at Lindenhoek, near Ypres, when he was killed by a German sniper on 12th March 1915.[19]

Laurence Helme

Laurence Helme was born on 24th June 1912 in Millom, Cumberland, the second son of Richard and Annie (née Taylor). In Q3 of 1938 he married Mary Hargreaves and they lived in Mollington; he joined the RAFVR and in 1942 was a Flight Sergeant in 39 Squadron which had been based in India since 1928, later moving to Egypt. From early 1942

a detachment was based in Malta, equipped with Bristol Beaufort torpedo bombers. Laurence was the observer in Beaufort DD875 which took off from RAF station, Luqa, Malta at 6.30 pm (local time) on 30th November 1942, together with two other aircraft, for an operational flight laying mines in Bizerta harbour, Tunis.[17] Nothing was heard from the aircraft after take-off and it did not return to base; searches failed to reveal any trace of the missing plane or crew and in 1949 it was formally recorded that the four crew had lost their lives at sea and had no known grave;[18] their names are commemorated on the Malta Memorial, outside the entrance to Valetta. His widow Mary re-married at Backford church in April 1948.

Hugh Humphreys

Although recorded as Hugh on the war memorial and on the family grave in Backford churchyard, his birth name was Richard Humphreys and the CWGC website lists him as such. He was born on 7th May 1919 and baptised at St Oswald's church on 24th August, the youngest son of Thomas and Margaret (née Gray) of The Nook, Backford. He was a pupil at Backford school from 1924 to 1933 although he spent over a year away from school because of defective eyesight.[20] The family grave in Backford churchyard records that he died in Lahore on 22nd April 1943 while serving with the RAMC. A little more information about him is given in a newspaper report of his death, which says that he had served in the RAMC for a little over a year and a half and before joining the army had been with Williams and Williams of Chester for a short time. Before that he had worked with his father (a gamekeeper) on the Backford Estate. The newspaper report also tells us that Hugh died of leukemia in the British Hospital in Lahore; he was buried in the Karachi War Cemetery.

John Harvey Hutchinson

John Harvey Hutchinson was born in Bebington on 16th October 1903, the elder son of William Hutchinson, a cotton broker and his wife Asta Carlotta (née Broadbent); he was christened at St Andrew's Church, Bebington on 22nd November. The family moved to Lea by Backford ca. 1914 and William served several terms as Churchwarden of St Oswald's Backford. John joined the RAF, was elected a member of the Royal Aero Club in 1925 and married Beatrice (Betty) Kendrick in Q1 1934 in Kensington; by this time his parents had moved to Finchampstead, Berkshire. He was promoted to Squadron Leader in April 1937 and became commanding officer of 812 Squadron,[21] which flew Swordfish aircraft on board HMS Glorious in the Mediterranean and also took part in the Coronation Review flypast at Spithead. He was promoted to Wing Commander in March 1940 and appointed Commanding Officer of RAF Pembrey in South Wales. During the later stages of the Battle of Britain, John was killed on 8th October 1940 when his Miles Magister P6347 hit the cable of a tethered barrage balloon at Langley near Slough. He was buried in St Illtyd's churchyard, Pembrey and there is a memorial to him in the Chapel at the RAF base; his name is also one of those listed on the Finchampstead war memorial.

John Pritchard

[I have narrowed this down to three possible servicemen and there were at least two Pritchard families living locally but I have so far been unable to establish a connection or identify who is named on the memorial.]

James Smith

James Smith was born in Mollington on 18th September 1903, the third son of seven children of Thomas and Elizabeth Smith. He was baptised at St Oswald's Backford on 25th October 1903 at which time the family was living at Lea Cottages, although they later moved to Parkgate Road. He was a pupil at Mollington School and for his last few years had a half-time exemption as he was working for Mr Farrell at Warren Farm (afternoons for milking). He married Rosemary Ann Ralph in 1936 in Uxbridge and they lived in Newcastle on Tyne. James joined the

RAF and was serving as a Warrant Officer with 45 (Transport) Group when he died on 23rd March 1945 and was buried in Rabat European Cemetery.

Walter Shone

Walter George Shone was born on 23rd January 1915 at Bickerton, the son of Walter and Emily (née Probin). He was serving as a Gunner with the 4th Maritime Regiment providing coastal defence artillery in Sierra Leone, where he died on 9th April 1944 and is buried in Freetown (King Tom) Cemetery. His father had died in 1927 and at the time of his death his mother was living in Ellesmere Port. Walter's name is also recorded on his parents' grave in Malpas cemetery.

John R Stevenson

John Stevenson was born in Q2 1922 in Whitchurch district, the eldest of four sons of William Edward and Alice Ena (née Clutton). The family moved to Mollington in the mid-1920s and are known to have been living at Overwood Cottage. John worked for Mr T. C. Clarke, haulage contractor in Wrexham before he joined up, and was serving as a Lance Corporal with the Royal Army Service Corps when he was killed in action during the North African campaign on 31st December 1942; he is buried in the Medjez-el-Bab War Cemetery, about 60 km. west of Tunis.

Campbell J Walker

Campbell James Cansdale Walker (known as 'Bunny') was born in Chester on 6th April 1917 and christened on 27 May 1917.[22] His parents were Campbell Gregory and Dorothy M (née Cansdale), who had married in Hartlepool in 1914 and then lived in Chester where they had two children, Campbell and Barbara (b. 1918). They later moved to live on Overwood Avenue in Mollington (ca. 1928) and Campbell was educated at the King's School, Chester from 1927 to 1934.[23] Early in the war he joined the RAFVR and on 5th December 1941 was promoted from Sergeant to Pilot Officer on probation (emergency) and posted to 248 Squadron, based at Bircham Newton in Norfolk, operating sorties against enemy shipping off the Dutch coast. On 22nd January 1942 he was the Wireless Operator/Observer in Bristol Beaufighter Mk IC T4786 which took off at 12.15 for a reconnaissance flight over the Dutch coast.[3] They were shot down by light flak from a port defence boat off Ijmuiden at about 14.30. Bunny was killed and is buried in the Amsterdam New Eastern Cemetery whilst the pilot, Flt Lt Joseph Blennerhassett (originally from Co. Kerry in Ireland) was listed as missing. Campbell senior was an accomplished artist and the Duchess of Westminster is reputed to have been one of his sitters. Bunny and his sister Barbara were also artists and she did the drawing of Mollington Hall on the Jubilee mug.

Edwin Weatherly

Edwin Weatherley was born in Saltney and christened on 26th May 1910 at St Mark's, Lache-cum-Saltney, the second son of William and Catherine (née Canderton). According to the 1911 census his father worked for the GWR as a carriage cleaner and Edwin had three brothers and a sister Lily; he was educated at the Wood Memorial School, Saltney. In 1932 he married Dilys Morgan and they had a daughter Edwina; the family lived at Tarrant Farm Cottage in Mollington, and his widow remained there until her death in 1958. From 1930 Edwin had worked as an attendant at the Deva Hospital and on the outbreak of war became an Air Raid Warden in Mollington;[4] he joined the RAF early in 1943 and by the end of the year was serving as a Sergeant (Air-Gunner) with 1667 HCU (Heavy Conversion Unit) at Faldingworth in Lincolnshire. He was one of the crew of Handley Page Halifax EB152 which went missing on a night navigational exercise on 21st January 1944[24] and is commemorated on the Runnymede memorial to the more than 20,000 airmen lost in WW2 from bases in the UK and North and West Europe and who have no known grave.

[Note: the correct spelling of his family name is Weatherley although it is recorded on the memorial as Weatherly.]

James Whitley

James Woodburn Whitley was born in Q1 1921 in Chorley, Lancs, the eldest of four children of Joseph Erle Whitley and Constance Mary née Walker, who later lived on Overwood Avenue in Mollington. After leaving school he enrolled at the Liverpool School of Architecture, hoping to follow his father's profession, but on the outbreak of war he joined the RAF and initially trained as a wireless operator. After serving with 100 Squadron he was transferred on 25th November 1943 to 550 Squadron based at North Killingholme near Grimsby, on its formation. Lancaster LM425 was delivered to the Squadron on 12th December 1943 and on the night of 30th March 1944 Sergeant Whitley was one of the crew (rear air gunner) when it took off at 9.45 pm to take part in a raid on Nuremberg.[25] On the outward flight it was hit by flak from batteries near Liege and exploded in mid-air near the Barrage de la Gileppe, 8 km. east of Verviers in Belgium. Three survivors managed to parachute to safety as the Lancaster blew up but Whitley and three others were killed and are buried in the Heverlee War Cemetery, near Leuven, whilst the three survivors were interned in PoW camps, one of them after hospitalisation. LM425 was one of two Lancasters of 550 Squadron lost that night, which saw the heaviest losses of the war for Bomber Command. A memorial was erected in 2010 in woodland to the south of Gileppe Lake, with a plaque giving the names of the crew members and including some fragments of the aircraft.[26]

Sgt James Whitley (at left) and crew of Lancaster LM425 By permission of RAF 550 Squadron and North Killingholme Association

Memorial to the crew of Lancaster LM425, near Gileppe Lake, Belgium. By permission of Ed van der Pas/ STIWOT

The radio operator on that ill-fated flight was Sgt Stanley Keirle and he has written about his memories of that night and his subsequent experiences in POW camps until he eventually made his way to Halle and was repatriated to the UK in May 1945.[27]

James' sister Doreen served in the ATS during the war,[4] married Lieut. Clifford Eriksen of the US Army at Backford church in October 1945 and emigrated to the USA in 1946 under the 'War Brides Act' which saw up to 100,000 GI brides leaving the UK.

Acknowledgements

I would like to thank those family members and others who have helped by providing photographs and other information, also the librarians at Sedbergh School and The King's School, Chester. Credit is also due to Brian Thaxter who first sparked my interest in this subject and set me off on what was to become at times a quite emotional journey.

References and Sources

1. Backford PCC minutes, Cheshire Record Office.
2. De Ruvigny's Roll of Honour 1914–18 (searchable online at findmypast.co.uk).
3. 'Progress' Lever Brothers house magazine October 1918.

4. Personal Communication.
5. The History of the King's Shropshire Light Infantry in the Great War 1914–18, Major W deB Wood, 1925.
6. Personal Communication, via Great War Forum.
7. Naval Casualties 1914 – 1919 (searchable on line at findmypast.co.uk).
8. Mollington School Logbooks, Cheshire Record Office.
9. British Genealogy.com.
10. Sedbergh School records.
11. USA 1910 census, searchable online at ancestry.com.
12. British Army WW1 Service Records 1914–20 (searchable online at ancestry.com).
13. Wikipedia entry for Joseph "Joe" Donnachie.
14. 'The Vanished Pubs of Chester' gallery at www.chesterwalls.info.
15. Obituary in Chester Chronicle, 21 October 1944.
16. Chester Chronicle, 22 August 1942.
17. http://www.rafcommands.com/archive/11603.php.
18. Navy List 1936, searchable at ancestry.com.
19. Lancing College War memorial website.
20. RAAF WW2 fatalities in RAF Beaufort squadrons. Author Alan Storr. Australian War memorial record RC09125.021.
21. National Archives of Australia, record A705, 163/59/88.
22. Backford school Registers, Cheshire Record Office.
23 History of 812 Squadron at www.hmstheseus.co.uk.
24. Information from King's School Chester.
25. RAF Aircraft EA100-EZ999, Air-Britain (Historians) Ltd. 2010.
26. www.aircrewremembered.com/raf1944.
27. www.550squadronassociation.org.uk.
28. www.rebecq-memorial.eu.
29. www.theoddbods.org.

Other information came from the following sources :

Commonwealth War Graves Commission website.
Electoral Rolls for Mollington.
British Army WW1 Medal Rolls Index Cards, on ancestry.com.
UK Soldiers died in the Great War, on ancestry.com.
Census returns for 1901 and 1911.
Cheshire Parish Records, searchable on findmypast.co.uk.

The Backford Parish Magazine

by John Peter Hess

This study divides naturally into two parts; firstly, the early days from 1935 to 1984, for which there are only a few magazine examples available and for which most useful information comes from PCC minutes; secondly, 1985 to the present, for which there is a continuous series of magazines available. For the former, a chronological narrative makes the best presentation, while for the latter a division into subjects will happily suffice.

Early History

The magazine was first published in 1935. Before that, news from Backford appeared only in the monthly Wirral Parish Magazine (going to twelve parishes), from which we have the entry for January 1918, giving news of war casualties and the church accounts for 1917.

On 8th December 1935 the vicar, Canon Blencowe, said at a PCC meeting that he felt a need for some form of publication: most news and church notices were being given from the pulpit and only those in church heard anything. He felt enough circulation could be created to cover costs. The PCC decided to produce a trial magazine for one year and then they would see. Messrs. Davies and Rowe were appointed as printers (W.F. Healey by September 1940) and advertisements were anticipated.

In fact circulation was two hundred by March 1936 and a profit of £6 was reported for the year to January 1937. The magazine would definitely continue.

Unfortunately the first copy to hand is from 1940 and there are no others available until 1969, although some information is given in PCC minutes. The 1940 copy has an attractive cover picture of the church with a list of church officers on the front. Inside are notices of various kinds relating to the church and to local groups associated with it. It does seem, however, that by 1939 there was a decrease in income and a small loss was being made. In 1945 the minutes record a year's deficit of £6, due to increased costs and reduced advertising, a trend which got worse in 1946, when print workers made a new agreement with their employers. At the end of that year the sale price for the magazine was raised from 2d to 3d a copy.

About this time it was decided to change the cover design, for which Mr. J.W. Clarke was asked to make a drawing of the church. This being accepted, it went into use in 1947 after old covers had been used up. He presented the block used for printing this drawing to the Church in 1948. (J.W. Clarke is the author of 'Mollington Hall', an article appearing in Journal of the Chester Archaeological Society, vol. 41, 1954. He was a teacher of art at Chester College and also an active member of Lancashire and Cheshire Antiquarian Society. He lived in Townfield Lane, Mollington, from 1939 to 1969, having been resident in Chester before that).

There was some discussion about changing the magazine's name to 'The Beacon', but this was not approved.

In the meantime the accounts still showed losses, so at the end of 1952 the sale price was raised to 4d. Rising costs were certainly becoming a problem, so the PCC appointed a sub-committee to investigate ways of making the magazine pay – its immediate answer, another price increase. The charge for advertisements was also put up. By 1965 the price was 6d a copy and a profit was being made.

A nationally distributed leaflet of religious news, the 'Sign', was being sent out monthly to parishes, and from 1961 that was stapled into Backford's magazine. Interestingly, that year Mr. Clarke was asked for a fresh drawing of the church. He responded so well that the result continued to be used most of the time up to 1995 – with his signature in the corner. That was long after he had died.

In 1964 Backford and Stoak were made into a joint benefice, so, for six years the magazine costs were shared, while Mr. Clarke created a cover picture of Stoak Church. It appears on a copy we have from 1969, though whether the two drawings alternated is not sure. Rosters of sidesmen and cleaners for both churches were certainly included. The 1969 magazine included a message from the vicar-designate, Sidney Weston, who began his ministry in 1970, and thus started as the joint benefice ended. After 1970 the 1961 cover drawing was again ubiquitous.

By 1970 the magazine had once more slipped into loss, with higher printing costs and falling sales leading to a deficit of £105. The sale price per copy was raised to 5p (50p a year). Note the change in currency, which came in during 1970. But deficits were also recorded for 1971 (£105), 1972 (£131) and 1973 (£121): plainly more radical ideas were needed. Accordingly, in 1975 the magazine format was changed to include more secular items of general interest, not always connected with the church. In addition both 'Sign' and the local 'Chester Diocesan News' were included, while the price was increased to £1 a year and advertisements to £3 from January 1977.

It is not clear when the magazine size was enlarged, but a copy from 1982 measures 12" x 8.2", as opposed to the old size of 7" x 5". The cover design was (temporarily) changed to show a fresh, though unattributed, drawing of the church, itself replaced again by the 1961 drawing by February 1984. Equally, the date a Gestetner printer was obtained so the magazine could be printed in house is unsure, but must have been by 1982. This move, too, was aimed at reducing cost.

The Progress of Magazine Content

From the beginning the magazine was intended to give church notices – those that the vicar would have made from the pulpit. A monthly letter, a list of church officers and services, rosters of sidesmen and cleaners, etc. Groups associated with the church were included; ACF, WI, Mother's Union and Evergreens.

In 1975 many more secular events began to appear, as mentioned above: parish council minutes, notices and reports on fundraising in the church and out, Village Hall activities and so on. Requests were made in print for items of interest and stories to be contributed. 1985 was a good year: the Hospice of the Good Shepherd opened then and its activities have appeared in the magazine regularly. The Flower Festival of 1985, involving the Church and Village Hall, was another event to fill space that year. It is worth mentioning that Capenhurst parish was joined to Backford in 1985. The magazine was thus ensured of a larger market and the costs could be shared too.

One might pick out 1988, which provided a first mention of the Backford War Memorial Trust, while 1989 saw Backford PC advertising for a street cleaner. 1990 was an important year for the Diocese, which celebrated four hundred and fifty years of existence in a variety of articles. More locally, Backford's new churchyard extension featured strongly. Bellringers' reports began in 1991 and have become regular contributors since.

1992 was a year of appeals by the Church, with an organ fund starting and its progress being reported in the years following. Requests were also published for a new verger for the church and for more choir members. In 1993 the first dog show at the Village Hall was advertised, while extracts from the parish register first appeared.

However, 1995 was the year when Backford's magazine presentation really turned quite lively. This coincided with the new printer, from which much enhancement of looks and content might be expected. Many illustrations and even cartoons appeared. Altogether, the magazine became a better and more interesting production, though one which retained its basic purpose, the provision of church information and news.

1996 saw the first items on school affairs, a year when both Mollington's and Backford's old buildings were replaced by a modern up to date school for both ends of the parish. Indeed, from 1997 a children's page in the magazine was established.

1997 also saw the first announcement of Festival 2000, a celebration of the millennium, which filled much space in the years ahead. The millennium yews featured in 1999, while in 2000 the millennium window in church furnished its own eulogies.

The Church Fabric Committee began to report in the magazine during 1999, and the content of PCC meetings soon appeared too. In fact, the many different activities now coming into the magazine reflected the real change in its purpose made over the years: something to read rather than a book of reference; with its function of church voice retained, yet with much to interest the non churchgoer. Consider the monthly recipes, weather reports, cricket club and cinema club articles on the one hand, church tower repairs and the 2002 Golden Jubilee on the other.

The magazine itself noted that from June 2004 production for August/ September would be one magazine only in future, as would December/ January.

Finally, it should be observed that the magazine contents have become much more sober in recent years – those exciting illustrations brought on by the new printer in 1995 have more or less disappeared.

Printing and Distribution

Although the magazine was printed by a commercial firm from 1935, the rising costs of that policy suggested printing be done by the church itself. The Gestetner printer, a large, cumbersome apparatus, which produced cyclostyled sheets of a relatively poor quality, was installed at the home of Mr and Mrs. Kay in about 1982. Harry Kay carried out the printing himself.

However, runs of over 5,000 copies were necessary each month for the magazine and other leaflets had to be produced for the school and for church notices – a lot of work. By 1995 the Gestetner was worn out. Its replacement this time was leased, allowing cheaper paper to be used, but essentially making for a much better quality result, and with a greater versatility. All manner of illustration could now be introduced and was. The magazine became an interesting read, even for those not particularly involved in the life of the church.

In 1995 for the first time separate magazines began to be produced for Capenhurst and Backford, with their own appropriate advertisements. Some time after this the printer was moved to the vicarage and the actual printing work taken over by Andrew Harkness, Michael Richardson and the vicar.

By 2007 the leased equipment itself was reaching the end of its life. Mollington School helped temporarily, but the opportunity was taken to look at outside printing again and, rather surprisingly, it seemed economic to go for that option. Agreement was made with Nemus Design of Frodsham and from September 2007 they provided the magazine for £55 each month, the only difficulty being that someone from Backford had to collect the copies from Frodsham. (At least this was easier than collecting them from Liverpool, where they were printed in earlier days).

Unfortunately, Bruce Wood, the proprietor of Nemus, died in 2009. His assistant tried to carry things on, but was unable to continue much longer, and from March 2010 Cheshire West and Chester Council took the work on in their printing department. Although more expensive at £92 a month, it was made acceptable to Backford by giving up the subscription to 'Sign'. 'Chester Diocesan News' was retained, but from then on was contained as an enclosure rather than by stapling in.

Mentioning stapling is a reminder that Joan Salisbury had to stop stapling the magazine in 2005 – she had collated it single handed for many years, probably between forty and fifty. It took two new teams to replace her and the work was then carried out in alternate months at the homes of Andrew Harkness and John Hess. At first the collation was as it had been, but when the Council started printing, they did the stapling themselves. That left only the insertion of 'Chester Diocesan News'.

Distribution, which included Moston during the 1940s and 1950s, was always the job of a dedicated and long term group of volunteers, who continue to this day. In this context think of Helen Orry, who started distributing in Canon Blencowe's time, about fifty years before she finally retired in 2006.

The Editor

No editor's name appears on the early magazines, most of the work being carried out by Canon Blencowe himself. After a while he recruited additional help and in 1961 Mr. D. Venables was thanked for his efforts in acting as assistant editor for several years. The editor was still the vicar until Rex Buckley's time, when Marian Selby was asked to take it over. By 1985, therefore, from when there exists a continuous series, the editor was definitely Marian Selby, who held the position until 2002. When the vicar, Stephen Southgate, became editor himself then, he thanked Marian for 'twenty years' service'.

The new arrangement was only altered in 2003 by Chris Surfleet taking on the collection of material for the magazine, since when she has gradually assumed the whole responsibility. Typing the magazine had been carried out by Janet Thaxter for a long period, though that job, too, was eventually handed over to Chris Surfleet.

The Magazine Cover

The September 1940 magazine has a pleasant photograph of Backford Church on the front. This may have been used for some years, but seems only to have been changed when Mr. J.W. Clarke drew a picture for 1947's issues. No copy from that period has survived, nor has the block used by Clarke and presented to the Church. In 1961 he drew another picture by request, this one proving very acceptable and being kept in use, with some exceptions, until 1995, long after Clarke died (1971). His characteristic signature was always on the cover picture.

In 1964 the connection with Stoak came into being, allowing a separate drawing of Stoak Church to be introduced by Clarke for the joint magazine. Whether this was employed for all or some of the magazines then isn't known, but certainly Stoak appears on the December 1969 issue. (Incidentally, the list of church officers has by 1969 gone permanently inside the cover). From the 1970 separation of the Churches, the 1961 Clarke drawing was certainly used again.

By June 1982 the magazine size had been increased from 5" x 7" to 12" x 8.2" and a new cover illustration employed, still of Backford Church, but a different and unattributed drawing. It didn't last long. In February 1984 the magazine kept its size increase, but returned once again to the Clarke 1961 drawing.

In April 1985 the cover featured for the first time a large cross on which was printed 'Christ is Risen' and underneath 'Christ will come again'. This design remained conventional thereafter at Easter. For December 1985 another special cover picture appeared, showing a sketch of the Holy Family, Joseph, Mary and Jesus, and this also became established for Christmas, until December 1996, when a more finely drawn, more formal rendering of the Holy Family came into use. That second design has continued for December up to now (with the odd exception of December 2000, when it seemed to be forgotten, or possibly no correct sheets were available at the time).

The long-lived Clarke drawing of 1961 was replaced in May 1995 by a photograph of the church, as part of the dramatic improvement taking place then. New colours were introduced at the same time. Up to 1995 all covers had been pale pinks, blues, yellow or green. Now deep blue, bright green and strong red colours appeared; from 2002 mauve; and in 2008 an even more lively green.

Advertisements and Enclosures

Three pages of advertisements by local tradesmen were included at least from the 1960s, although, when the magazine size was increased in 1982, the same number of advertisements fitted two pages. An increase to three pages again took place in 2000, becoming four pages by 2009, when more tradesmen were taking part.

The two enclosures were 'Sign', information from the Church from a national point of view, and 'Chester Diocesan News', composed of more local facts and events. Both were welcomed in the 1960s. Normally they were stapled into the magazine, but from 2010, when printing at the Council began, the 'Diocesan News' was just slipped into it. 'Sign' was dropped in 2010 to save cost.

Magazine Pricing

Almost from the beginning the cost of producing the magazine was a problem. Price increases for 1946, 1952, 1965, 1970 and 1977 have been mentioned above, and there seemed almost a permanent problem of catching up with rising printing costs. The relative amounts were, of course, subject all the time to inflation. Sales (including advertisements) were £33 in 1942, with attendant costs just under £36. In 1970 sales, etc. were £77, costs £183. Some control was re-established in about 1982, when the Gestetner was installed, but the sale price still had to rise by 2p in 1985, another 5p in 1986.

The new printer of 1995, described above, improved sales – £1,062 in 1996, £1,631 in 2000 and £2,090 in 2005, and the magazine account was by now showing a regular profit. But price has been increased regularly and no doubt will always have to be carefully watched.

Magazine sale price	1946	2d	1986	15p
	1947	3d		
Per copy	1952	4d	1995	20p
	1965	6d	1996	35p
	1970	5p*	2003	50p
	1977	10p	2012	60p
	1985	12p		

*Note change to decimal currency

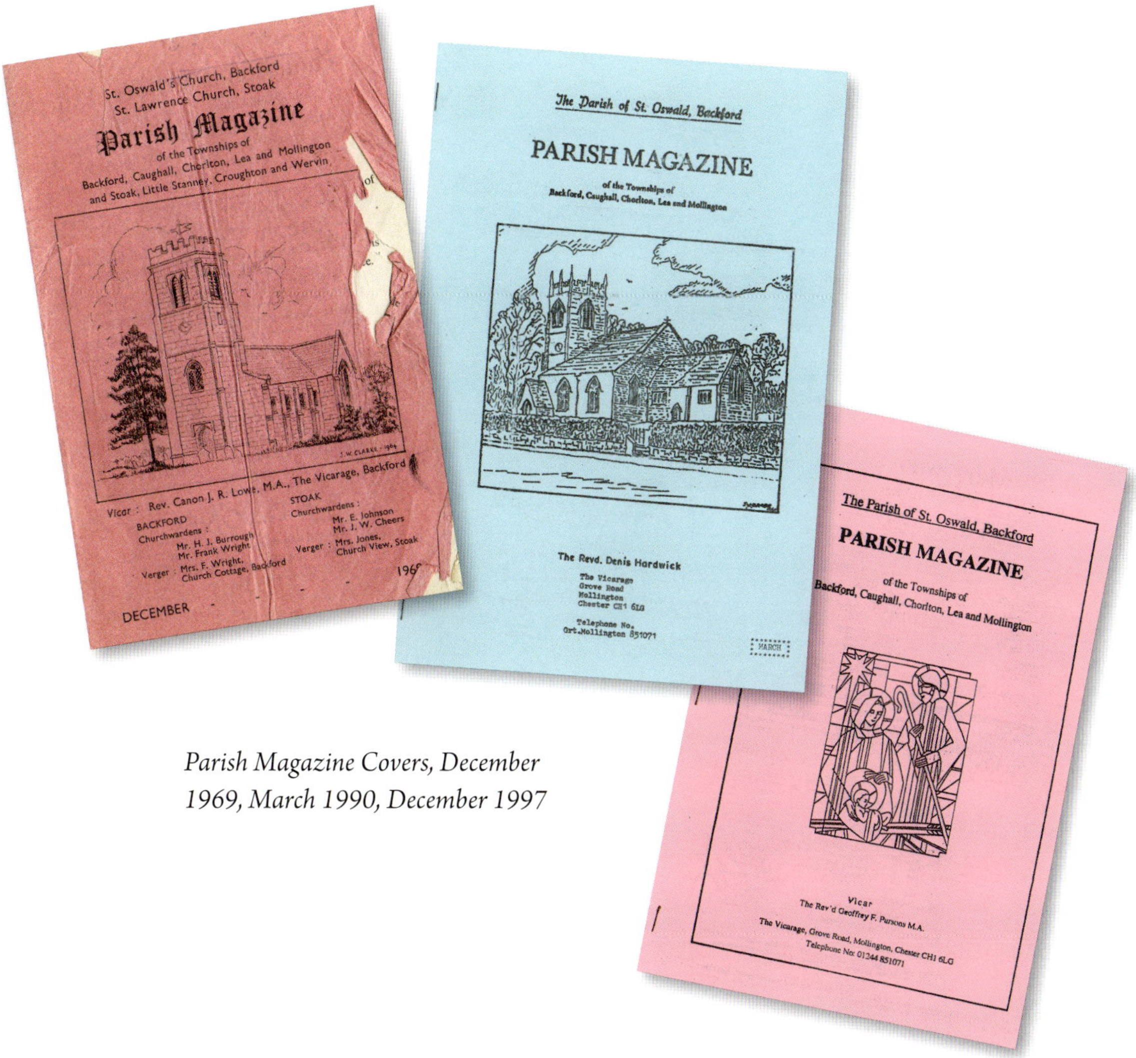

Parish Magazine Covers, December 1969, March 1990, December 1997

Edgar (Cobber) Kain – The First RAF Fighter Ace of World War II

by Carl Stagg

Introduction

It was 11 am on a quiet Sunday morning in late summer 2008 at home in Mollington, when the bell rang at the roadside front door of Rose Farmhouse. Opening the door there stood a middle aged man casually dressed in shorts. He introduced himself as Gavin Wilson from New Zealand. Gavin was on holiday touring the UK. In his hand he held a small file of papers and some photographs. He explained that whilst on holiday in the UK he was pursuing an interest he had in the life of the World War II pilot, Edgar 'Cobber' Kain. Kain was brought up near Gavin's home town in New Zealand and he had become acquainted with the Kain family including Edgar Kain's sister whom he had met. In New Zealand Cobber Kain is a Second World War national hero. I was eager to share and compare our notes on the war time events surrounding fighter pilot Flying Officer Kain and learn more about his short and dramatic life.

The RAF pilot, away from home in New Zealand, who made his home from home in Mollington, Chester.

Gavin's photographs of "Cobber" Kain at Rose Farmhouse had lain in the Kain New Zealand household for over 70 years. I copied the photos to add to my research material on the first RAF air ace of the 2nd World War. The photographs of Kain at our house were taken in April 1940; Gavin had tracked down our home address to gain more information on the RAF ace fighter pilot.

Kain used to visit and stay at Rose Farm, Mollington regularly. From the time of his arrival in the UK, and also as a future son in-law, he could be seen around the village. Mollington is not far from the war time training air base at Sealand where the various flying friends of the family used to fly up from around the

In the Lounge at Rose Farmhouse

country to Chester. Sometimes they would fly up from Sealand and 'beat up' the house, swooping low across the fields at the back. This barn-storming, showboating activity would not now be allowed. I had previously encountered the connection with Rose Farmhouse and Cobber Kain when I was researching the past history of our old farmhouse. Little did I know what facts and events were to unfold!

It was late 1939 and the first part of 1940, that Edgar Kain RAF fighter pilot, became widely internationally known. He was recognised and fêted by the press, by the general public at large, everywhere he went, across France, the UK and known about across most of the free world. He enjoyed, or as some would say suffered, celebrity status and was widely recognised everywhere he went. When he did become a celebrity, wherever he went he was followed by members of the Press, particularly Noel Monks, war correspondent of the Daily Mail, and Charles Gardner the war time BBC news reporter. His military and social exploits were well publicised, this included his engagement to

Cobber with Graham Phillips and Titch (April 1940) walking down Townfield Lane, Mollington outside Rose Farm House

Joyce Phillips the young actress daughter who lived with her family at Rose Farmhouse, Mollington.

Kain trained as a fighter pilot in 1937–38 during the time when the RAF was developing as a much larger military force. As a fighter pilot he went on to take part in battle operations in France during the Phoney War of 1939 and early 1940, and in the six weeks from the 10th May 1940 during the Battle of France. He was acknowledged as the first RAF air ace of the Second World War. The term "ace" (l'as in French) was first coined by the French in World War I and came to refer to an airman who had destroyed five or more enemy aircraft in aerial combat.

The Early Years

Edgar Kain was the fourth of five children. He was born on 27th June 1918 near Wellington, New Zealand. Edgar's father Reginald, a self made business man, sent him to the Croydon Preparatory School in Wellington; this school was to provide him with his formative education. Kain's secondary schooling in the early 1930s was as a boarder at Christ's College, Christchurch NZ. He was better at sports than academic work. He left college early in 1935 without taking the standard exams, but it was at this time that he showed his keen interest in flying, watching aircraft from the nearby Royal New Zealand Air Force station at nearby Wigram.

In 1936 when Kain was 18 he joined the Wellington Aero Club. After only 7 hours of instruction he was flying solo and it wasn't long after that he gained a pilot's private licence at the Wigram air station. Kain worked as a clerk in his father's merchant business, but flying was his first interest, and entry to the Royal Air Force in the UK his one main ambition.

In late 1936 Kain with his father, mother and sister sailed to England via Australia when his father was coming to the UK on business. On arrival, as planned, Kain approached the Air Ministry for a short-service commission in the RAF, but the journey had not suited him; initially he failed the medical. To get himself in better health he worked for a time as a farm labourer. He then reapplied and was accepted into the RAF in December 1936. Kain's father knew the Phillips family in

Trainee Pilots – Kain in the White Scarf

Mollington from his business connections and the Kains were regular visitors to Mollington and Rose Farmhouse.

Kain's basic military flying training was at a civil training school at Brough, Humberside, after which he was promoted to acting pilot officer on 21 December 1936. Following ground training at RAF Uxbridge, he started advanced flying training at Sealand and then at Ternhill. Training then was in bi-winged Gloster Gladiators. He gained his full pilot's wings in June 1937 and in November 1937 he was posted to the recently reformed No 73 Squadron based at Digby, Lincolnshire. In this period just before the war Kain showed what a natural he was at aerobatics with an exhibition in a Gloster Gladiator bi-plane at the 1938 Empire Air Day show at Hendon.

Hurricanes, Spitfires and Messerschmitts

In July 1938 he began flying the RAF's new Hawker Hurricane fighter that was starting to be delivered to a number of squadrons. In July 1939 he was again promoted to the rank of Flying Officer. All of Kain's battle actions were to be flying the new Hawker Hurricane.

The early history of the Hurricane is an interesting parallel in many ways with that of the Spitfire with which it was to form an immortal partnership. While the Spitfire was an entirely new concept based on specialized experience, the Hurricane was the logical progressive development of a long line of fighting aircraft. Although the two airplanes broadly met the same requirements, they represented very different approaches to the same problem in fighter design. The two approaches were reflected to an interesting degree in their respective appearances; the Hurricane workmanlike, rugged and sturdy, the Spitfire more slender and streamlined.

The Hurricane development was the work of Sydney Camm, chief designer of Hawker Aircraft, who began its design in 1934. The prototype first took to the air at Brooklands in November 1935, and the initial production Hurricane type I entered RAF service in December 1937, initially with No 111 Squadron. Powered by the famous Rolls-Royce Merlin engine, it became the first RAF monoplane fighter with an enclosed cockpit and retractable undercarriage and was the first RAF fighter monoplane capable of exceeding 300 mph in level flight whereas the Gloster Gladiator could muster a top speed of only 257 mph.

During the early design phase of the Hurricane, Sydney Camm learned of the work being undertaken by Rolls-Royce to develop a powerful new engine. At that time, the Hawker design team had been working on a fighter project known as the Fury Monoplane which had been designed around the 660 hp Rolls-Royce Goshawk steam-cooled engine. As the new Merlin engine offered a substantial improvement in performance, the projected fighter was re-designed for the new engine. For its first flight on 23rd October 1935 the fighter was powered by a Merlin engine, which drove a two-bladed, fixed-pitch wooden propeller. By the time war was declared on 2nd September 1939, nearly

73 Squadron at Digby Air Field, 1938. Courtesy of National Library of New Zealand

Gloster Gladiators at Digby 1938. Courtesy of National Library of New Zealand

500 Hurricanes had been delivered and eighteen squadrons had been equipped. These were all of the Mark I type, armed with eight 0.303-in. machine-guns. The Hurricane, weighing 7,127 lb., possessed a maximum speed of 325 mph, a range of 700 miles, a ceiling of 36,000 feet, and the ability to climb to 20,000 feet in 9 minutes.

The Spitfire was of similar specification although it weighed only 5,280 lb. and its maximum speed was 362 mph, it could climb to 20,000ft in 9.4 minutes. Its combat range was only 395 miles. Standard armament again was eight 0.303-in. Browning machine-guns with 300 rounds of ammunition to each gun. Deliveries of the Spitfire I began later than the Hurricane, in June 1938.

Kain flying Hurricane 'P'

The German battle opponent, the Messerschmitt Bf109e weighed 4685 lb., had a maximum speed 343 mph, a ceiling height 34,500 ft. but a range of only 410 miles. The speed of the Spitfire I was marginally higher than that of its principal opponent, the Luftwaffe's Messerschmitt Bf109e and it was infinitely more manoeuvrable than the German fighter. The Bf109e could out-climb and out-dive the British fighters and its shell-firing cannon had a longer range than the Spitfire and Hurricane Browning machine-guns.

On balance, from a technical standpoint, the Hurricanes used by the squadrons based in France during the earlier months of the war were inferior to the Messerschmitt Bf109e 3s that were stationed just across the border from them. Many of the aircraft were still fitted with wooden "Watts" two bladed propellers, had fabric covered wings, lacked cockpit armour for the pilot, with only a WW1 design vintage ring-bead gun sight. On the positive side, the Hurricane was an exceptionally steady gun platform and capable of withstanding substantial battle damage. UK plane production rose from 158 aircraft per month in April 1938 to nearly 800 per month by the outbreak of war.

The Outbreak of War

The Battle of France in May 1940 was possibly one of the lesser publicised and shortest, but decisive, battles of the Second World War. It is against the background of this 6 week period and the preceding 8 months, from the 3rd September 1939, a period known as the Phoney War, we follow and explore the events and exploits surrounding the RAF's first declared fighter ace of World War II: Edgar "Cobber" Kain of 73 (Hurricane) Squadron.

Kain is sometimes incorrectly credited as being the first Allied ace of the Second World War. However, this distinction actually went to Stanisław Skalski, of the Polish Air Force, with 18+ kills.

On 24th August 1939, with war approaching, No 73 Squadron was mobilised in response to a request from the French government for 10 fighter squadrons to provide air support. Air Chief Marshal Sir Hugh Dowding, Commander-in-Chief of RAF Fighter Command, insisted that this number would deplete British defences severely, and so initially only the four squadrons of Hurricanes, numbers 1, 73, 85 and 87, were relocated to France, keeping Spitfires back for "Home" defence. The movements of 73 Squadron both before and at the start of the war are well documented:

November 1937–September 1939: Digby

September 1939: Le Havre/ Octeville

September–October 1939: Norrent Fontes

9 Oct 1939 Rouvres… 73's main base during the Phoney War.

On 3rd September 1939, when war was declared with Germany, there was a long standing agreement between Britain and France that would see the British rapidly dispatch a substantial armed force to the continent; this force was known as the British Expeditionary Force (BEF). From an RAF standpoint it was comprised of two distinct elements. The first of these was the Advanced Air Striking Force (AASF) formed on 24th August 1939 and made up of bombers, Fairey III's and Blenheim IV's. So, after war was declared, the AASF was dispatched to France, close to the German border to allow its medium and light bombers to come into range to strike Germany. These squadrons were tasked with strategic bombing operations and initially had no dedicated fighter cover from Fighter Command as the French Air Force was initially responsible for protecting these bombers.

The second element was to operate closely with the ground forces of the BEF which consisted of the whole of No.22 Group (mostly Lysander II's) and some Blenheim Bombers plus initially four Hurricane fighter

73 Squadron September 1939, Le Havre

squadrons. The four Hurricane Squadrons, numbers 1, 73, 85 and 87, were to become part of No. 60 Wing.

The first squadron to fly to France was 1 Squadron on the 7th September. On 9th September, 73 Squadron, comprising 16 Hurricanes, flew across the channel to Le Havre-Octeville, France to join 1 Squadron. In all, in the ensuing period there were initially about 500 fighter and bomber planes involved in moving across to France.

The AASF was an independent command from the British Expeditionary Force and at first reported directly to the Air Ministry in London. However, this arrangement proved to be inadequate and on 15th January 1940 it was placed under the command of the British Air Forces in France headquarters. That headquarters also took the Air Component of the British Expeditionary Force under its command. Air Vice-Marshal 'Ugly' Barratt commanded these British Air Forces in France.

The Phoney War

The great powers of Europe had declared war on one another in September 1939, yet neither side had committed to launching a significant attack, and there was relatively little fighting in the air or on the ground. During late September 1939, following a series of losses of Fairey Battle bombers during armed recognisance missions into Germany, senior air force commanders within the BEF realised that the medium bombers of this strike force could not operate independently of dedicated RAF fighter escorts over enemy territory. The promised French fighter escorts had not proved up to the job. The more so as the French Anti-Aircraft regularly shot at British planes of 1 and 73 squadrons. Consequently, on 10th October 1939 these squadrons were transferred from the Air Component covering the BEF to these strike force bomber units, forming no. 67 Wing. Pilots within both units were happy with this news as up to this point all they had been doing was performing convoy patrols in between long periods of rain. No 1 squadron moved to Vassincourt (50 miles east of Rheims) whilst Kain with 73 squadron went to Rouvres which was even closer to the German border. Action for both squadrons followed almost immediately, although the first encounter with combat involved avoiding over-zealous French fighter pilots who on several occasions attempted to shoot down patrolling Hurricanes. It is difficult to imagine how it seemed to these young pilots so near the German border, muddy make-shift airfields, inadequate billets with the onset of winter and long periods of rain in that very wet and cold autumn and winter of 1939.

The winter of 1939/40

The adverse conditions of the 1939/40 winter in France are well described by one of these pilots on the front, Flight Lieutenant George Purslow DFC: "In 1938 I joined the Royal Air Force as a wireless operator/air gunner. On 3rd September 1939, I was posted to France to join number 12 Fairey Battle Squadron, just behind the lines at a place called Berry-au-Bac near Rheims in the Champagne Area. When I joined this squadron it was the period known as "The Phoney War. During that time from Sept. 1939 until the German invasion in May, we had long training periods and we became accustomed to the territory over which we would be attacking the enemy. The Fairey Battle was obsolete and should never have been used in the war at all as it was far too slow, but at that time Britain was not well equipped for a war and so we had to fly in these ancient aircraft.

Rouvres Air Field Shelter before the snows of 1939 (Kain in the balaclava) © IWM (C173)

In the Autumn of 1939, the rain was unceasing and the airfield soon became a sea of mud. Army engineers were called in to construct metal grids to make runways, thus preventing our planes from sinking, but after a few take offs by the aircraft, these constructions had sunk deep into the mud. We had dug-outs, and the dug-outs too were flooded. Flying was restricted and almost impossible under these conditions.

It is during the Phoney War period that the press were hungry for news. Nothing was happening and there was nothing to report for the war correspondents that were based just up the border at Rheims which had become the HQ of the RAF in France.

Fighting Techniques

Before the war, Fighter Command decided their main task was to defend England from attack by bombers. It was also believed that these German bombers would have to fly from bases in Germany, and would thus be without fighter escort. Having created the theoretical scenario on German tactics, the RAF then created the "ideal" tactics to counter it. These were called "Fighting Area Tactics" which would have been perfect during the First World War, which itself may be explained by the fact that the senior officers who formulated them were ex-RFC flyers. Their thinking was based on their own experiences of almost a quarter of a century before, rather than the current reality, where aircraft speed had increased two-fold and armament had increased four-fold! By contrast, German tactics were developed by front-line flyers such as Adolf Galland and Werner Moelders in the Spanish Civil War. So far ahead were they in their thinking that over seventy years later their basic formations and tactics are still used today,

One aspect demanded by the command in the RAF was rigid control over their pilots; discipline and holding tight formations was a key requirement. With radio came the potential to control whole squadrons from the ground, but without any means of assessing the tactical situation in the air such rigid control soon proved impracticable. RDF (radar and ranging) was greeted with enthusiasm because it enabled this control to be used, and generally to some effect. Radio also allowed the squadron leader to rigidly control his own squadron in the air. In WWI, close formation flying was required for communication by hand-signals, but once battle was joined it was every man for himself. In the RAF, radio meant even tighter formations could be flown by ordering stragglers to close up, or to direct formations to perform pre-planned manoeuvres. In the Luftwaffe it meant the opposite, formations being opened out as the radio replaced the hand as a communication medium, and tactical flexibility replacing rigidity.

Going into battle

On 10th September 1939 Kain flew his first operational patrols along the French German border without making contact with the enemy. On the 9th October, 73 Squadron was moved to Rouvres close to the German Border; Rouvres aerodrome had been built by the French Air Force in 1937. From there they flew Bloch-131 tactical reconnaissance aircraft. It was then, when World War II began, that the Royal Air Force moved in, flying the Hawker Hurricanes of 73 Squadron.

On 30th October, the Hurricanes saw action over France. That day, Pilot Officer "Boy" Mould of 1 Squadron, flying a Hurricane, shot down a Dornier Do17. The German aircraft, sent to photograph Allied airfields close to the border, fell in flames about 10 miles west of Toul. "Boy" Mould was the first RAF pilot to down an enemy aircraft on the continent in the Second World War.

Kain at Lubey inspecting the remains of the Dornier

Dennys Phillips (brother of Joyce) with the Dornier Machine Gun in the back garden of Rose Farm

Flying Officer E. J. "Cobber" Kain, was responsible for 73 Squadron's first victory on 8th November 1939, while stationed at Rouvres. His first victory occurred on this day during a defensive patrol. Kain had spotted a Dornier Do17 from a reconnaissance unit, above and ahead of him and as the Do17 began to climb to 27,000 ft with Kain in pursuit, he made two attacks but initially saw no result. This was the

"Cobber" and Graham Phillips inspecting the machine gun (younger brother of Joyce)

highest altitude for a dogfight in the history to date of aerial warfare. With his Hurricane showing signs of strain, he attacked again and hit the Dornier which dived steeply. Kain followed but pulled out when he saw fabric peeling off his wings. The Dornier crashed into the small village of Lubey northwest of Metz, exploding on impact and killing the crew.

A machine gun recovered from that aircraft features as part of the *Outbreak 1939* exhibition at the Imperial War Museum. This gun was photographed in the garden at Rose Farmhouse in 1940.

It was RAF policy not to acknowledge individual scorers, or officially use the term "ace" to describe a successful pilot. Because of the strict and disciplined formation flying, individuals were not singled out for praise and their achievements were not publicized. This was to discourage any undisciplined breach of standing policy by "glory-seekers". Also, it was thought that to make too much of the fighter pilots' exploits would be to ignore the less-glamorous but vital work of Bomber, Coastal, Transport and Training Command pilots and crew.

Returning fighter pilots were debriefed and their claims totalled with an aim to assess total enemy losses and not to give them individual credit. However, Fighter Command could not prevent unofficial totalling of scores, especially when these led to flying award recommendations which became public knowledge when granted. The names of these pilots were soon well-known as these events were reported abroad and every kill was avidly reported.

On 23rd November, near Conflans, Kain shot down his second plane another Dornier 17. The winter of 39/40 closed in and both the Germans and the allies were unable to fly effectively and so the patrols became fewer and the German reconnisance flights were also greatly curtailed.

Creating a legend

During the first months of the war, when there was little action in the air, Kain became popular with the war correspondents, who were hungry for exciting news or indeed any news. Kain was over six feet tall, and just 21 years old he was an ideal candidate to profile.

The remains of "kill" Number 2

It wasn't until the 22nd December 1939 when a number of 3-bladed, variable pitch propeller equipped Hurricanes arrived in France. Their increased performance, both in terms of rate of climb and straight line speed, helped even out the planes' performance against the German fighters. At the start of the war, the Merlin engine ran on standard 87 octane aviation spirit. From early 1940, increasing quantities of 100 octane fuel imported from the U.S. became available. In February 1940, Hurricanes with the Merlin engines began to receive modifications to allow for an additional supercharger boost. This extra boost, which increased engine output by nearly 250 hp, gave the Hurricane an increase in speed of 25 mph.

Due to bad weather there was little flying in December, January and February. It would be difficult to imagine how Kain and his colleagues would have felt and handled the situation in such a threatening and unfamiliar setting. Make-shift living conditions, a constant threat of attack, cold dark muddy winter conditions and an unenviable lonely task at hand. On 23rd February, Kain, as the Squadron's star flyer, received a Mention in Dispatches. He was by now the centre of a blaze of publicity and his was a household name. As spring broke, activity stepped up with more combats recorded and successes starting to build up.

On 1st March 1940, Kain fought an action with two Messerschmitt Bf 109 fighters. His Hurricane was already damaged when he shot down the first Bf 109 in flames although the second fighter attacked him, stopping the Hurricane's engine with a cannon shell but then flew off, leaving Kain to glide 30 miles from 20,000 feet to reach French territory. When his engine caught fire, Kain prepared to bail out but had to re-enter the cockpit when he realized his parachute strap was not in position. Fortunately the flames went out and Kain glided on to a forced-landing at Metz aerodrome.

Later in March 1940, Kain was awarded the Distinguished Flying Cross for a particularly daring action. While flying on operations, he sighted seven enemy Bf109 fighters 5,000 ft above him, immediately giving chase, and while pursuing them back towards the German lines Kain discovered another enemy fighter on his tail. Attacked from behind, and with his own Hurricane fighter badly damaged, he engaged the enemy and shot it down. With his cockpit full of smoke and oil, he managed to bring his Hurricane down behind the Allied lines. The citation for the award referred to "the magnificent fighting spirit Kain displayed in outmanoeuvring his enemy and destroying him." In some ways it was the news that people wanted, Pilot Officer E.J. "Cobber" Kain DFC, a New Zealander and the first fighter pilot to receive the DFC in WWII, thus also became Britain's first and widely-known air ace of the war. Kain himself put the adulation down to his nationality, which he thought was being used to promote recruitment in the Dominions, and felt that another pilot of 73 Squadron, Flying Officer H "Fanny" Orton (who he thought was shooting down even more enemy aircraft) should have been receiving some of the attention.

On 26th March, Kain destroyed a Bf109 and probably a second Bf 109 of JG 53, an elite German fighter squadron, but then with his own engine on fire he bailed out, with shell splinters to his left leg, a bullet-grazed left hand and burns to the face. Kain went on leave to England for 10 days, and his every move was followed and reported on by the national press. On 2nd April and before he returned, his engagement to Joyce Phillips of Rose Farmhouse was announced with a wedding to take place in the second week of June.

Back with the squadron on 23rd April he damaged a Messerschmitt Bf 110. Orders to 73 Squadron were a little erratic and they kept having to relocate their base as the pressure built until the German invasion of France. When the base was moved, along with the pilots and planes, support and ground crew of over 350 men were uprooted.

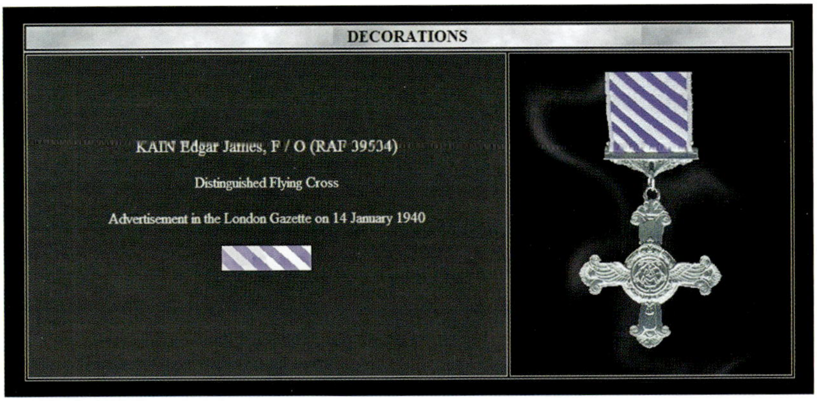

Celebrity status – being presented with a Movietone film of himself in France April 1940 with his fiancée Joyce. Courtesy of Peterborough Museum and Art Gallery'

Further relocations of 73 squadron base were made up until the invasion:

11th Apr 1940 Rheims/Champagne (the Norway panic)

19th Apr 1940 Rouvres (panic off)

10th May 1940 Rheims/Champagne (the German Offensive).

The Battle of France

On 10th May 1940, the German forces launched the blitzkrieg through the Low Countries and France; in the next 10 days, Kain destroyed five more enemy aircraft including an unusual Do17 victory on 15 May

Kain with fellow Ace "Fanny" Orton May 1940 © IWM (C1564)

where the enemy crew was seen to bale out when Kain had attacked in a head-on pass. He probably destroyed or damaged another five.

The Allied forces had deployed about 3.3 million men (2.2 million French), 5,800 tanks and self-propelled guns and 14,000 units of artillery. British Squadrons 3, 79 and 504 reinforced the earlier units as the German offensive gathered momentum, so on 13th May 1940, a further 32 Hurricanes arrived. All 10 Hurricane squadrons were now operating from French soil and felt the full force of the Nazi offensive.

As early on as the 16th May, the French positions on the ground and in the air became desperate. They pressed the British to commit more of the RAF fighter groups to the battle. Hugh Dowding, C-in-C of RAF Fighter Command refused, arguing that if France collapsed, the British fighter force would be severely weakened. After the German attack in May 1940, No 73 helped to cover Allied airfields and bases, falling back as its airfields were overrun by enemy columns. By 17th May, the end of the first week of fighting, only three of the squadrons were near operational strength, but despite their heavy losses the Hurricanes had managed to destroy nearly double the number of German aircraft. The British Air Forces in France now were fighting a rearguard action almost from day one, retreating from airfield to airfield as the Panzers rapidly sped westwards. This air battle has largely been overshadowed by the Battle of Britain which followed, yet the Battle of France was even more costly in lives and planes lost.

73 Squadron movements 10 May 1940 – June 1940 during the retreat across France:
10 May 1940 Rheims/Champagne
11 May 1940 Rouvres
14 May 1940 Rheims/Champagne
16th May 1940 from Rheims/Courcy to Villeneuve(Vertus).
18th May 1940 to Gaye.
3rd June 1940 to Eschemines.
7th June 1940 to Ruaudin.
15th June 1940 to Saumur/Bagneux, then Nantes/Château Bougon.
16th June 1940 to Saumur/Bagneux.
18th June 1940 to Church Fenton.

Each and every flight of Kain's is recorded in detail and the resultant activity, except during the later part of the battle, as the odds became overwhelming and the recording of combats and kills became less relevant in the pilots' fight for survival.

The Allies enjoyed a clear numerical superiority on the ground but were inferior in the air: the French Armée de l'Air had 1,562 aircraft in total, and RAF Fighter Command eventually committed 680 aircraft. Bomber Command could contribute some 390 aircraft to operations along with flights from across the channel. Most of the Allied aircraft were obsolete

Hurricanes refuelling at Rouvres in the Battle of France

May 12th Post-Combat Briefing
© IWM (C1548)

types; among the fighter force only the 130 British Hawker Hurricane and the French Dewoitine 520 could contend with the German Messerschmitt Bf109 on something approaching equal terms. In May 1940 the Luftwaffe could call on 1558 bombers and 1290 fighter planes.

The Luftwaffe virtually destroyed the Armée de l'Air during the campaign and inflicted heavy losses on the RAF contingent that was deployed. It is estimated the French had 1,274 aircraft destroyed during the campaign; the British suffered plane losses of 960 including over 450 fighters. The allies were not totally humiliated; the battle for France had cost the Luftwaffe a large proportion of its front line strength, some 1,428 aircraft destroyed and a further 488 were damaged.

Kain was in the thick of the action, destroying three enemy aircraft between 10th and 12th May, and claiming two more on the 19th May. In those ten days Kain destroyed five enemy aircraft and probably destroyed or damaged another five. During the Battle of France, word got out about a pilot who was scoring regular victories, and enterprising newsmen discovered his identity, thus enhancing his celebrity status.

As the original surviving squadron members were all suffering extreme fatigue, on 22nd May Kain was posted back to England. With other pilots he left early on the 23rd but on arrival in Britain, because of the desperate situation, Kain and another pilot were ordered to report back at once to 73 Squadron in France. Because of battle fatigue, they were put on administrative duties and Kain did not fly again until the 25th May, when he destroyed a Do17 but had to make an emergency landing in his damaged Hurricane. He destroyed a HS 126 (Henschel observation plane) on the 26th and another DO17 on the 27th. The Dunkirk evacuation of the BEF which 73 Squadron supported was between 26th May–3rd June.

Kain continued to fly as his unit retreated from one airfield to the next. It was during the last days in France, on 5th June, that Flying Officer 'Cobber' Kain, whose 73 Squadron was one of the few fighter units left on the Continent, engaged in what was to be his last combat mission and shot down a Messerschmitt Bf109 near Rheims.

The final Act

By early June 1940 he had probably downed 17 German aircraft and was to be rested from operations. Two days later on the 7th June he was ordered to return to England again, immediately from Echimenes; he was to be married the following week to Joyce Phillips. The following morning a group of the squadron gathered to bid him farewell as he took off in his Hurricane to fly to Le Mans to collect his kit. To mark his departure, as was the tradition, he flew an aerobatic display over the aerodrome. He was carrying out aerobatics at a low level when a wing-tip of his Hurricane touched the ground and the machine cart-wheeled across the airfield and was wrecked. Whether he felt that those watching below expected him to put on a last show will never be known but he completed the two low-level rolls and was attempting a third when he crashed onto the airfield. The Hurricane broke up and Kain, fatally injured, was thrown out of the aircraft and killed. He was not yet 22 years old!

During the early months of the war, when there was little activity in the air, Kain's exploits received phenomenal publicity in the press and he was acclaimed as the Empire's first air ace of the Second World War. This distinction still appears well justified and there is ample evidence that Kain's fine offensive spirit, together with his outstanding ability as a fighter pilot, was an inspiration not only to his fellow pilots but also to thousands of young men in his own country and, indeed, throughout the world.

The events from mid-May 1940 and into June can be followed in the log record of another pilot of 73 Squadron. "Kain's official score is fourteen confirmed victories but was more likely to be between fifteen and twenty. Whatever the true facts may be, 'Cobber' Kain – as the first Allied ace of the war – had ensured his place in history".

He was buried in Troyes cemetery. After the war his remains were moved to the Allied section of the Choloy war cemetery in France. Many tributes were paid to Kain by the world's media. Popular with his fellow airmen, he had shown himself to be a combat pilot of remarkable skill, and had achieved almost legendary status in the early months of the war.

From the records of fellow pilot Legge:

> 7th June ... this was to be a very sad day for the squadron as 'Cobber' Kain was killed whilst attempting a 'flick-roll' over the airfield. He was due to get married the following week and his mother in his place attended Buckingham Palace to collect his well deserved DFC from the King.

All told, between 3rd September, 1939 and 24th June, 1940, the RAF lost 1,127 airmen, of whom 415 paid the supreme sacrifice. Their names, and the cemeteries where they lie or the memorials where they are commemorated, are listed so their memories are not forgotten.

They were – as Squadron Leader Hall of 73 Squadron describes them – "the First of the Few."

Bibliography

Richard Stowers, Cobber Kain, Kiwi Fighter Ace Extraordinaire.
Michael Burns, Cobber Kain. Auckland, 1992.
Tony Holmes, Hurricane Aces 1939–40 Osprey 1998.
Noel Monks, Squadron Up World 1942.
(Anonymous) Paul Richey Fighter Pilot Batsford 1941.

Harrison, Paul, 'Kain, Edgar James 1918–1940'.
Dictionary of New Zealand Biography.
Minterne, D., The history of 73 Squadron, RAF. Part 1, 1917 to 1940. Dorchester, 1994.
Thompson, H. L., New Zealanders with the Royal Air Force. Vol. 1. Wellington, 1953.
http://www.aviation-history.com/hawker/hurrcane.html.
Aviation History online Museum.
http://www.aviation-history.com/hawker/hurrcane.html.

Lea & Mollington Residents' Association

Number 147

December 2009

OPEN LINE

Newsletter of LEMRA (for private distribution)

Message from the Chairman

A Happy Christmas and every Good Wish for the year 2010. On behalf of the LEMRA committee I would like to thank all residents for the help and cooperation we have received during this past year to maintain the standards in the area where we all enjoy living.

There are many challenges arising which need attention during the coming year. New members are always welcome to join the committee and/or part time assistance with special skills would be appreciated. Hoping this will interest you—please ring Janet Thaxter on 851328

With our Best Wishes to you and your families at this festive time.

Gordon Edwards

Gordon Edwards,
Chairman

Quiz Night and the Hospice of the Good Shepherd

We have received a letter from Mrs Olive Minors, Chair of the Mollington & Backford Support group thanking us for our "generous donation of £200.00". This money results directly from all those who attended our annual Quiz Night at the Village Hall so we in turn thank you all.

A Look at LEMRA

by Nick Nichols

The 1970s saw the rapid expansion of motorways in Britain and also many projects which had been delayed owing to the Second World War and the period of austerity afterwards. In 1972 it was announced that there would be a rubbish disposal burial ground established in the Lea Valley, involving massive soil removal, and that the Mid-Wirral Motorway would have a spur leading from Hooton and extending through Lea-by-Backford. Fortunately the latter project was called off, but there was considerable alarm in the area and this led to the founding of the Lea and Mollington Residents' Association (LEMRA) that year.

The leading spirit in this protest movement was Harold Cooper of Lea. During the war Harold had commanded a small boat delivering agents to the south of France and supporting the D-Day landings. He was always modest and courteous but he was never afraid to make a firm stand when he thought it justified. Harold became the first Chairman of LEMRA which had as its aims the provision of input to local authorities structure plans, the monitoring of actual developments, the lobbying for improvements to road safety and preserving and enhancing village amenities. Also established was a newsletter, the "Open Line" delivered to every householder in Lea and Mollington and encouraging the provision of leaflets entitled "Welcome to Mollington" which set out the various services etc. available in the two villages.

The LEMRA Committee met frequently, usually the first Thursday of the month in one of its members' homes and the Annual General Meeting was held, most often in May or June, at the Village Hall. It was the custom to have a speaker on various relevant subjects to address the meeting after the LEMRA annual reports had been presented. Among the topics were home security, planning and development both locally and countywise, recycling, prospective changes in local government, advice on deterring burglars and the comments of a leading judge on crime in the area.

In 1982 LEMRA launched the Home Watch movement, a local crime prevention organisation which rapidly spread across the land and now numbers some 130,000 groups covering five million households in England and Wales. This system was based on a similar set-up in the USA.

During Harold Cooper's chairmanship the LEMRA Committee was formed into functional groups specialising in Home Watch, Planning, Environment, Welcome to Mollington, and Community Affairs. The latter under Marie Hughes organised various social events of which the annual Quiz parties proved to be the most popular. There were also wine-tasting sessions and even a mediaeval banquet on occasion. Much of the money raised at these events was donated to charities such as the Hospice of the Good Shepherd at Backford and the Village Hall on the outskirts of Lea. These social events won substantial support from many residents of Backford, Lea, Mollington and beyond. Many active charity fund raisers, such as Olive Minors of Well Lane, also helped in the organisation of these functions.

The planning group on the Committee was run for many years by the duo Harry Kay and Norman Gould who examined every application for development of any property in our area and commented on it to the District Council. Their example was followed on their departure by their successors including latterly by Ken Owen of Mollington.

Campaigns were also fought to keep open the village shop and post office but economic circumstances were too much and sadly this fight was lost. There was also a battle to make the roads in the villages safer and success was gained in improving the dangerous junction between the A41 and Station Road by the Village Hall. LEMRA also has run and provided cash prizes for a successful Garden Contest held each year.

In early 2006 there was a threat that the owner of Mere Farm was planning to sell thirty, two-acre plots for gypsy sites. Although this would not be given planning permission in the Green Belt, there was a real possibility of pre-emptive development. The enforcement action to force actual removal could have taken years. The potential consequences caused consternation to residents and an informal committee, including the LEMRA Chairman Gordon Edwards, was formed to investigate alternatives. A public meeting to discuss this threat and possible actions was held at Mollington Golf Club. In the event, a local resident (anonymous at the time) was found willing and able to buy the land. The meeting was assured that the purchaser would keep it as it was and ensure restrictions on future use.

Cordial relations have been maintained with the local parish councils of Lea and Mollington and many members of the LEMRA Committee have also served on these councils.

At first there was a levy for LEMRA membership of 50p per household per annum and this was raised to £1 in 1990. However, thanks to the help offered by Shell UK which printed our documents for free, we were able to abolish this charge and every household received the LEMRA newsletter free of charge. This is issued some four or five times a year and is delivered by a team of some 11 or 12 residents each one responsible for a specific street or stretch of road. 'Open Line' had the aim of ensuring that every household in Lea and Mollington was kept fully aware of what was happening in the villages, particularly with regard to crime and development. The early issues were edited by Nick Nichols who at that time was the Editor of the Shell house journal for Company employees and pensioners at Stanlow Refinery and Thornton Research Centre in Ellesmere Port. Later editions were prepared by Ken Owen who had a more up-to-date computer and was well versed in its working. Nick who was in the Public Affairs Section of Shell UK, approached the Company who kindly agreed to print 'Open Line'. Thanks to this help and also to LEMRA generating funds from its social events, the organisation was able to issue its newsletter to every household in its area free of charge. It is hoped to continue this service after the demise of LEMRA in November 2010.

Harold Cooper retired from the Chair in 1989 becoming President until his death in 2007. He was succeeded by Carl Stagg (1989–1991) and Gordon Edwards, also of Mollington (1991–2010). Among those who served as Vice Chairman over the years were David Braithwaite, John Barker, Harry Kay and Charles Charlesworth. Among the Treasurers were Carol Fraser, Carl Stagg, Ailsa Sumner, Roger Cash and Charles Minors. The post of Secretary was filled at various times by Nick Nichols, Charles Charlesworth and Janet Thaxter.

With the growth in the role of parish councils, the departure of many stalwarts to live outside the area and the difficulty to replace them it was decided to stand down LEMRA in November 2010. However, some of its functions will be carried on by the parish councils and volunteers are thankfully available to continue the production of "Open Line" and the "Welcome to Mollington" leaflet.

LEMRA has been the work of devoted volunteers and besides those listed above mention should be made of Charles Charlesworth for his work on planning and the various county and rural development schemes, Roger Cash for his determination to improve the environment, Ken Owen for his contribution to planning, Maria Gillespie for her good work on environmental matters and Marie Hughes for arranging the many social occasions. Norman Gould and Harry Kay were assiduous in their work on planning matters. Harry Kay eventually became Vice President until his passing in 2007.

WELCOME TO LEA AND MOLLINGTON

A short guide to the area prepared by the Lea and Mollington Residents' Association (LEMRA)

Appendix 1: Sale Catalogue of Building Materials from the Demolition of Mollington Hall 1937

TO BUILDERS AND CONTRACTORS, FARMERS, &c.

Mollington Hall,

2 miles from Chester on the Parkgate Road.

PERRY and PHILLIPS, LTD.

in conjunction with

LEONARD WRIGHT & CO.

will SELL by AUCTION, on the Site,

On MONDAY, 13th SEPTEMBER, 1937

A LARGE QUANTITY OF EXCELLENT

BUILDING MATERIAL

Arising from the Demolition of the above Mansion, including:
100 Pine Panelled Doors, 4 Pairs Garage Doors, 50 Glazed Windows

200 TONS USEFUL TIMBER

comprising. 10,000 feet of 12 × 3, 9 × 3, 7 × 3 Joists,
10,000 feet of Pine Flooring, 15,000 feet of Spars, Baulks,
Timber, etc.;

12,000 BLUE WELSH ROOFING SLATES

Pair Half-glazed Mahogany Entrance Doors, Wrought Iron Piping,
"Eeeston" Domestic Boiler, Galvanized Tanks;

500 Sheets Galvanised Corrugated Iron

Quantity of Firewood, Garden Ornaments, 5 Tons Coping Stone

20 TONS OF ROCKERY STONE

40 Tons of Tun Slates, Steel Girders, 8 Tons of York Stone Paving,
etc., and many other interesting lots.

SALE TO COMMENCE AT 10.30 O'CLOCK PROMPT.

Printed by R. S. Fallows, "Journal" Office Bridgnorth.

CATALOGUE

LOT	
1	136ft. joists, 5in. × 3in.
2-5	300ft. joists, 4in. × 3in.
6-8	220ft. spars, 3in. × 3in.
9-10	220ft. spars, 3in. × 2in.
11-19	220ft. spars, 3in. × 3in.
20-28	160ft. spars, 3in. × 3in.
29-30	136ft. joists, 9in. × 3in.
31-33	112ft. joists, 9in. × 3in.
34-42	110ft. pine joists, 9in. × 3in.
43-46	180ft. T. and G. boards, 6in.
47-50	180ft. ditto
51-53	Stack of short boards
54	36ft. baulk timber, 14in. × 14in. and 9in. × 6in.
55-56	80ft. baulk timber, suitable for gate posts
57-59	100ft. pine joists, 6in. × 6in.
60-63	114ft. ditto, 6in. × 6in.
64	150ft. ditto, 6in. × 6in.
65	180ft. ditto, 6in. × 6in.
66	96ft. ditto, 11in. × 4in.
67-70	140ft. ditto, 11in. × 3in.
71	160ft. ditto, 9in. × 3in.
72	120ft. ditto, 10in. × 3in.

4

LOT

73 54ft. pine baulk timber, 9in. × 6in.

74 66ft. baulk timber

75-93 Stack of wide boards

94 A LARGE DECORATED COMPOSITION VASE, WITH MASK AND SCROLL DECORATION, 4ft. HIGH, ON A PEDESTAL AND BASE 5ft. HIGH

95 100ft. joists, 11in. × 4in.

96 96ft. joists, 8in. × 4in.

97 120ft. pine baulk timber, 10in. × 6in.

98 70ft. timber ,6in. × 6in.

99-100 60ft. timber, 6in. × 6in.

101 110ft. timber, 6in. × 6in.

102 Stack of partitions and boards

103-105 Stack of short boards

106-109 200ft. pine flooring boards

110-113 200ft. T. and G. matchboards

114-118 Stack of short spars

119-124 130ft. spars

125-132 160ft. ditto

133-134 90ft. joists, 5in. × 3in.

135-136 130ft. joists

137-143 96ft. pine joists, 7in. × 3in.

144-149 100ft. ditto , 7in. × 3in.

150-156 Stack of wide pine flooring boards

5

LOT
157-158 250ft. T. and G. matchboards

159 300ft. ditto ditto

160-162 200ft. T. and G. flooring boards

163 Stack of shutters

164-167 Stack of short boards

168 110ft. joists, 6in. × 3in.

169 135ft. joists, 6in. × 3in.

170 100ft. joists, 6in. × 3in.

171 110ft. joists, 5in. × 2½in.

172 100ft. joists, 5in. × 2½in.

173 88ft. joists, 7in. × 3in.

174 150ft. timber, 5in. × 2in.

175 130ft. pine timber, 4½in. × 3in.

176 Stack of spars

177 Stack of useful timber

178 Ditto ditto

179 Stack of useful posts

180 Ditto ditto

181 Ditto ditto

182 Ditto ditto

183 Ditto ditto

184 4ft. 12in York stone coping

185 Quantity 2in. wrought iron piping

186 Quantity 1in. ditto

6

LOT

187 PAIR OF HALF-GLAZED MAHOGANY ENTRANCE DOORS WITH LEADED LIGHT PANELS

188-194 Four pine panelled doors (at each)

195-201 Six glazed windows (at each)

202-205 Stack of rockery stone

206 36ft. 14in. stone coping

207 Large stack of tun slates (at per ton)

208 Stack of firewood

209 Stack of short spars

210 Stack of short planks

211 Three pine panelled doors (at each)

212 Two ditto ditto

213 Two ditto ditto

214 One ditto ditto

215 One garden door

216 Four doors

217 Four ditto

218 Four ditto

219 Eighty ridge tiles and stack of slates

220 Two York stone sills

221 Stack of York stone paving

222-227 Stack of stone paving

228 Stack of crazy paving

7

LOT

229 SEVEN LENGTHS WROUGHT IRON GARDEN FENCING

230 70ft. 14in. stone coping

231 Garden bird bath

232 " BEESTON " DOMESTIC BOILER

233 TEN OLD MILLSTONES, WITH GLASS CENTRE PANELS, SUITABLE FOR GARDEN ORNAMENTS

234 Stack of firewood

235 Ditto

236 Two galvanized tanks

237 Two ditto

238-246 200 TUN SLATES (at per 100)

247 Twenty-six ridge tiles and stack damp-course slates

248 Pair garage doors, 8ft. × 8ft.

249 Four doors (at each)

250 Four ditto

251 Four ditto

252 Five ditto

253 Glazed door and frame

254 Two glazed windows

255 Five glazed windows (2 oak frames)

256 Four ditto

257 Four ditto

258 Two ditto

8

LOT				
259	Three rolled steel joists			
260-265	STACK OF YORK STONE PAVING			
266	Large stack baulk timber			
266a	Stack of oak beams			
267-268	Pair garage doors, 12ft. wide × 11ft. high			
269	Pair	ditto	8ft. 6in. × 8ft.	
270	Pair	ditto	8ft. × 8ft.	
271	Three half-glazed doors			
272-276	Four pine panelled doors (at each)			
277	8 galvanized corrugated iron sheets, 10ft. (at per sheet)			
278	10	ditto	7ft.	,,
279	20	ditto	7ft.	,,
280	10	ditto	6ft.	,,
281-285	20	ditto	6ft.	,,
286-288	20	ditto	5ft.	,,
289	13	ditto	5ft.	,,
290-293	4 pine panelled doors (at each)			
294	7 doors (various)			
295	Stack of panelling and mantelpieces			
296-297	Stack of short spars			

9

LOT

298 1,300 BLUE WELSH ROOFING SLATES, 24in × 14in.
(at per 100)

299 1,000 ditto 24in. × 14in.
(at per 100)

300 1,270 ditto 24in. × 12in.
(at per 100)

301 1,000 ditto 24in. × 12in.
(at per 100)

302 1,000 ditto 24in. × 12in.
(at per 100)

303 500 ditto 24in. × 12in.
(at per 100)

304 620 ditto 20in. × 12in.
(at per 100)

305 1,200 SLATES, 20in. × 10in. (at per 100)

306-309 1,000 BLUE WELSH SLATES (at per 100)

310-315 200 tun slates (at per 100)

316 130 slates

317 2,000 slates (various)

318 A GALVANIZED SEMI-CIRCULAR ROOF STOCK SHED, 25ft. × 28ft., WITH IRON PRINCIPALS AND STEEL STANCHIONS ON BRICK WALLS; ONE END AND PART OF SIDE ENCLOSED BY BRICK WALL AND WOOD PARTITION

END OF SALE.

GENERAL CONDITIONS.

1.—The highest Bidder shall be the Purchaser and if any dispute arise between two or more Bidders, the lot in dispute shall be put up again and re-sold. The Auctioneers may, at their discretion, refuse any bidding, and reserve the right to make biddings for each Lot, and to alter the lotting as may be considered necessary.

2.—Purchasers shall give their names and place of abode, on the slips provided for such purpose on the inside cover of Catalogue, and shall pay a deposit of twenty-five per cent. in part payment, or the whole of the purchase money IF REQUIRED, on or before the conclusion of the day of Sale on which their purchase or purchases have been made. No Lot shall be removed, or taken away, until full cash payment is made.

3.—Transfer of Purchasers' names in the Sale Book cannot be recognised.

4.—The sizes stated are believed to be correct, and are given as a guide to Purchasers, **but no guarantee is given as to Exact Measurements,** and any difference arising between the actual measurements, and those advertised, will not be allowed to vitiate or affect the Sale of any Lot.

5.—**No Goods can under any circumstances be removed during the Sale.**

6.—Upon failure of complying with any of the above conditions the money deposited shall be forfeited, and all Lots unpaid for at the conclusion of the day of Sale on which their Purchase has been made may be sold by Public or Private Sale, without any further notice to the Purchaser at this Sale and the deficiency (if any) attending such re-sale shall be made good by the defaulter.

7.—Whilst every care will be taken to avoid accidents, neither the Vendors nor the Auctioneers will hold themselves responsible for any such accidents which may occur during the inspection, auction, or removal of the goods.

PERRY & PHILLIPS, Ltd.,
'Phone 2248. Auctioneers, 59, High Street, Bridgnorth.

LEONARD WRIGHT & CO.,
Auctioneers, Newgate Street, Chester.

Appendix 2: The Lost Door of Mollington Hall

By Ann Marie Curtis

Mollington Hall was pulled down during the period 1937–38. In 1937 there was a sale of items such as fireplaces, timbers, staircases and doors. Most were bought by building firms or builders merchants and few of the items have been traced. The fate of the doors of Mollington Hall have been shrouded in mystery ever since.

A letter was sent to the Observer newspaper, in 1953, stating that the door of Mollington Hall had been bought by a Canadian, Mr. J. W. Connell and had been donated by him to the 'Musée des Beaux-Arts' in Montreal. It was reputed to be the work of Abraham Swan an internationally known maker of mainly doors and staircases whose most prolific period was the mid 1700s when Mollington Hall had its big Georgian makeover by Thomas Hunt III.

I contacted the 'Musée des Beaux-Arts' in Montreal and asked if the door was in their possession and if so would it be possible to have a photograph of it. The registraire-archiviste sent me a photograph of the door and also gave the provenance which they had concerning it. The door was 'attributed to Abraham Swan' and the provenance was not very compelling. The archiviste asked if I could provide any more details.

The first stage was to consult Raleigh Trevelyan Esq. who is the last person alive to have lived at Mollington Hall, the home of his grandparents, Thomas and Beatrice Gibbons Frost. Raleigh, who lived there only as a young child, did not recognise the picture of the door at all and had no information as to the wooden fittings in the Hall generally. Raleigh gave some photographs of the exterior of Mollington Hall to our archives and the door in the Montreal Museum does not appear to be the front door of the Hall, as shown on these photographs.

The second stage was to contact the auctioneers of the Mollington Hall sale, Perry and Phillips Ltd. in conjunction with Leonard Wright

The Mollington Hall door. Reproduced by kind permission of the Museum of Fine Arts, Montreal.

& Co. They had no data concerning the sale, as a fire in their store rooms in the 1980s had destroyed any relevant information which they may have had. However, we have a copy of the sale catalogue in our archives and the door in the Montreal Musée des Beaux-Arts may be one of four pine panelled doors specifically mentioned as lots 188–194, just after the entrance doors (lot 187).

The third stage was to consult the article about Mollington Hall, by J. W. Clarke in Vol. 41, Journal of Chester and North Wales Architectural, Archaeological and Historic Society, of 1954, in Ellesmere Port Reference Library. The fireplace and doors of the lounge (drawing room) were said to be by Robert Adam and also the fireplace in the dining room. No specific mention was made as to the other doors except to say that some may have been brought from elsewhere. The door in Montreal does not resemble an Adam door but does resemble an Abraham Swan door. Clarke states that the Hall was built by Chester builders, but does not state which.

The fourth stage was to search through Abraham Swan patterns. The first book of patterns which I obtained was the following:

1757 London Abraham Swan: A Collection of Designs in Architecture, containing New Plans and Elevations of Houses, for General Use. (There are further editions in 1758 and 1768).

So far my investigations had not yielded much success. However, in 2012 events took a turn for the better. In September 2012 I visited family in Montreal and took the opportunity of obtaining an interview with the registraire-archiviste at the Musée. The staff there were very helpful to me and very interested in the material which I had taken on Mollington Hall. They had been under the impression that there were no photographs or illustrations of the Hall and were delighted to find out that this was untrue. Unfortunately I was unable to view the door itself as it is stored in pieces, off-site. The last time it was on display was in 2001. However, we compared the designs in this pattern book with another, better, photograph of the door in the Musee. Both the archiviste, Mme. Daniele Archambault and I were convinced that the door was indeed the work of Abraham Swan. Mme. Archambault also permitted me to have access to all the normally undisclosed paperwork pertaining to the door. I have been able to summarize this, as follows:

The door was bought, probably direct from the auction of Mollington Hall artefacts at the Old Mill Auction Rooms in Bridgnorth, Salop, by Mr. Sydney Burney, who had a gallery in London. He was a reputable antiquarian dealer and Mme. Archambault feels that he was probably there in person to buy the door, (and possibly the other three similar ones) though it is also possible that he had appointed an agent who bought on his behalf. Burney was one who enjoyed the comforts of life and did not travel so far north unless it was for a special purchase or for some important personal reason. The door was kept by Burney at a London warehouse, until he had a buyer.

Cleveland Morgan was the first curator of the Art Gallery in Montreal. He was from a wealthy local family and being a philanthropist, worked practically every morning at the Gallery without salary. Sydney Burney, who had supplied the Montreal Gallery with artefacts in the past, approached this valued customer. However, the Gallery was short of funds at that time and though Morgan wished to purchase the door and was constantly 'nattered' by Burney to do so, he was not able to commit to the purchase. Burney then indicated that there might be other buyers in the pipeline and so Morgan approached his friend and fellow philanthropist, John W. McConnell.

Jack McConnell was another Anglophone Montrealer, who was generous with his fortune. McConnell had previously made endowments, particularly of land, to McGill University, Montreal. Passing through the campus, I noticed that the J.W. McConnell, Engineering Building was named in recognition of this fact. Morgan persuaded McConnell to buy the Mollington Hall door and leave it on permanent loan to the Gallery, which is now the Musée des Beaux-Arts/Museum of Fine Arts, Montreal.

So, the Mollington Hall Door was bought by J.W. McConnell, from Sydney Burney, for the sum of £150 and shipped to Montreal. It was unloaded at the old port and stored in a customs warehouse before being sent up to the Gallery. Although the sum for which it was bought does not seem enormous, the cost of the preservation and storage of the door, together with the deployment of a dedicated assembly team each time it goes on display, have meant that the overall cost of the door to the Musee has been much more than that sum. However, the treatment it has received in Montreal has been of the highest quality and it is good to know that at least one artefact from the Hall is preserved in such a special environment and can also be appreciated by members of the public. I wonder what Abraham Swan and the Hunts, the Feildens and the Frosts, who lived successively in Mollington Hall between 1699 and 1937, would think of this story.

Index

Taken from text, appendices and notes, but not from illustrations. Pages from notes followed by n.

Persons of interest pages

Places and Subjects of interest